Free Speech, Scholarly Critique and the Limit
Proceedings of the 9th AMI Contemporary Fic

C000140667

Proceedings of the AMI Contemporary Fiqhī Issues Workshop

VOLUME 3

Free Speech, Scholarly Critique and the Limits of Expression in Islam

Proceedings of the

9th AMI Contemporary Fiqhī Issues Workshop

1–2 July, 2021

Edited by

Liyakat Takim

AMI PRESS

Free Speech, Scholarly Critique and the Limits of Expression in Islam
proceedings of the 9th AMI contemporary fiqhī issues workshop, 1–2 july 2021

© AMI PRESS 2022

ISBN 978-1-915550-01-9

All rights reserved. No part of this publication may be reproduced, stored in a retrieval system, or transmitted in any form or by any means without the prior permission in writing of AMI Press, or as expressly permitted by law, by license, or under terms agreed with the appropriate rights organisation. Inquiries concerning reproduction outside the scope of the above should be sent to AMI Press, 60 Weoley Park Road, Selly Oak, Birmingham B29 6RB.

Printed in the United Kingdom

CONTENTS

List of Contributors vii

Introduction 1

Liyakat Takim

The Primacy of the Freedoms of Thoughts and Expression within the Existential Framework: Implications on Sharīʿa Regulations, Rights and Freedoms 10

Arif Abdul Hussain

Free Speech as Ethical Speech in Islam: An Essay in Ethnographic Moral Theology 40

Ali-Reza Bhojani and Morgan Clarke

Dangerous Definitions: Free Speech Implications of Legal Definitions of Racism, Antisemitism and Islamophobia within the UK 56

Rebecca Ruth Gould

Intellectual Media: Jurisprudence and the Books of Misguidance 72

Haidar Hobballah

Free Speech and Critique of Religion in Contemporary Islam 131

Mohsen Kadivar

Ghazālian Insights on Scholarly Critique and Freedom 152

Ebrahim Moosa

Freedom of Expression or Freedom to Ban: Delineating Boundaries in Islam 169

Liyakat Takim

Arif Abdul Hussain

Shaykh Arif Abdul Hussain founded the Al-Mahdi Institute in 1993 and currently serves as its Director. He lectures in *uṣūl al-fiqh* and Muslim Philosophy. For over twenty years, Shaykh Arif has been at the forefront of developing and delivering advanced Islamic studies, tailored toward training students capable of addressing the needs of contemporary societies. Shaykh Arif was educated at the Madrassah Syed al-Khoei, London where he graduated with Honours and then taught grammar, logic, Islamic law and *uṣūl al-fiqh*. He then pursued Post-Graduate Islamic studies in Iran and attended private training and research studies with leading scholars of the Qom seminary. After founding the Al-Mahdi Institute he continued his graduate (*khārij*) training in *uṣūl al-fiqh* and *fiqh* under Ayatollah H. Amini, a student of Ayatollah Khoei.

Ali-Reza Bhojani

Dr Ali-Reza Bhojani is Teaching Fellow in Islamic Theology and Ethics at the University of Birmingham's Department of Theology and Religion. A graduate of the Al-Mahdi Institute, his research, teaching and writing focuses on intersections between Islamic legal theory, theology and ethics. His doctoral study, conducted at Durham University, was published as *Moral Rationalism and Shari'a* (Routledge, 2015) and he has held academic posts at the Al-Mahdi Institute, the University of Nottingham, the University of Oxford and the Markfield Institute of Higher Education. More recent publications include the co-edited volume *Visions of Sharīʿa* (Brill, 2020).

Morgan Clarke

Morgan Clarke is Professor of Social Anthropology at the University of Oxford. He is the author of *Islam and New Kinship: Reproductive Technology and the Shariah in Lebanon* (Berghahn, 2009) and *Islam and Law in Lebanon: Sharia Within and Without the State* (CUP, 2018). His research centres on the anthropology of law, ethics and Islam, through fieldwork in Lebanon and the UK.

Rebecca Ruth Gould

Rebecca Ruth Gould is a Professor of Islamic World and Comparative Literature at the University of Birmingham, working at the intersections of literary, political, and legal theory. Her developing and current interests include free speech and comparative legal cultures. Prior to joining the University of Birmingham in 2017, she taught at the University of Bristol and Yale-NUS College (Singapore). Rebecca Ruth Gould's books include *Writers and Rebels: The Literatures of Insurgency in the Caucasus* (2016), *The Routledge Handbook of Translation and Activism* (2020, co-edited with Kayvan Tahmasebian), and *The Persian Prison Poem: Sovereignty and the Political Imagination* (2021).

Haidar Hobballah

Dr. Haidar Hobballah specialises in Quran and *ḥadīth* sciences, jurisprudence, and Islamic legal theory as well as Christian theology and the study of comparative religions. He has twenty-six years of experience as a teacher in the Islamic seminary of Qom and has taught a variety of courses at Al-Mustafa University and the University of Religions and Denominations in Iran. He is the founder and editor-in-chief of multiple journals and has authored more than twenty books and numerous journal articles in Arabic. He holds a PhD in Christian Theology and Comparative Religions from the University of Religions and Denominations and a Master's degree in Quran and Ḥadīth Sciences from the Faculty of Fundamentals of Religion in Iran.

Mohsen Kadivar

Mohsen Kadivar (b. 1959) is a contemporary Shīʾī theologian and jurist and a research professor of Islamic Studies at Duke University (Durham, NC, US). His interests span both classical and modern Islamic thought with a special focus on Islamic philosophy and ethics, Shīʾī theology and jurisprudence, Quranic studies, Shīʾī political thought, and Islam and human rights. He has authored twenty-nine books in Persian and recently published his English monograph *Human Rights and Reformist Islam and Blasphemy and Apostasy in Islam: Debates in Shīʿa Jurisprudence* (Edinburgh University Press, 2021). He has contributed several articles and book-chapters, the most recent of which include "Democracy and Ethical values from Islamic Perspective" (March 2020), "Genealogies of Pluralism in Islamic Thought: Shi'a Perspective" and "Toward Removing the Punishment of Apostasy in Islam" (both March 2021).

His forthcoming books include *Governance by Guardianship: Rule and Government in the Islamic Republic of Iran* (Cambridge U. Press) and *Islamic Theocracy in the Secular Age: Revisiting Shi'ite Political Thought of Islamic Republic of Iran* (University of North Carolina Press).

Ebrahim Moosa

Ebrahim Moosa (PhD, University of Cape Town 1995) is Mirza Family Professor of Islamic Thought and Muslim Societies in Notre Dame's Keough School of Global Affairs and Department of History. Moosa co-directs Contending Modernities, the global research and education initiative examining the interaction among Catholic, Muslim, and other religious and secular forces in the world. Moosa's interests span both classical and modern Islamic thought with a special focus on Islamic law, history, ethics, and theology. His book *What Is a Madrasa?* was published in 2015 by the University of North Carolina Press. Moosa also is the author of *Ghazali and the Poetics of Imagination*, winner of the American Academy of Religion's Best First Book in the History of Religions (2006) and editor of the last manuscript of the late Professor Fazlur Rahman, *Revival and Reform in Islam: A Study of Islamic Fundamentalism*. Other publications also include the co-edited book T*he African Renaissance and the Afro-Arab Spring* (Georgetown University Press, 2015).

Liyakat Takim

Professor Liyakat Takim is the Sharjah Chair in Global Islam at McMaster University in Canada. He is the author of more than one hundred and thirty scholarly works which have been published in various journals, books, and encyclopaedias. He has written on a wide range of topics such as reformation in Islam, the role of custom in shaping Islamic law, Islam in the Western diaspora, Islamic fundamentalism, Islamic mystical tradition, Islamophobia, the treatment of women in Islam law and many other topics.

Introduction

The present volume represents a collection of seven papers delivered at the ninth Contemporary Fiqhī Issues Workshop held at Al-Mahdi Institute (AMI), Birmingham, UK, in July 2021. The theme of the workshop, Freedom of Thought and Expression, is certainly topical and one of the most hotly debated issues in contemporary times. This book is an important contribution to the assiduous Muslim contention that human rights, freedom of conscience and expression are integral to Islam. Such claims have come under increased scrutiny and debate especially after the Salman Rushdie controversy in 1989 and also in light of fatwas issued by various Muslim scholars against those deemed to be apostates and blasphemers.

Many have compared Muslim claims of dignity and freedom for all citizens living in its domain with the Universal Declaration of Human Rights and have found that such claims are not substantiated especially given the tendency to curtail freedom of conscience and expression in many parts of the Muslim world. Moreover, the rise of various fundamentalist groups like the Islamic State of Iraq and the Levant (ISIS), al-Qaeda, the Taliban and their treatment of women, non-Muslim minority groups, and Muslim dissenters has further exacerbated the situation.

Indeed, many Muslims claim that notions such as human rights, egalitarianism, human dignity and a notion of public conscience based on freedom of worship and expression smack of Western intellectual and cultural imperialism. They also see these concepts as an imposition of secular ideals under the guise of inclusiveness and universalism on religious traditions that are radically different from the West. Thus, many contemporary Muslim scholars have reiterated and supported the laws on apostasy, blasphemy and freedom of speech as pronounced by previous generation of scholars.

The challenge for contemporary Muslims is to find a balance between their claims of dignity and freedom for all within the inherited traditions, often located in Muslim sacred sources, and how to respond to those who dare challenge traditionally held beliefs on human rights and freedom of conscience. This was one of the main topics discussed at the AMI workshop.

As will become apparent in this volume, the papers presented at the workshop also challenge the sources, hermeneutics and methodologies that traditional

Muslims invoke to respond to apostates and blasphemers. The papers also claim that the time has come to revise some of the long-held and often archaic punitive measures meted out to dissenters.

The papers in this volume deal with a variety of issues connected to human rights and freedom. Drawing on the Ṣadrian principles of ontology, Arif Abdul Hussain's paper argues that the concepts of freedom of thought and expression are integral to human growth and progression. This is because growth is a natural process of self-realisation, and as such, is the inner impetus that inexorably drives beings towards completion. As he explains, Sadra's notion of continuous movement towards perfection and completion assumes an intrinsic state of human self-awareness by virtue of sharing in God's existence and the yearning to unite with the origin. It is this longing that is the cause for continuous movement towards completion.

The growth process and drive towards perfection entails the constant negation of and liberation from all restrictive impediments. Freedom of thought and expression are essential ingredients to the growth process, for they are necessary prerequisites for rational and moral progression. Stated differently, according to Abdul Hussain, Islam's theological, moral and normative imperatives are subordinate to the innate desire for growth. Moreover, there cannot be a 'sacred' space that is exempt from rational deliberation and critique. This means there are no theological beliefs, moral precepts, regulations of 'Islamic' socio-economic systems and political governance, and human rights that are beyond scrutiny.

Abdul Hussain utilises various principles enunciated by the Shīʿī mystic-cum-theosophist Mullā Ṣadrā Shīrāzī to argue for the intrinsic capacity for growth within human beings. Growth, in his understanding, also necessitates the primacy of reason in determining normative behaviour and rules. For Abdul Hussain, freedoms of thought and expression are fundamental prerequisites for growth that is intrinsic in humankind. Since every soul desires self-enhancement and perfection; the desire to acquire knowledge of the nature of things becomes an integral feature of the soul's inbuilt teleology. The process of growth and the desire for self-completion also necessitates both the soul's critique and rejection of its own established ideas and beliefs, and its freedom to challenge the ideas, beliefs and norms of the status quo, which it views as being restrictive.

Abdul Hussain further maintains the Sharīʿa has to assist in the actualisation of the growth process by promoting freedom in all its aspects. More specifically, the Sharīʿa has to be liberating and growth promoting rather than constrictive. To help the growth process in the post-revelatory period, the Sharīʿa has to be malleable and open to adjustment based on the existential aptitudes and circumstances of the time. In this process, reason plays an indispensable role in assessing the efficacy of revelation and can, in certain contexts, abrogate them should circumstances demand. Hence, reason must have complete freedom to critique and modify the Sharīʿa. Without saying so explicitly, he seems to suggest the preponderance of reason over revelation. Abdul Hussain further claims that freedom of thought and expression cannot be curtailed by the Sharīʿa because the latter offered laws that were moral, rational and in accordance with the contexts and aptitudes of its audience based on the telos of growth.

His contention that reason can ascertain the feasibility of the application of regulations stated in the sacred sources is not new. His statement that reason can abrogate them as Sharīʿa regulations formulated in seventh-century Arabia may have lost their efficacy for contexts that differ vastly is certainly contentious and needs much more in-depth exploration given reason's inability to provide conclusive proof of the Lawgiver's intent. Abdul Hussain qualifies his advocacy for freedom by claiming that whereas freedom of thought is absolute, freedom of expression is not because the latter is contingent upon situational contexts and the customs and aptitudes of the community. His paper, based on the Ṣadrian notion of innate tendency for growth, and the primacy of reason in this movement, will certainly raise many eyebrows.

In their paper, Ali-Reza Bhojani and Morgan Clarke approach the topic of freedom of speech through the lens of ethical speech. They examine the experience of a Muslim (more specifically the Khoja) community in the UK based on ethnographic data obtained from the daily religious practices of the community. They dichotomise their analysis between the need to avoid communal harm, on the one hand, and to share knowledge with community members, on the other. The paper focusses on the community's practices of banning speakers who engage sensitive topics that could possibly confuse and mislead the masses. Ayatollah Sistani is quoted as stating that 'specialist issues wherein the audience has no grasp of the prerequisites of the issue as per the required academic standards should not be discussed from the pulpit or other public platforms'.

Bhojani and Clarke polarise the duty not to conceal results derived from an intellectual engagement of the sacred sources with the possible harm that could result in divulging such conclusions. It is clear from their investigations that, especially within the community, the question of free speech is not absolute and may be guided by many factors, including the possible impact on and welfare of the community. For some, the more important duty (protecting the community from possible harm) should be prioritised over the less important right (freedom of speech). The move towards a more ethnographic approach to shaping expert engagement with the Islamic tradition – an Islamic 'ethnographic theology' as the authors call it – deserves greater study.

Their conclusion that 'in *fiqhī* terms at least, the admittedly reasonable urge to protect communities, and society more widely, from possible harm through restricting scholarly expression ought to be trumped by the need to preserve the more important duty of free reasoned scholarly expression' will be refuted by many scholars who see the welfare of the community as being more important than exposing it to intellectual discussions which the masses may not be able to grasp. Thus, for them, the public has to be shielded from topics that might confuse and possibly lead them astray.

On a different note, Rebecca Ruth Gould's paper is critical of government-sponsored definitions of Islamophobia in the UK. She argues that efforts by a government to define Islamophobia may have the detrimental effect of increased surveillance and the targeting of Muslims. She cites the example of the International Holocaust Remembrance Alliance (IHRA) and demonstrates how government-sponsored censorship can alienate minority groups within a religion while constricting the boundaries of permissible speech.

For Gould, every religion must define itself on its own terms. By defining Islamophobia and censoring Islamophobic speech, the government may be negligent of some of the detrimental impacts of its action, that is, the effects of its securitising policies. Such manipulations, Gould argues, restrict the capacity of Muslims to define Islam on their own terms. Government-imposed definitions could also coerce minority groups within the Muslim community to affiliate themselves with larger Islamic sects and accept particular versions of Islam that they might find unpalatable.

A democratic state, Gould argues, must uphold foundational principles such as the freedom of worship and speech rather than defining Islamophobia based on its own understanding of Islam. She also claims that through its arbitrary definition of extremism, the British government presupposes the inferiority of 'Islamic values' to 'British values', even while claiming to protect them.

In defining a group's characteristics, the state further increases that group's vulnerability by placing it under greater extensive surveillance and censorship. As Gould says, 'Most institutions and most individuals in positions of authority have not hesitated to compromise on free speech when under pressure to conform to the government's (convoluted) policy. While definitions can help to identify harms, when used to silence controversial speech, government-backed definitions may also undermine democratic governance.'

Haidar Hobballah raises important questions regarding what falls under the rubric of misguidance and if books or media outlets that could conceivably be construed as misguiding should be proscribed and/or their authors prosecuted. Importantly, he couches this discussion under the subject of freedom of thought. Historically, charges of misguidance have been used to silence those upholding variant or opposite views and beliefs. Hobballah explains that books on misguidance or blasphemy were initially discussed by the early Shīʿī scholars who probably coined the term. Later on, books and titles that could fall under this domain were added to. Hence the list of misguided books expanded exponentially.

Adopting the dialectic approach of Islamic seminaries, he examines various Qur'anic verses and arguments that could be used to prohibit misguidance. He discusses and refutes various interpretations to prove that Qur'anic verses on misguidance do not refer to scholarly discussion on a controversial topic; rather, they pertain to frivolous or deliberate attempts to mislead the masses. Hobballah contends that most of the verses cited to proscribe controversial books are not relevant to the topic of misguidance. Often focussing on the letter rather than intent of the verses, Hobballah categorically states that the Qur'an does not address the legal dimensions of dealing with the intellectual and cultural media.

Moreover, he states, it is not possible to apply the Qur'anic framework of misguidance to include scholarly disagreement or views that may unintentionally misguide others. In particular, he is critical of those who extend the purport of Qur'anic verses to vindicate the seizure of what are deemed to be misguided works, the closure of centers, the burning and destroying books of misguidance, or preventing movements from expressing their distinctive opinions.

Concerned to promote freedom of thought and expression, Hobballah meticulously examines various traditions cited in Shīʿī sources and refutes them claiming that many are transmitted by narrators who are deemed to be weak or that the purport of the traditions cited do not pertain to the topic under discussion. To underscore the point, Hobballah claims that although Imām Riḍā debated with deviant sects and groups he did not call for the proscription or banning of other schools of thought. Furthermore, the Shīʿī Imāms did not denounce the translation movement in philosophy and other fields, nor were they critical of the ruling powers for permitting it. Although traditions forbid the wilful misguidance of people, the texts are silent on the legal procedures to enforce the proscription.

While he agrees that reason determines whether it is necessary to confront misguidance and disbelief, Hobballah states that reason is also silent on the method of confronting it. He also claims that reason rules that, in conformity with Islamic law, it is impermissible to confront misguidance through killing and incarcerating. Restrictions imposed by Islamic law prevent us from recourse to such methods in efforts to confront misguidance.

Hobballah concludes from his rhetorical discourse that there is no textual proof that enunciates methods to deploy in responding to books or the media for misguidance; and that reading or keeping such books does not mean agreement with their contents. As he astutely observes, 'had it been the case, it would eventually hinder the intellectual advancement of the Islamic communities.' While he concedes that some books of misguidance are prohibited, he insists that the sacred sources do not prescribe any punishment for keeping or reading them. He carefully goes through different forms of misguidance ranging from publishing, distributing, to reading misguiding material and concludes that jurists are not always consistent when deeming what is misguidance and that principles of conflict, priorities and the weighing of public interests have to be balanced when countering misguidance.

Mohsen Kadivar's paper focuses on the decriminalisation of the laws of apostasy and blasphemy. He claims that religious freedom and freedom of expression are embedded in the Universal Declaration of Human Rights (UDHR) and International Covenant on Civil and Political Rights (ICCPR). However, in the charter on the Cairo Declaration on Human Rights in Islam (CDHRI), such notions are interwoven to the Sharīʿa. This inevitably curtails freedom of speech and imposes severe punishments on apostasy and blasphemy.

Kadivar strongly argues that Islam grants people freedom of conscience and recognises the diversity of religions and beliefs. Traditions that oppose this principle must therefore be rejected. As he states, 'there is no reliable proof from the Qur'an, Sunna, consensus (*ijmāʿ*) or reason that can establish the validity of executing anyone accused of apostasy or blaspheming the Prophet.' Traditional jurists, by employing *ijtihād*, have arrived at this judgement and claimed consensus by relying on 'isolated' *ḥadīth*s (*khabar al-wāḥid*). The ruling on killing apostates and blasphemers is incorrect and should not be carried out. In stating this, Kadivar is clearly challenging long-held juridical prescriptions against blasphemers and apostates. He presents various *uṣūlī* and rational arguments to support his thesis. The reforms in Islamic law that he suggests will not accepted by many conservative *ʿulamā'*. Kadivar also calls for a critique of Islam in Muslim-majority countries, stating that Islam's logic is that of demonstration and proof, not one of force and coercion. A critique would lead to a revision of many hotly contested laws. He also advocates for open and public debates regarding basic Islamic beliefs.

Kadivar stresses that Islamic jurisprudence should be revisited in the light of questions on freedom of expression and religious freedom. This is because the Qur'an and the traditions of the Prophet and the Imāms support these notions. Without elaborating on it he also stresses the need to re-examine traditional principles and foundations of *ijtihād* so as to exercise it in a new form, which he calls 'structural *ijtihād*'. Such views are important in emphasising that the laws on blasphemy and apostasy were, in all probability, tied to political contingencies in early Islamic history and are not universally binding.

In his paper, Ebrahim Moosa states that the concept of freedom has to be discussed based on how it is perceived in different societies. Freedom in slave societies, for example, was viewed very differently from those that had abolished slavery. Early Islamic societies valorised both free individuals and slavery, whilst encouraging manumission and freedom. Moosa goes on to cogently argue that in early and medieval Islam, the idea of an individual possessing rights that cannot be infringed would be a rarity. Similarly, notions of dignity and freedom were viewed differently in the past. Appeals to human rights in the pre-modern world could not abrogate or abolish slavery, nor could appeals to dignity equate believers and non-believers, nor make women equal to men. To be sure, the past had limits on what we today perceive as freedoms or the right to dissent. Thus, we need to be careful when using categories and concepts that had very different resonances in the past rather than merely replicating and transplanting them into the present especially as they are transposed on contemporary societies that are deeply secularised.

Moosa's paper also explores the notion of freedom in the early and medieval Islamic period by focusing on al-Ghazālī and his views on Muslim philosophers. For al-Ghazālī, the philosophers had portrayed God as speaking in different tongues to different audiences. At the same time, the philosophers claimed to speak to the elite and claimed that their language was the truth. Al-Ghazālī deemed the philosophers' hermeneutics to be so dangerous that they threatened basic Islamic beliefs. In his critique of the philosophers, al-Ghazālī emboldened theology so that it could ostracise and anathematise ideas that it deemed unacceptable. Thus, freedom of thought was curtailed especially for those who dared to challenge normative beliefs. Henceforth, scriptural authority could trump philosophical reason, and generate its own tradition or authority-constitutive reason. Ironically, al-Ghazālī found some of the literalist postulates to fundamentally clash with some of his own metaphysical propositions.

Whilst critiquing al-Ghazālī's efforts to mark theological red lines Moosa argues that it is essential to revise the unofficial ban on questioning the boundaries of theological dissent. He expresses concern that the stifling of intellectual thought in Muslim societies had frightened Muslim scientists and dissuaded them from pronouncing their views especially if these could challenge Muslim theological doctrines like that of evolution and the creation of the universe.

Moosa argues that to have freedom at the political and theological centre means the need to completely overhaul the dominant Muslim political theology from an obedience-centred worldview to one that is a freedom-centred polity and theology. Here, he seems to advocate al-Ghazālī's views of theological truths and convictions based on a more expansive scale of acceptable interpretative possibilities. As he states, 'To energetically pursue pluralism and toleration we need to ensure that the knowledge system contemporary Muslims pursue is capacious enough to include the experiences of the varieties of Muslim practices and beliefs as well as the shared experiences with people who retain different commitments to ours.'

Moosa seeks to broaden the circle of tolerance and acceptance by proposing a system that advocates freedom within a communitarian ethos of individual and communal liberty. Stated differently, there could be communitarian modes of liberty that value freedom, responsibility and the centrality of the community. This would create space for discussion and debate among Muslims on various topics without being accused of blasphemy or heresy.

In his paper on freedom of expression, Liyakat Takim claims that pluralism is inherent in Islamic law and that the law is discursive and open to a multiplicity of interpretations. Due to this, Muslims can hold divergent and, at times, opposite views on a particular topic. Despite this, through various forms of hermeneutics, boundaries limiting freedom of thought, conscience and expression have been constructed by scholars. Dissenters have been accused of blasphemy and heresy. Delineating boundaries is important because they limit unorthodox reading of texts.

After citing various examples of scholars who have held unorthodox views, Takim argues that boundaries of what constitute acceptable or unacceptable views are often fluid and subject to the proclivities of and manipulation by a scholar and the customs of the time. He then considers the laws on blasphemy and claims that, although the Qur'an denounces different genres of blasphemies, it does not prescribe any temporal punishment for them. Similarly, the early texts do not state that blasphemy against the Prophet and his Companions is a punishable crime. This phenomenon is a much later development in Islamic intellectual history. Later, with the emergence of different factions and sects, scholars added to the list of blasphemous views and practices. Takim attempts to prove this by exploring the association of blasphemy with apostasy and argues that the punishment for these crimes was subject to much scholarly disagreement and debate. He concludes that boundaries were constructed, contested and then rigidly applied even though initially there were none. Punishments were imposed even though none was prescribed in the scripture. These were often applied to curtail people's freedom of speech. In the process, freedom to express was replaced by freedom to ban and silence.

ARIF ABDUL HUSSAIN

The Primacy of the Freedoms of Thought and Expression within the Existential Framework: Implications on Sharīʿa Regulations, Rights and Freedoms[1]

Drawing on the existential principles of Ṣadrian ontology, this paper surmises that the freedoms of thought and expression are integral to human growth and progression.[2] In other words, when analysing such freedoms humankind accords to itself from an existential perspective, it is clear they are the outcome of and congruent with the existential state of evolutionary growth enjoyed by existence at large.[3] Growth is an evolutionary process of self-realisation, and as such it is the inner telos and dynamism by which all entities gradually actualise their potential. This growth process entails the constant negation of, or liberation from, previous restrictive forms and states and the emergence of newer ones. In humankind, the growth process manifests as the incessant drive

1 The existential framework is a legal methodology being developed by the author. For more information, see Arif Abdul Hussain, 'The Conflict between the Actual and Apparent Regulations – Part 2: The Solution of "The Existential Framework"', Shaykh Arif, www.shaykharif.com/blog/the-conflict-between-the-actual-and-apparent-regulations. The term 'existential' is an adjective denoting either (a) the notion of 'pertaining to existence', or (b) the philosophical school of Mullā Ṣadrā, in particular its ontological principles. Hence, the existential framework is called as such because it presupposes Ṣadrā's ontological principles as the ontological foundations of Sharīʿa regulations. Thus far, the focus of the existential framework has been the sciences of 'the principles of jurisprudence' (*uṣūl al-fiqh*) and 'jurisprudence' (*fiqh*); however, there is potential to extend its scope of influence to the other Islamic sciences, which would also have the reciprocal effect of developing it as a philosophy further. The author is grateful to Riaz Walji for kindly editing and referencing the paper, Dr Wahid Amin and Mohammad Reza Tajri for their patience and encouragement and colleagues at Al-Mahdi Institute for organising the workshop in which an early draft of this paper was presented and for their efforts in getting this paper to publication.

2 It should be noted that 'Ṣadrian' is an adjective for the philosophical thought of the Islamic philosopher Ṣadr al-Dīn Shīrāzī, commonly known as Mullā Ṣadrā (d. 1636).

3 The phrase 'from an existential perspective' also means 'according to the existential framework'. The adjective 'existentially' can also be used in its stead to convey the same meaning.

to progress, or actualise itself, both rationally and morally. This is because the nature of humankind is to be rational and moral and actualise its potential both rationally and morally. Since rational and moral progression constitute the evolution and growth of humankind, the freedoms of thought and expression are fundamental to the growth process, for they are necessary prerequisites for rational and moral progression.[4] Hence, the freedoms of thought and expression are existential in themselves, because they are growth-promoting essentially, and as such, they are knowable intuitively and subsequently justifiable rationally, that is, they are known and justified by the soul's faculties of intuition and reason, respectively. This will be explained in due course. To ensure the continued growth of both human reason and morality, it is necessary to constantly scrutinise all restrictions placed on the individual and collectivity vis-à-vis the freedoms of thought and expression, remove those that become impediments to growth and increase access to knowledge as and when possible and so long as it is conducive to growth.

Accordingly, successful systems of governance are those endeavouring to maximise these freedoms constantly (for such freedoms are necessary for the actualisation of the potential inherent in their respective human subjects). Restrictions on the freedoms of thought and expression can only be envisaged as momentary impositions due to the existential limitations of the human collectivity.[5] This is because the purpose of such curtailment is to facilitate the collective growth process and increase freedoms inevitably. Although the freedom of expression is a natural consequence of the freedom of thought, only the former can be restrained meaningfully for a time deemed necessary. It is impossible to curb the freedom of thought directly, for thinking in itself is an integral part of being human and does not have any outward expression.

4 Steven J. Heyman, 'Righting the Balance: An Inquiry into the Foundations and Limits of Freedom of Expression', *BUL Rev.* 78 (1998): 1326.

5 'Existential limitations' refers to (a) the limitations of the existential context, that is, of any given time and place; and (b) the limitations of the existential aptitudes, that is, of the psychological, cognitive and moral aptitudes, of the human individual and collectivity of any given time and place. The term 'collectivity' (pl. 'collectivities') refers to every type of human grouping, irrespective of whether it is natural and/or based on an ideology, philosophy or otherwise. It refers to the family, tribe, community, society, nation and global human community. It can be used to refer to any one, some or all of them. For more information on the notions of 'existential aptitudes' and 'collectivities', see the foreword and lectures 8 and 9 in Arif Abdul Hussain, *Islam and God-Centricity: Plurality and Mutability of Religion* (Birmingham: Sajjadiyya Press, 2022).

It is no surprise therefore that the whole endeavour of the Prophet was to liberate souls restricted and constricted by the 'sacred' theologies of the time.[6] The Qur'an's persistent questioning of the truth and value of many of the pagan practices and beliefs appealed to its initial audience intuitively;[7] thereafter their faculties of reason justified this intuitive knowledge regarding the status quo, and in time, everything barring them from growth was either rejected or modified. In fact, the primary effect intended by the famous proclamation of the Oneness of God (*lā ilāha illā Allāh* – there is no god other than God) was to remove the obstacles impeding the freedom of thought so that souls could realign themselves with their existential inclination to grow rationally and morally.[8]

Therefore, the initial success of the Qur'an and the Prophet was in realigning minds with the existential telos of growth (*iflāḥ*). This means their message, which is that the religion of Islam is a means for the actualisation of the human potential, had to be in line with the nature of existence of necessity and by priority. In other words, Islam's theological, moral and normative formula-

6 For instance, see Qur'an 53:21–23 and 26–30.

7 For instance, see Qur'an 46:4, 10, 28, 50:6–11, 52:32–43 and 53:19–20.

8 This import can be gleaned from the Prophet's statement, 'O humankind, say: "There is no god other than God"; you will be successful or saved (*tufliḥū*).' For reference to the Prophetic report, see al-Faḍl ibn al-Ḥasan al-Ṭabarsī, *Majmaʿ al-bayān fī tafsīr al-Qur'ān* (Beirut: Mu'assasat al-Aʿlamī li-l-Maṭbūʿāt, 1995), 10:476. The root of the verb *tufliḥū* – the verb *falaḥa* – is commonly used to refer to the act of 'cultivating' something, especially crops, and so 'success' (*iflāḥ*) was understood by the Arabs in terms of 'cultivation' and 'growth'. Thus, the signification of the Prophet's statement is that should the pagan Arab be able to proclaim, 'There is no god other than God', then it would result in *falāḥ* (success or salvation), that is, it would result in the internal growth of the proclaimer. This is because their ability to proclaim it indicated they had recognised on some level (that is, either intuitively, rationally or both) that the gods they had been worshiping – and all the patriarchy, hierarchy and injustice they represented – were false and illusory, and hence were obstacles impeding internal growth. Indeed, the mere fact of proclaiming, 'There is no god other than God', for such Arabs would have been an extremely cathartic moment if not kenotic. It should be noted that salvation as per the Qur'an is predicated on growth. For instance, see Qur'an 91:9, where the verb *zakkā* signifies the act of purifying and growing. For etymology of the derivates of the verb *zakā* and their usage in the Qur'an, see Arif Abdul Hussain, 'A Functional Interpretation of *Zakāt* and the Inclusion of Contemporary Taxation as Its Legitimate Form', in *The Efficacy of Financial Structures for Islamic Taxes and Dues: Proceedings of the 7th AMI Contemporary Fiqhī Issues Workshop*, ed. Wahid M. Amin (Birmingham: AMI Press, 2020), 21–24.

tions are subordinate to the existential feature of growth and not vice versa.[9] The corollary of this – that is, of Islam being subordinate to existence – is the primacy of reason over revelation despite revelation being the most superior mode of the knowledge of the Truth. This will be examined further below.

The implication of this is that Islam as a system of beliefs, morals and norms has to be open to critique by insiders and outsiders alike, just like any other system of beliefs, morals and norms: rational critique is the only means for both insiders and outsiders to verify its truth, increase faith and bring about reform. Being salvific, Islam requires the wilful surrender to God, which itself presupposes the evaluation of its content to ascertain whether it is meaningful and growth promoting. Thus, there cannot be a 'sacred' space within religion exempt from rational deliberation and critique. This means there are no theological beliefs, moral precepts, regulations of 'Islamic' socio-economic systems and political governance, and human rights that are beyond scrutiny.

This paper utilises the Ṣadrian principles of the unity of existence (*waḥdat al-wujūd*), individuality (*tashkhīṣ*), the gradation of existence (*tashkīk al-wujūd*), and the alignment of revelation (*waḥy*), intuition[10] (*al-ʿaql al-kullī*) and reason (*al-ʿaql al-juzʾī*) to argue for the inherency of the existential telos of growth within humankind and it being the basis for (1) the freedoms of thought and expression; (2) the primacy of reason in determining the efficacy of normativity; and (3) the contextual nature of restrictions upon the freedoms of thought and expression.

---

9 The existential telos of growth can be inferred whenever the Qur'an utilises the verbal and nominal derivatives of the root verb *falaḥa*, which means to cultivate and grow (see note 8). The notion of the primacy of the existential telos of growth over theological, moral and normative formulations can be extrapolated from verses such as Qur'an 91:9, 'He indeed is successful [or has grown], who purifies it [the soul],' where 'purification' (*tazkiya*) of the soul is the purpose (telos) of all religious formulations (for instance, see Qur'an 62:2). In fact, the utility of the verbal and nominal conjugates of the verbal noun *tazkiya* (purification) in the Qur'an has the connotation of 'growth' too, and hence the existential telos growth can be inferred from their usage too.

10 Other translations of *al-ʿaql al-kullī* (which are synonyms of 'the faculty of intuition') include 'the Universal Intellect', 'the Spirit' and 'the Heart'. See Zailan Moris, *Revelation, Intellectual Intuition and Reason in the Philosophy of Mulla Ṣadrā: An Analysis of the al-Hikmah al-ʿArshiyyah* (London and New York: Routledge, 2012), 33–36.

1. Ṣadrian Ontological Foundations

Ṣadrā's synthesis of Ibn Sīnā's principiality of existence (*aṣālat al-wujūd*), the Suhrawardian notion of the gradation of Light and Ibn al-ʿArabī's notion of the unity of existence and its perpetual dissolution and re-creation in every moment (*al-labs baʿda al-khulʿ*) gives rise to an ontology that is unitive and evolutionary.[11] Since the nature of existence is oneness, his system does not allow for any 'real' distinction between God and His attributes, on the one hand, and the existence of God and the world, on the other. All such distinctions are merely 'apparent' in themselves, for in 'reality', existence is just one and gradated.[12] All manifested existence emanates from the mind of God and is encompassed by it; manifested existence is the result of the realisation of the content of His mind in a causative scheme in which the effect is nothing more than the expression of its cause.[13] Existence is gradated in a hierarchy in which lower gradations are the effects of higher gradations. Successive levels of gradations in descending order have greater privation of existence, the lowest being this realm of corporeality wherein forms manifest with matter and hence have potentiality to grow.[14] Thus, there is incessant motion in the realm of corporeality in which all entities that descended and manifested via causation therein begin to actualise their latent potentials and reascend to

11 Seyyed Hossein Nasr, 'Mullā Ṣadrā: His Teachings', in *History of Islamic Philosophy*, ed. Seyyed Hossein Nasr and Oliver Leaman (London and New York: Routledge, 2003), 643–48.

12 Fazlur Rahman, *The Philosophy of Mullā Ṣadrā (Ṣadr al-Dīn al-Shirāzī)* (Albany: SUNY, 1975), 37–41, 141–42.

13 See Muḥammad Ḥusayn Ṭabāṭabāʾī, *The Elements of Islamic Metaphysics* (London: ICAS Press, 2003), 70–71; Mullā Ṣadrā, *The Wisdom of the Throne: An Introduction to the Philosophy of Mulla Ṣadrā*, trans. James Winston Morris (Princeton: Princeton University Press, 1981), 74.

14 See Mahdi Dehbashi, *Transubstantial Motion and the Natural World: With a Translation of Volume III, Stage 7, Chapters 18–32 of the* Asfar *of Mulla Sadra* (London: ICAS Press, 2010), 33–34; Sajjad H. Rizvi, *Mullā Ṣadrā and Metaphysics: Modulation of Being* (Oxon: Routledge, 2013), 45–46. It should be noted that the philosophical notion of prime matter is the outcome of logical deliberation and merely signifies the hypothetical gradation of pure potentiality and non-existence, or the gradation in which there is the absolute privation of all existence. See William C. Chittick, *The Heart of Islamic Philosophy: The Quest for Self-Knowledge in the Teachings of Afḍal al-Dīn Kāshānī* (New York: Oxford University Press, 2001), 91, 93.

their point of origin by the attainment of greater degrees of existence.[15] Based on the understanding that effects are merely the expressions of the proximate and ultimate causes, Ṣadrā's notion of motion towards completion assumes a state of self-awareness enjoyed by all existent entities: all things are self-aware by virtue of sharing in God's existence and yearn constantly to re-join their origin.[16] This existential yearning is the cause for the incessant motion towards completion.[17]

The notion of existent entities being vested with potential and motion towards actualisation implies that an inherent telos resides within each of them driving each along its trajectory of completion. Furthermore, since life and self-awareness are concomitants of existence qua existence, it follows that things move towards their completion consciously; hence, this consciousness is either 'essential', as in the case of human and animal souls, or 'accidental', as in the case of minerals.[18] Therefore, the source of dynamism in existence is the inherent telos embedded within existence; in other words, its source is from within as opposed to without.

The next section discusses the existential nature of the freedoms of thought and expression.

2. The Existential Nature of the Freedoms of Thought and Expression

According to Ṣadrā, the human soul is bodily in its origination and spiritual in its subsistence. The soul is an incorporeal substance in itself, yet due to its connection with a body, it is subject to motion and growth. The soul enables and facilitates the evolutionary growth of its corporeal material constitution. It gives things their forms, and enables and facilitates their motion and growth from a state of potentiality to actuality; without it, things would not have forms, nor would they move and grow. For the duration the soul supplies the forms of things and facilitates their motion and growth, it is subject to motion and growth itself. This motion and growth of the soul is also evolutionary insofar

15 Mullā Ṣadrā, *Divine Manifestations: Concerning the Secrets of the Perfecting Sciences*, trans. Fazel Asadi Amjad and Mahdi Dasht Bozorgi (London: ICAS Press, 2010), 83.

16 Rizvi, *Mullā Ṣadrā and Metaphysics*, 84–85.

17 Mullā Ṣadrā, *The Elixir of the Gnostics*, trans. William. C. Chittick (Provo: Brigham Young University Press, 2003), xxix–xxx.

18 Rahman, *The Philosophy of Mullā Ṣadrā*, 200–202.

as it is moving continually from a state of potentiality to actuality. The fact that entities move and grow towards their objective, actualising their inherent potential, in a direct and consciously driven manner, is indicative of the existence of their souls and their innate telos. The objective towards which the human soul is moving and growing incessantly, unlike its bodily locus, is the completion of itself by the expansion and internalisation of knowledge.[19] This is true for all human souls irrespective of the soteriological issue of salvation and damnation. Therefore, every soul naturally wishes to complete itself by acquiring knowledge, for the desire to acquire the knowledge of the nature of things is an integral feature of the soul's inbuilt teleology.

As mentioned, the process of completion entails, as a general rule, the constant departure from former restrictive forms and the emergence of newer ones, and the human soul is no different in this respect to other evolving existent entities: its forms are constantly being renewed, reformed and modified. Hence, in the domain of knowledge, the soul continuously endeavours to build upon its knowledge base as part of its process of self-actualisation. This self-actualisation, which includes the renewal, reformulation and modification of knowledge, necessitates the soul be in a state of freedom to learn, encounter and entertain newer ideas. The process of learning entails both the soul's critique and often rejection of its own established ideas and beliefs, and its freedom to challenge the ideas, beliefs and norms of the status quo, which it views as being restrictive, by appropriate and effective means of expression.

Human history is a testament to the innate telos of growth within the soul. Human thought and consciousness have evolved by the process of challenging, renewing, reformulating and modifying the ideas, beliefs and norms of the status quo continually. The result has been paradigm shifts in all domains of knowledge, rights, modes of governance, socio-economic systems and technology. At every stage of human development, human thought has undergone constant revision and refinement resulting in either the abandonment of ineffective systems and regulations or their optimalisation by modifying them. The Qur'an often references the restrictive systems, beliefs and practices of the pagans and invites its audience to reflect upon them and review whether they make sense, that is, whether they are rational and moral.[20]

Of course, the assessment of pagan cultures and theologies, as exhorted to by the Qur'an, was to be carried out both in terms of their internal logic and

19 Ibid., 195–200, 202–6.

20 See notes 6 and 7.

coherency, and their effectuality.[21] The content of the Qur'an critiquing the status quo and inviting its audience to ponder and challenge its foundations, beliefs and norms presupposes the freedom of expression, albeit on the part of the divine agencies, and the freedom of thought of its audience, that is, their right to exercise thought freely. During the Meccan period of the revelatory era, the Qur'an affirms the effectivity of its approach of rationally challenging and changing the status quo thus: 'he [the Prophet] lifts the burden off your shoulders and unshackles you'.[22]

In view of the above, it is clear that the freedoms of thought and expression are existential. This is because they are fundamental prerequisites for growth in the domain of human knowledge, which means they are essential in facilitating the actualisation of the telos of growth innate in humankind. Therefore, a successful system of governance in essence is not only one that champions the freedom of thought and defines the appropriate degree of the freedom of expression, but one that encourages the active removal of ignorance. This conclusion raises several issues, such as the detrimental effects of the freedom of thought to the growth of humans incapable of discerning the accuracy of their thoughts vis-à-vis the information they encounter. A possible recent example is the anti-vaccination campaigns against the COVID-19 vaccine.[23] Similarly, the absolute freedom of expression (of one's thoughts) can be disruptive and detrimental both to the individual and collectivity. Examples include conspiracy theories and radical ideas potentially leading to extremism. Such problems pertain to existential limitations, such as the lack of aptitude in discerning things accurately or the susceptibility of the human mind to believe misinformation. However, they do not contravene the thesis that the freedoms of thought and expression are absolute existential prerequisites essential for the growth of humankind via knowledge. Thus, it is undeniable that limits have to be placed on the freedoms of thought and expression due to existential limitations, such as those mentioned above.[24] The extent of the limitations are determined by the degree of rational and moral growth of the collectivity, that is, they are contextual and not essential. The freedom of thought can only be limited

---

21 See notes 6 and 7.

22 Qur'an 7:157.

23 Usha M. Rodrigues and Jian Xu, 'Regulation of COVID-19 Fake News Infodemic in China and India', *Media International Australia* 177, no. 1 (2020): 125–31.

24 Daniel Overgaauw, 'The Paradoxes of Liberty: The Freedom of Speech (Re-)considered', *Amsterdam Law Forum* 2 (2009): 27–28.

indirectly by restricting access to certain information, for it is not possible to bar humans from thinking and holding personal opinions. As for the freedom of expression, every collectivity will define its limits in accordance with the existential aptitudes of its individuals, which are continually evolving, and with a view to facilitating their growth. The freedom of expression should never be limited to the degree that the expression of certain ideas is barred from being discussed absolutely, that is, in every conceivable context, for then they cannot be proven to be defective or effective. Moreover, any form of unconditional restraint or coercion of rational thought will be defied by the soul and ultimately proven to be counterproductive, for to limit the application of human reason absolutely contravenes the natural disposition of the soul.[25] The most effective form of restraint is the restraint that is wilful and maximises freedom. This will be discussed in the forthcoming sections.

It should be noted that the epistemic distinction between statements of fact and value, and the problem of the unbridgeable gap between the two, is premised on the assumption that either existence qua existence is value-less in itself or that there is a fundamental epistemological doubt as to whether existence qua existence has any value. However, the problem of the fact-value distinction ceases to be relevant, significant and even operative when existence qua existence is assumed to be conscious, dynamic and evolving. This is because existence qua existence is then unitive, self-manifesting and self-actualising, which means it is simultaneously 'being' and 'becoming', the implication of which is that 'fact' is 'value laden' inherently.[26]

Moreover, the fact that things are evolving by virtue of the innate telos of growth means that evolution is the nature of things and that things naturally evolve so long as they are allowed to do so. In the human domain, where there is a multiplicity of possible actions in any given moment, and where will and freedom of choice are functional, every possible action will differ with respect

25 For references to the defiant and disobedient tendency of the soul, see Qur'an 4:14, 33:36 and 72:23.

26 For a substantive and philosophically rigorous treatment of the problems of the assumptions underlying the fact/value dichotomy (such as the analytic/synthetic proposition dualism), see Hilary Putnam, *The Collapse of the Fact/Value Dichotomy and Other Essays* (Cambridge, MA: Harvard University Press, 2002), 7–45. It should be noted that from the time of Aristotle until Hume, most philosophers thought that 'fact' being 'value laden' was a given. Undoubtedly, the distinction is useful as a tool to aid philosophical understanding and inquiry. It was only in the twentieth century that it became established as an absolute dualism by the logical positivists. See ibid.

to the others in the degree to which it accommodates growth and evolution. Hence, questions of 'ought' become pertinent for humans, for they are able to distinguish between different courses of action and determine which course of action 'ought' to be taken on the basis of which accommodates growth the most.[27] In light of the dynamic nature of existence and its perpetual growth, the knowledge of the value of things in relation to humans, and the statuses of actions based on that knowledge, is in a state of flux.[28] It is possible for humans to know the value of things in relation to themselves, and the statuses of actions based on that knowledge, in and for a particular existential context infallibly, that is, such knowledge may be 'correct' and 'best' in and for a particular context, and hence, it may be termed as being 'contextually infallible'; however, beyond the immediate context, all such knowledge is to be designated as 'fallible' in itself, for such knowledge always carries the possibility of not being 'correct' and 'best' in and for other contexts.[29] The notions of the 'infallibility' and 'fallibility' of such knowledge, and the statuses of actions based on that knowledge, will be discussed in the following sections. In view of this (that is, the ability of humans to know the value of things in relation to themselves in any given context, and the fact that everything is in flux) and the fact that human knowledge is subject to expansion in accordance with the telos of growth innate in existence, humans have the capacity to review and revise their knowledge. This capacity for revision is a manifestation of an inbuilt mechanism of self-rectification within existence, which is itself a necessary concomitant of the telos of growth.[30] Thus, even though humans are bound to

---

27 Of course, the question of what constitutes substantial growth and the actualisation of the rational and moral potential innate in humans needs to be delineated; however, it is beyond the remit of this paper to discuss this issue.

28 For more information on the dynamic nature of existence, see Abdul Hussain, 'The Conflict between the Actual and Apparent Regulations – Part 2', 3–13. The phrase 'the status of actions' refers to the five types of normative regulations (*aḥkām taklīfiyya*): the obligatory (*wājib*), the encouraged (*mustaḥabb*), the permissible (*mubāḥ*), the discouraged (*makrūh*) and the prohibited (*ḥarām*). See Muḥammad Bāqir Ṣadr, *Durūs fī 'ilm al-uṣūl* (Qom: Markaz al-Abḥāth wa-l-Dirāsāt al-Takhaṣṣuṣiyya li-l-Shahīd al-Ṣadr, 2005), 1:65.

29 See Abdul Hussain, 'The Conflict between the Actual and Apparent Regulations – Part 2', 13–25.

30 The following is an explanation of how the 'inbuilt mechanism of self-rectification within existence' is 'a necessary concomitant of the telos of growth': The existential property and telos of growth means that existence is continually negating and liberating itself from its current states and forms, which are restrictive and limiting in and of themselves, and consequently manifesting newer ones. In other words, existence is

get things wrong, they will inevitably tweak their understanding and acquire a more accurate course.

Since there is a constant change in human aptitudes resulting from growth and evolution, the designation of infallibility can never be ascribed to any form of governance or system of rights absolutely.[31] The fallibilism of all inductive-based human knowledge of regulations, rights, duties and freedoms is a concomitant of the growth process, for human endeavour is in itself to struggle ceaselessly to arrive at the optimal state.[32] Furthermore, since the discourse on rights is predicated on the existential principle of justice, which postulates that justice is to give everything its rightful due in accordance with its existential aptitude, it is not possible for any system of rights to be optimal indefinitely, that is, beyond its own existential context, given that perpetual growth is a property of existence.[33] Thus, fallibilism is a property of all inductive-based knowledge of regulations, rights, duties and freedoms, and as such, it cannot be circumvented. Therefore, in light of the evolutionary nature of existence, the meta-norms to be abided by during the formulation of regulations, rights, duties and freedoms include:

- The principle of justice, which asserts that everything be given its rightful due.

constantly revising and updating itself so that previous forms are modified, and their limitations and defects are rectified.

31 This is because both the form of governance and the degree to which rights are limited and granted is contingent upon existential aptitudes of individuals and their collectivities.

32 The following is an explanation of how 'the fallibilism of all inductive-based human knowledge of regulations, rights, duties and freedoms is a concomitant of the growth process': Since things, contexts and aptitudes are in perpetual flux, the knowledge of regulations, rights, duties and freedoms also fluctuate in accordance with the changes of the statuses of things in relation to humans, and changes in contexts and aptitudes. This means it is possible for any given inductive-based formulation of a regulation, right, duty or freedom to be 'contextually infallible'; however, in essence, that is, in itself, it will always be fallible. Hence the existential property of growth necessitates that all inductive-based formulations of regulations, rights, duties and freedoms are 'essentially' fallible. For more information on the fallibility and 'no finality' of any type of regulative formation, see lectures 7 and 8 in Abdul Hussain, *Islam and God-Centricity*.

33 The following is the reasoning for this: (1) Rights are formulated on the basis of the principle of justice. (2) Justice is to give everything its rightful due in accordance with their existential aptitudes. (3) Existential aptitudes are subject to perpetual flux. (4) Therefore, justice demands that rights fluctuate in accordance with changes in existential aptitudes

- The removal of restrictions as per the existential context, resulting in the increase of freedoms, which is a necessary prerequisite for the actualisation of the existential telos of growth.

The next section addresses the question of whether sacred teachings can be subject to evaluation and critique. As stated above, Islam liberated its initial audience by questioning the logic of the theologies and norms of the status quo in its own existential context. However, can its own teachings – be they in the form of the revelation or the broader Sharīʿa which includes the Sunna – be subject to the same scrutiny? This question, which the next section addresses, is difficult for Muslims to entertain because the Qur'an is the Word of God, that is, it is the Word of the One who has complete knowledge of all things and communicates guidance accordingly and truthfully, and the Prophet is divinely inspired and protected from making mistakes when providing the exegeses of the theology and normativity of the Qur'an.

3. Sacred Space and the Freedoms of Thought and Expression

In essence, religion (*dīn*) is God-orientation by wilfully surrendering to Him (*islām*), according to the Qur'an.[34] The end of religion is the completion of the soul, that is, a soul in which godliness culminates, and it is the outcome of personal reflection, purification, devotion and surrender.[35] The Qur'an detests blind imitation of the practices and beliefs of one's collectivity, and constantly exhorts critical evaluation; hence, it asserts non-coercion as the fundamental norm vis-à-vis one's religion.[36] Individuals are expected to evaluate religious teachings critically prior to embracing Islam. This is the import of many of its verses, such as, 'And if We had so willed, We could have given every soul its guidance.'[37] The Qur'an emphasises non-coercion in religion because any form of coercion in the domain of belief is counterproductive ultimately; it is not possible for a coerced soul to yield to God, which is contrary to His objective.

34 For instance, see Qur'an 2:211–12 and 4:123–25.

35 For instance, see Qur'an 50:31–33, 79:40–41, 89:27–30 and 91:1–9.

36 For instance, see Qur'an 2:170, 7:172–73, 31:21, 34:43 and 43:22–25 for references to forefathers, and Qur'an 2:256, 185, 4:28, 5:6 and 22:78 for references to the norm of 'non-coercion'. See notes 6 and 7 for Qur'anic references exhorting critical evaluation.

37 Qur'an 32:13.

Therefore, Islam cannot be accepted and efficacious as a religion without some form of prior understanding of its content and the individual's attestation to it rationally, all of which presupposes the freedom of thought.

However, since the religion of Islam is based upon the final communication of God and its divinely inspired exegeses in the actions, speech and instructions of the Prophet, the individual immediately adopts the attitude of its sacredness and infallibility. Such an assumption renders the freedom to critique its content problematic, for the very act of engaging in such activity contravenes the premise that God knows what is best for all humankind and has conveyed it in His final communication and the person of the Prophet (that is, in the bodily actions and interactions, the morality, and the spirituality of the Prophet); in other words, critiquing the religion of Islam is tantamount to the rejection of the thesis of the 'finality' of the Qur'an and Sunna.[38] Therefore, the freedom of thought is curtailed to confirming the content of religion prior to accepting it; thereafter, the freedom to critique its content and express contrary religious beliefs is generally meaningless for the insider, that is, one who is part of the 'faithful'.

That said, the faithful have the right to exercise the freedoms of thought and expression in the domain of the human interpretations of the regulations of the Sharīʿa. This is because such critique is not of the Sharīʿa per se; rather it pertains to its exegeses, understandings and interpretations, which are the products of non-divinely inspired minds. An example of this is the regulation of apostasy.[39] It can be dismissed legitimately because the Qur'an does not make any reference to it and the *ḥadīth* literature is inconclusive and in opposition to the Qur'anic principle of non-coercion.[40] Similarly, it is permissible for the insider to critique the theological understandings of the texts of the Sharīʿa on the basis that they are human interpretations of texts sufficiently ambiguous to allow for plurality. The right to critique also extends to political systems of governance and socio-economic models founded on the interpretations of the texts of the Sharīʿa.

38 For information on the significance of the notion of 'finality', especially regarding the regulations of the Qur'an and Sharīʿa, see lectures 7 and 8 in Abdul Hussain, *Islam and God-Centricity*.

39 For instance, see the jurisprudential (*fiqhī*) discourse on apostacy in Muḥammad Ḥasan Najafī, *Jawāhir al-kalām fī sharāʾiʿ al-Islām* (Qom: Mu'assasat al-Nashr al-Islāmī, 2012), 42:946–95.

40 For *ḥadīth* literature, see ibid.

However, the Qur'an and *ḥadīth* literature have normative texts that by today's standards are either non-egalitarian, such as those pertaining to the rights of women and those inconsistent with human rights generally (for instance, those pertaining to slavery), or they are inhumane, such as those texts prescribing draconian punishments.[41] Here, the issue is not one of interpretation per se; rather it is with the Qur'anic regulations themselves; for while Qur'anic theology (for example, the events of the hereafter and the nature of God and creation) can be philosophised over and made sense of, and ultimately accepted as infallible due to the superior knowledge of God, the same cannot be said of Sharīʿa regulations or rights derived from the Qur'an directly, irrespective of whether the regulations are devotional or societal. To elaborate, theological doctrine, such as the nature of God and human purpose, is theoretical, which means its objective is merely to reiterate truths and emphasise the necessity of self-actualising the potential within and liberating oneself from restrictions. Thus, the theological teachings of the Sharīʿa are universal, essential and stable. However, the same is not true of Sharīʿa regulations because they are concrete formulations facilitating the self-actualisation of the potential within individuals of a particular existential context.

Generally, it is assumed that Sharʿīa regulations facilitate the human soul's natural telos of growth towards completion. This understanding of the function of Sharīʿa regulations is implicit in the *ʿadliyya* notion of regulations having intrinsic value.[42] Additionally, the context-based manner in which the revelation supplied and modified regulations for its immediate audience, as evinced by the chronological reading of the Qur'an, attests to the fact that regulations were prescribed and instituted in accordance with the degree of growth of the individual and collectivity, and the demands of the existential context.[43] The implication of this – that is, the fact that regulations are contingent upon the degree of growth of the individual and collectivity, and the demands of the existential context – is that regulations are subject to change, and hence in need of constant scrutiny. However, since the notions of 'infallibility' and 'finality'

41 For instance, see Qur'an 4:34, 5:38 and 70:29–31.

42 See Arif Abdul Hussain, 'The Conflict between the Actual and Apparent Regulations – Part 1: The Theoretical Foundations of *Uṣūl al-Fiqh* and the *Uṣūlī* Resolutions', Shaykh Arif, www.shaykharif.com/the-conflict-between-the-actual-and-apparent-regulations, 1–4. The term *ʿadliyya* refers to the Shīʿī Imāmī school of theology and jurisprudence (*uṣūl al-fiqh*) due to the tenet of 'the justice of God' being the defining feature distinguishing it from other schools.

43 See Abdul Hussain, 'A Functional Interpretation of *Zakāt*'.

have been ascribed to Sharīʿa regulations due to their being formulations of Qur'anic and Prophetic prescriptions, the ethos of critiquing regulations with the possibility of revising them has become a sacrilegious act. It should be noted that the application of the notion of 'finality' to Sharīʿa regulations derived from Qur'anic and Prophetic prescriptions is premised on an ontology that is stable, that is, the nature of existence is static, fixed and immutable, which means that regulations based on the knowledge of the relations of things to humans in the mind God are also static, fixed, immutable and eternal.[44] The natural consequence of this is that regulations derived from Sharīʿa texts based on the conventional/literal meaning of the texts (*aṣālat al-ẓuhūr*) are assumed to be *eternally* efficacious in facilitating the human growth process.[45] In other words, the existential telos of growth responsible for evolutionary motion of humans towards their completion is to be facilitated by unchanging regulations despite the ever-changing existential aptitudes and contexts of humans.

Of course, this opposes the fact that existence is evolutionary at the level of the corporeal world, and normativity is contingent upon the existential growth and contexts of humans. The phenomena of successive Sharīʿas superseding earlier ones throughout history and the process of Qur'anic abrogation presuppose the evolutionary nature of existence, and the contingency of normativity upon human existential aptitudes and contexts that are always changing.[46] The different revelations of God are in conformity about the nature of God, the necessity of acquiring virtues and the prescription to establish justice by giving everything its rightful due; they only differ in their formulations of what constitutes justice and how to attain virtues on account of their differing existential contexts and the different existential aptitudes of their respective audiences (that is, their respective regulative formulations differ because of the different degrees of growth of peoples of different times and places). The chronological reading of the Qur'an is a testament to the reformulation of norms as and when the existential aptitudes of the faithful increased and circumstances changed.[47]

To state that the unambiguous regulations stemming from the Sharīʿa of the Prophet Muḥammad in seventh-century Arabia can be critiqued and revised is an audacious claim, for it grants primacy to human understanding, assumes

44 See Abdul Hussain, 'The Conflict between the Actual and Apparent Regulations – Part 2', 1–6.

45 Ibid., 3–6, 14–18.

46 Ibid., 5; see also note 6 in ibid.

47 See Abdul Hussain, 'A Functional Interpretation of *Zakāt*'.

reason can abrogate 'Sharīʿa' regulations and hence seems to be challenging the wisdom of God. In order to make sense of this, a prelude is necessary on the nature of normativity generally.

Based on the Ṣadrian notion of substantive motion, all things have an inherent telos of growth driving them towards their completion, as stated previously.[48] Completion is a progressive process in which the potentiality innate in things is actualised gradually.[49] From this, it is surmised that the purpose of normativity is to assist humans in their growth process. Hence, regulations are relevant so long as they are effective in facilitating the attainment of the existential telos of growth, which means normativity is subordinate to existence.[50] Therefore, since normativity is contingent upon human existential aptitudes and contexts, and since the latter are subject to continual change, then the former is also subject to perpetual flux. A corollary of this – that is, the fact that normativity is contingent upon fluctuating human aptitudes – is that normativity itself is on an evolutionary trajectory, which means greater levels of rights and responsibilities are to be afforded to humankind as and when there is growth.[51]

In view of this, the assumption of the Sharīʿa being a stable, fixed and an unchanging normative system of regulative forms is erroneous.[52] As alluded to previously, flux in normativity is evident throughout the Meccan and Medinan periods of the revelatory era as attested to by the chronological reading of regulations of the Qur'an. Just as the evolution and flux in normativity occurring throughout the revelatory era is due to its contingency upon the changing existential aptitudes and contexts of the Prophet Muḥammad and his followers, the same is true of normativity beyond the revelatory period; in other words, it follows suit and does not cease being contingent upon existence. It should be noted that meta-norms, such as the principle of justice and the protocol of removing restrictions as per the existential context, are fixed, stable and eternal; collectively, such meta-norms constitute the means of furthering moral and rational growth in an evolutionary scheme.

---

48 Sayeh Meisami, *Mulla Sadra* (New York: Oneworld, 2013), 75–76.

49 Ibid.

50 See Abdul Hussain, 'The Conflict between the Actual and Apparent Regulations – Part 2', 9–10.

51 This is because as humankind becomes increasingly more rational and moral as a result of the existential telos of growth, it will warrant the bestowal of more freedoms and rights, which will itself be the means to further growth.

52 See Abdul Hussain, 'The Conflict between the Actual and Apparent Regulations – Part 2', 3–14.

The contingency of normativity to existence means that 'no finality' and 'fallibility' are essential properties of regulative forms in and of themselves, that is, taken in isolation of their immediate existential contexts or those similar to them. Consequently, the optimality and infallibility of the regulative forms of the Sharīʿa, derived from the words of the Qur'an and Prophet delivered at and for a particular point in time, are confined to their original context, for 'eternality' (or 'finality') cannot be ascribed to any regulative form in an evolutionary ontology. In other words, the 'optimality' and 'infallibility' ascribed to regulative forms are contextual and relative. It should be noted that the ascription of the notion of 'infallibility' to a regulation simply means that a regulation is universalizable to a particular existential context should it reoccur in history (that is, in different times and places) and the most appropriate and optimal in facilitating the growth of the individuals and collectivities of that context (that is, given the existential limitations of the individuals, collectivities and context). This does not preclude the fact that optimal regulations may be subject to abuse or that they may have loopholes; rather 'infallibility' means that a regulation is congruent with a particular existential context and the existential aptitudes of the individuals and collectivities of that context, and hence optimal in facilitating their growth.[53] To reiterate, the infallibility of a regulation lies in its being 'the most appropriate' and 'optimal' for the people of a particular time and place and nothing more. Hence, regulations are infallible contextually and relatively, but fallible essentially.[54] Therefore, since 'no finality' and 'fallibility' are among the essential properties of all regulative forms including those of the Sharīʿa, regulative forms are in need of constant scrutiny and revision as and when necessary to ensure they are optimal, and the only means of scrutinising and revising regulations in the absence of revelation is the faculty of reason.

The root of the problem is the assumption that the Sharīʿa is an independent body of normativity, and its texts (namely, the Qur'an and *ḥadīth* literature) are

53 For more information on the notions of regulative 'fallibilism' and 'infallibilism', see Abdul Hussain, 'The Conflict between the Actual and Apparent Regulations – Part 1', 17–20; Abdul Hussain, 'The Conflict between the Actual and Apparent Regulations – Part 2', 21–25.

54 Despite the theoretical possibility of the formulations of regulations, rights and freedoms being 'contextually infallible', one can only ever be confident in ascribing the regulations of the Qur'an and the Prophet as 'contextually infallible'; the regulations of all other contexts will be ascribed with the expressions of 'most appropriate' and 'optimal' alone, and not 'infallibility', due to the fact that every regulation (in itself) is essentially 'fallible'.

independent epistemic sources of normativity.[55] In reality, the Sharīʿa was the most appropriate and optimal body of regulations for a particular existential context only, and its texts were sources prescribing the most appropriate and optimal regulations for the audience of that context.[56] Since the texts of the Sharīʿa were the sources of normativity for a particular existential context in accordance with the existential property and telos of growth, it follows that they and the Sharīʿa itself are subordinate to the existential property and telos of growth. In fact, all just regulative forms, religious or otherwise, are contextualised renderings of particular essences of growth.[57] These regulative essences are thus contained within them (that is, within the regulative forms), and hence are extractable and re-formulable.[58] They are universal, and hence 'no finality' is their essential property.[59] Furthermore, since the confirmation and acceptance of the just-ness and optimality of the Sharīʿa regulations of the Qur'an and the Prophet by their audience was contingent upon the faculty of reason, the initial formulation of the Sharīʿa regulations themselves, albeit by the divine agencies and/or the Prophet, had to be based on a rational assessment of the existential context and aptitudes of the people it was addressing.[60] Thus, those Sharīʿa regulations were rational and moral, and hence the 'most appropriate' and 'optimal', in and for their own context. Consequently, it would not have been possible for an insider to challenge them in their own context on the basis of reason, morality, appropriateness and optimality. However, beyond their context, all such Sharīʿa regulative forms can be critiqued by the faculty of reason legitimately as to whether they are still moral, appropriate and optimal in facilitating the growth of individuals and collectivities of other different existential contexts.

Despite the primacy of reason, it must be admitted that the human soul is unable to have knowledge of material entities qua physical phenomena absolutely. Its knowledge of such things is limited, contextual, relative and

55 Noel J. Coulson, *A History of Islamic Law* (Edinburgh: Edinburgh University Press, 2004), 2, 55–58.

56 See Abdul Hussain, 'The Conflict between the Actual and Apparent Regulations – Part 2', 7–10.

57 See lecture 9 in Abdul Hussain, *Islam and God-Centricity*.

58 See Abdul Hussain, 'The Conflict between the Actual and Apparent Regulations – Part 2', 16.

59 Ibid.

60 For instance, see Qur'an 6:151–53.

predicated upon assumptions.[61] This is evinced by the paradigm shifts in science.[62] An indefinite period of time would be necessary for the faculty of reason to understand the nature of physical existence absolutely and that too assumes that the physical aspect of reality has a fixed nature. However, if physical existence is assumed to be conscious, not subject to any coercion, and hence able to behave when and how it chooses, then to understand its nature accurately, let alone absolutely, is an impossible task altogether. Yet despite human knowledge of physical phenomena being limited, the faculty of reason has been very efficacious in enabling humankind to (a) create crafts traversing the far regions of the solar system and (b) predict many future occurrences of natural phenomena correctly. Humankind has been able to do this due to reason's accurate appreciation of the stable workings of nature albeit within limited contexts. Similarly, the faculty of reason has always had the capacity to distinguish between societal regulations that are growth promoting in any given existential context and those that are not. In today's existential context, slavery, concubinage, child marriages and wife-beating are inconsistent with human rights, and the unequal share of inheritance for women in collectivities in which the woman is an equal contributor to the family and society (that is, the woman contributes to the same degree fiscally as the man) is unjust. Similarly, modes of governance and socio-political systems that were efficacious in the past have been either modified or abolished because the faculty of reason judged them not to be the most appropriate and optimal for collectivities that had evolved beyond a particular degree of growth vis-à-vis their collective existential aptitude.[63]

---

61 Kwasi Wiredu, 'Knowledge, Truth and Fallibility', in *The Concept of Knowledge: The Ankara Seminar*, ed. Ioanna Kuçuradi and Robert S. Cohen (Dordrecht: Kluwer, 1995), 139–43.

62 Thomas S. Kuhn, *The Structure of Scientific Revolutions* (Chicago: The University of Chicago Press, 2012), 6–12.

63 The following should be noted vis-à-vis the existential nature of the hermeneutical tools of *binā' al-ʿuqalā'* (the convention of wise/rational people) and *ʿurf* (local convention and custom) in post-Anṣārī *uṣūl al-fiqh*: The *ʿadliyya* presupposes that Sharīʿa regulations are value based, that is, the values innate in such regulations are rationally discernible in principle. This position is encapsulated in the school's famous dictum, 'whatever is dictated by the faculty of reason is dictated by the Sharīʿa, and whatever is dictated by the Sharīʿa is dictated by the faculty of reason'. In practice, however, the role of the faculty of reason is negligible beyond its assistance in extrapolating Sharīʿa regulations from religious texts, which comprise most regulations Muslims adhere to. This is because it is maintained that the faculty of reason cannot actually grasp the values

Since both existence and divine communications emanate from One Source,

innate in Sharīʿa regulations due to its incapacity to fully appreciate the values entailed within *God's* regulations which He has formulated based on His unlimited knowledge as 'the Lawgiver'. Thus, aside from it being able to understand a few universal moral statements independently of the Sharīʿa, such as 'justice is good' and 'oppression is reprehensible', reason as a faculty of the soul is subordinate to and dependent upon the religious texts of the Sharīʿa and their regulative formulations. Hence in *uṣūl al-fiqh*, the faculty of reason is a hermeneutic tool that is effectively limited to interpreting the religious texts of the Sharīʿa in practice.

As for the notion of *binā' al-ʿuqalā'* (the convention of wise/rational people), it includes the behaviours, judgements and conventions of rational people qua rational people, and hence it is not restricted to any particular locale, for the behaviours, judgements and conventions of rational people qua rational people are universalisable spatially at the very least if not temporally (since such conventions result from rational perspectives shared by rational agents). However, in view of the aforementioned deliberations on the limited scope of the role of the faculty of reason in *uṣūl al-fiqh*, rational convention (*binā' al-ʿuqalā'*) functions as a disclosive tool in relation to pre-existing Sharīʿa regulations at most. In other words, rational convention can give a sense of what the Sharīʿa regulation was or is; however, it cannot initiate a novel Sharīʿa regulation.

As for the notion of *ʿurf* (local convention and custom), it includes the behaviours, judgements and conventions of local people qua local people, and hence they are not usually universalisable. This means the *ʿurf* (convention) of any given locale will almost certainly be unique to the culture of that locale and not others, and hence it will have the sense of being *prima facie* arbitrary and non-rational. In *uṣūl al-fiqh*, the role of the *ʿurf* (convention) of any given locale is subordinate to and dependent upon the religious texts of the Sharīʿa and their regulative formulations. If the notion of *ʿurf* qua convention is extended to include the knowledge-based understandings of the natural and social sciences, it may be possible to argue that it can define/stipulate the subject (*mawḍūʿ*) of certain pre-existing Sharīʿa regulations at most; for instance, current medical convention may define the status of being pregnant contrary to how it was defined previously. However, even *ʿurf* in this extended sense cannot formulate regulations independently of the religious texts of the Sharīʿa without recourse to further argumentation. According to the existential framework, the faculty of reason, together with the faculty of intuition, is a hermeneutical tool for understanding existence itself. Hence, in addition to understanding reality qua natural, social and intellectual sciences, it is able to extrapolate the essences of regulations and formulate new regulations independently of the religious texts of the Sharīʿa within the domain of societal regulations. With regards to *ʿurf* (local convention and custom), the existential framework posits that all such seemingly arbitrary and non-rational conventions and customs have emerged as a result of the response of the faculty of reason to temporal factors, such as socio-economical, climatical and geographical. Therefore, it considers both *binā' al-ʿuqalā'* (the convention of wise/rational people) and *ʿurf* (local convention and custom) to be like non-devotional Sharīʿa regulations: they are all instances of interpretations of the relations between human beings and things in light of the existential property of growth in particular contexts.

namely God, it is understood that the divine communications are mirrors reflecting existence to the faculty of reason in order to prompt it (reason) to facilitate the soul's awakening to its faculty of intuition.[64] Based on this, Ṣadrā asserts that revelation, the soul's faculty of mystical intuition, and the soul's faculty of reason are aligned vis-à-vis their respective knowledge.[65] Revelation is the most superior mode of knowledge, followed by illuminative intuition, and finally the judgements of reason.[66] He employs the word *revelation* mainly in the sense of the Sharī'a, which is the body of knowledge crystallised in the divine communication and the teachings of the infallible, as opposed to a mode of knowledge. He uses the phrase *illuminative intuition* to refer to the 'presential knowledge' (*al-'ilm al-ḥuḍūrī*) of the faculty of intuition that mystics awaken to by the process of purifying the soul. Finally, he understands the faculty of reason to be a tool for rational deductions and the expression of knowledge as facts and norms, which is in line with Ibn Sīnā's conception of human reason.[67] Undoubtedly, Ṣadrā would concur that all Sharī'a regulations must of necessity be rational and hence understandable and affirmable by the faculty of reason; however, he dedicated his scholastic career to the formulation of arguments for higher truths, such as the existence and nature of God, the nature and teleology of existence and the nature of eschatology and soteriology.[68] Hence, revelation as 'a body of knowledge' (rather than as a mode of knowledge) occupies the most superior position theologically and philosophically speaking because its Author is the Author of existence per se, it corroborates the Truth as it stands in itself most accurately and it informs of the details of the nature of many phenomena hitherto unknown.[69] Presential

Thus, according to the existential framework, all three – Sharī'a regulations, rational convention (*binā' al-'uqalā'*) and local convention (*'urf*) – emerge and are formulated on the basis of the existential property of growth, and as such they all can be said to be contextual interpretations of the status of existential growth in a given time and place. The author hopes to discuss these notions more fully in a subsequent treatise. For information on the notion of *binā' al-'uqalā'*, see Muḥammad Ṣanqūr 'Alī, *al-Mu'jam al-uṣūlī* (Qom: Dār al-Mujtabā, 2001), 639–44; and on the notion of *'urf*, see ibid., 752–61.

64 See Seyyed Hossein Nasr, *The Heart of Islam: Enduring Values for Humanity* (New York: HarperCollins, 2004), 12, 15.

65 Moris, *Revelation*, 174.

66 Ibid.

67 Ibid., 155, 168–70, 174–77.

68 Ibid., 75–81.

69 Examples of phenomena, the details of which were hitherto unknown, include the angels, jinn, the life prior to this one in the realm of spirits (*'ālam al-arwāḥ*), the Final

knowledge is received by the heart (*al-ʿaql al-kullī*) for it is a receptacle of the higher truths as they are.[70] There are degrees of presential knowledge due to its contingency upon the degree to which a soul has purified itself; hence, the manifestation of presential knowledge either as judgements of reason or as symbolic representations of the imaginative faculty (either in dreams or in visions during the waking state) are deemed to be limited.[71] Finally, the faculty of reason confirms and justifies revelatory knowledge and illuminative intuition at a philosophical level, and then expresses coherent arguments linguistically.[72]

It must be noted that the confirmational role of revelation qua Sharīʿa with respect to the knowledge of the faculty of intuition is restricted to the higher truths only, that is, revelation confirms the knowledge of the faculty of intuition regarding the higher truths only. Its confirmational role does not extend to intuitive knowledge about physical existence and normativity; in other words, revelation qua Sharīʿa does not confirm the insights of the faculty of intuition on the nature of the physical aspect of reality, such as those pertaining to the domain of sub-atomic particle physics, and all its normative insights, such as its ethical deliberations in the domain of AI. If the contrary were true (that is, if the confirmational role of revelation qua Sharīʿa did extend to intuitive knowledge about physical existence and normativity), there would be no value to the existence of the faculty of intuition and its insights beyond it confirming and being confirmed by revelation qua Sharīʿa. An implication of this is that there would not be any increase in knowledge beyond what is in the revelation qua Sharīʿa.[73] From the existential perspective (or in other words, given the unitive nature of existence and its telos of growth), the faculty of intuition functions, at a very basic level, as a receptor within the soul that is able to discern the factors of growth, and their contraries, prior to rational appraisal.[74] Hence, the revelation's methodology is one of questioning the minds of its audience.[75] The Qur'an questioned its audience frequently as to whether

Day and the hereafter.

70 See note 10.

71 Moris, *Revelation*, 159–63.

72 Ibid., 168–70, 174–77.

73 Here, 'revelation qua Sharīʿa' refers to the revealed and contextualised rendering of *al-kitāb al-mubīn* (the Clear Book), that is, the Qur'an, which obviously does not contain all facts and norms. In itself, *al-kitāb al-mubīn* is the overwhelming reality that does contain them all. For instance, see Qur'an 6:59, 12:1–2 and 43:1–4.

74 Moris, *Revelation*, 168–70, 174–77. See also Qur'an 91:1–9.

75 See note 5.

certain pagan beliefs and practices made sense and served any beneficial purpose.[76] Such questioning resonated with the audience and prompted them to reason with the issues raised. Here, intuitive knowledge is the immediate but unreasoned sense of knowing stemming from the existential level of the soul that is able to apprehend whether norms, regulations, duties and rights are growth promoting or not. Thereafter, the faculty of reason evaluates and confirms the validity or invalidity of a proposition constructed on the basis of that intuitive knowledge.[77] It should be noted that reason only entertains propositions resonating at an intuitive level, otherwise it does not generally.[78] Hence, when the Qur'an questioned certain pagan beliefs and practices, some of its listeners were prompted to think and subsequently verified its teachings, whereas others who rejected it were unable to provide counter-arguments.[79]

Furthermore, the Qur'an's methodology of questioning the minds of its audience about their beliefs and practices, and prompting them thereby to think, presupposes the principiality of the faculties of intuition and reason. This means the Sharīʿa never enjoyed primacy in the domains of normativity and rights because primacy belongs to moral intuition and reason in these domains. All it did was offer regulations that were moral, rational and in accordance with the existential contexts and aptitudes of its audience. In other words, it merely supplied the most appropriate and optimal regulations in and for the context of its audience based on the existential property and telos of growth. Therefore, since the domains of normativity and rights are governed by moral intuitions and reason-based analyses, essentially it is the role of their respective faculties (that is, of intuition and reason) to postulate regulations for any given context. In other words, the faculties of intuition and reason institute regulations in light of the particularities of the existential aptitudes and contexts of the individuals and collectivities they are legislating for. This means regulations pertaining to the same subject matter will differ for peoples

76 Moris, *Revelation*, 168–70, 174–77.

77 Ibid.

78 A patently absurd proposition, such as 'jumping from a height of fifty meters to the ground is a good form of exercise', would be deemed by intuition immediately to be false and unproductive. Hence, the faculty of reason would not entertain such a proposition unless it was necessary to demonstrate its absurdity.

79 Hence, the pagan Arabs resorted to name-calling and slandering; for example, see Qur'an 46:7–8, 52:29–30, 68:1–6, 69:40–43 and 74:24–25. The only justification offered by the pagan Arabs for the validity of their practices was that they were part of the tradition of their forefathers; see note 36 for references to Qur'anic verses.

of different times and places; hence, normativity is relative and contextual.[80] With growth in existential aptitudes and contexts, the optimality of current regulative forms will lessen, which will be detected by the faculty of intuition. Thereupon, it is the task of the faculty of reason to extrapolate the essences of the sub-optimal regulative forms and reformulate them into newer optimal forms.[81] As stated previously, the existential telos of evolutionary growth entails that regulations are fallible essentially, which means there has to be constant monitoring of regulative forms to ensure they are the most productive in facilitating the self-actualisation of the inherent potential within humankind.

Therefore, Sharīʿa regulations were formulated in and for the existential contexts and aptitudes of the followers of the Prophet in seventh-century Arabia, and hence certain regulative forms may have lost their efficacy in and for contexts that differ vastly, such as today's. Despite this, the essence of growth that the sub-optimal regulative forms sought to fashion endures and needs reformulation.[82]

In view of this prelude and the discussions preceding it, the following are the conclusions of this paper thus far:

- Essentially, the freedoms of thought and expression cannot be curtailed by the Sharīʿa.[83] Just as individuals are free to embrace the religion of Islam, so too are they free to leave it.

- There is no sacred space within the Sharīʿa that cannot be questioned, and as such, inquiries by insiders are not tantamount to the rejection of the Sharīʿa. The appropriate expression of differences must be accommodated, as will be explained in the final section, for it is the right of every believer to be able to express him or herself. This is because surrendering to God depends upon it being wholesome and wilful, and because the methodology of the Qur'an itself is to challenge and question. Individuals may wish to question, not question, express their understanding, or not to express it. This is entirely their prerogative.

---

80 See Abdul Hussain, 'The Conflict between the Actual and Apparent Regulations – Part 2', 7–9.

81 Ibid., 15–26.

82 Ibid.

83 For the notion of 'absolute individual freedom' in Islam and the Sharīʿa's role in facilitating it, see Mahmoud M. Taha, *The Second Message of Islam* (Syracuse: Syracuse University Press, 1996), 64–77.

- The faculties of intuition and reason have primacy in assessing and formulating normativity, and not the status quo in any of its many iterations. This does not mean all regulations and rights of the status quo must be abandoned; on the contrary, it simply means the faculties of intuition and reason are the assessors of the optimality of all regulative forms.

- Therefore, as a general rule, the governing system of any collectivity has to be open to appraisal and must cultivate an atmosphere of constant questioning and critique.

To reiterate, there is no sacred space lying beyond the freedoms of thought and expression. Thus, regulations curbing the freedoms of thought and expression – such as those of apostacy and blasphemy, and those removing individuals from the sphere of faith due to their interpretations of certain articles of faith deemed by the majority to be erroneous – have to be considered as either distortions of the Sharīʿa or as contextual impositions due to existential limitations. Having said this, there are differing degrees of aptitudes of individuals, and other societal considerations, within every collectivity warranting (a) the limitation of the freedom of thought by withholding access to information, and (b) the curtailment of the freedom of expression by criminalising certain expressions, both of which are necessary for the growth of the collectivity. The final section examines the existential dynamics within every collectivity necessitating the restriction of the freedoms of thought and expression, and whether it is possible to overcome them.

4. Contextual Limitations

The growth of humans is gradual, for it is subject to the existential property of growth according to which all things actualise their potential in an evolutionary manner. Based on this, one may extrapolate that the freedoms of thought and expression are contingent upon a certain degree of rational maturity, requiring training of the faculty of reason, its mandatory exposure to a base level of education and its acquaintance with societal cultures, norms, regulations and rights. Hence, individuals not having acquired that degree of rational maturity must have their freedom of thought curtailed by restricting access to knowledge, and thereby limiting their freedom of expression also. This seems to set the status quo beyond scrutiny, irrespective of whether it is religious, secular or a combination of both. However, it must be noted that the actualisation of rational maturity is itself contingent upon increasing the degree of the freedom of thought gradually during the training and education of the faculty of reason in accordance with what is just, equitable and optimal in facilitating the growth of individuals in any given collectivity.[84] Increasing the freedom of thought incrementally in this manner is true of all collectivities, even primitive ones, because both justice and optimality are understood intuitively and rationally by one and all as giving everything its rightful due in accordance with its existential aptitudes.

The freedom of thought is absolute in and of itself, whereas the freedom of expression is contingent upon the existential contexts and aptitudes of the individual and collectivity. The scope of the freedom of expression is limitable explicitly, and it is usually defined by and for a given collectivity, such as the specific legislation instituted for a people of a particular time and place penalising certain forms of hate speech.[85] In contrast, the scope of the freedom of thought is not limitable explicitly; it can only be curbed indirectly. However, both are principial essentially and fundamental existentially, for together they constitute the vehicle of growth of humankind; hence, they are both the means and markers of the growth of humankind.[86] The degree of their curtailment is based on the degree of growth of the existential aptitudes of the individual and collectivity, and the regulations curtailing them are formulated and enforced with a view to actualising the individual and collectivity further. The problems of drawing wrong conclusions, and the dissemination of inaccurate information, are plausible grounds for curtailing the scope of the freedom of thought by dissuasion, denying access to information and instituting punitive measures for expressing ideas detrimental to the harmony and cohesion of the collectivity and its individuals.[87] However, all such measures must be viewed as temporary until access to all the relevant information is made available. As for the freedom of expression, all speech compromising the safety of other individuals and/or their collectivities must be curtailed.[88]

---

84 For the importance of the freedoms of thought and expression in rational, moral, political and social education, see Ross Scanlan, 'Freedom, Knowledge, and Public Speaking', *Quarterly Journal of Speech* 35, no. 3 (1949): 313–14. See also Overgaauw, 'The Paradoxes of Liberty', 25–27.

85 Heyman, 'Righting the Balance', 1345.

86 Scanlan, 'Freedom, Knowledge, and Public Speaking', 313–14.

87 Heyman, 'Righting the Balance', 1329–44.

88 Jim Murdoch, *Freedom of Thought, Conscience and Religion: A Guide to the Implementa-*

It must be emphasised that granting the absolute freedom of thought and its expression to individuals and collectivities irrespective of their existential aptitudes (such as age, cognitive abilities and psychological experiences), by permitting access to all information, poses a serious threat to the growth of both. Indeed, history testifies to the wrongs committed by wayward ideologies being expressed and followed by individuals of collectivities en masse.[89] Such catastrophic moments in history are the unavoidable consequences of the fallibilism entailed within an evolutionary scheme so long as the danger of desiring growth outwardly and for the few, at the expense of growth inwardly (that is, moral and rational growth) and for all humankind, is an actualisable possibility.[90] However, given that the existential telos of humankind is to grow by actualising the potential inherent within itself, it has a self-correctional mechanism whereby it puts itself back on the trajectory of growth inevitably.[91] Nonetheless, in order to mitigate the possibility of the recurrence of such catastrophic events, the bestowal of the freedoms of thought and expression must be qualified in accordance with the existential aptitudes of individuals and their collectivities.

In view of today's existential context, which is termed 'the Information Age', Sharīʿa proscriptions attempting to curtail the freedoms of thought and expression of the faithful by designating certain genres of literature as 'books of misguidance' (*kutub ḍalāl*), or barring certain people from utilising public platforms to express their ideas, are counterproductive.[92] Today, people generally should be granted access to relevant information so that a culture of mature expression and exchanging of ideas is engendered throughout society. Only in extreme circumstances should access to literature be denied, such as when suitable platforms to present and discuss those ideas are not available. However, it must be reiterated that such restrictions must be viewed as momen-

tion of Article 9 of the European Convention on Human Rights (Strasbourg: Directorate General of Human Rights, Council of Europe, 2007), 26.

89 Onder Bakircioglu, 'Freedom of Expression and Hate Speech', *Tulsa Journal of Comparative and International Law* 16, no. 1 (2008): 2–3.

90 In other words, since it is not possible to restrict the private movement of thought inside the souls of people, humankind will continue to face such catastrophic events, until it realises a level of rational and moral maturity where the possibility of such occurrences being effected by the freedoms of thought and expression is nullified.

91 See note 30.

92 For arguments against censorship, see David O. Brink, 'Millian Principles, Freedom of Expression, and Hate Speech', *Legal Theory* 7, no. 2 (2001): 122–25.

tary measures, the implementation of which are necessary whilst accurate and researched information is made accessible, and suitable platforms created.

Aside from prescribing regulations, another method employed by the Qur'an to prevent thought from venturing into areas deemed to be dangerous was to ask its audience to wilfully restrain themselves from thinking and questioning in those areas, and to trust the wisdom of God and the divine authorities in issuing such admonitions. For instance, it advised the faithful to refrain from asking questions to the Prophet during the periods in which the verses of revelation were being revealed to him, for they ran the risk of not being able to bear the responses to their questions and losing their faith.[93] However, the Qur'an did not prohibit the faithful from asking questions outright; it merely admonished them. Similarly, the Prophet advised the collectivity not to inquire into the nature of God, and the Imāms admonished their followers not to delve into the topic of free will and predestination for the fear of losing their faith.[94] Again, neither the Prophet nor the Imāms stated it was a sin and a punishable crime to think about such theological issues; they were simply admonitions. The only instance in which curtailing access to information unrestrictedly is justified and legitimate is in the case of minors and individuals with learning difficulties, for they do not possess the existential aptitudes to assimilate and understand certain genres of information.[95] They should only be permitted access to such information if and when they acquire the requisite existential aptitudes.

Undoubtedly, both religious and non-religious authorities have encroached and will continue to encroach upon the freedoms of thought and expression of their followers and subjects by appealing to the justification of the latter's lack of aptitude in assimilating and understanding certain information, thereby

---

93 See Qur'an 5:101.

94 See *ḥadīths* 5704–8 of the Prophet in ʿAlī ibn ʿAbd al-Malik al-Hindī al-Muttaqī, *Kanz al-ʿummāl fī sunan al-aqwāl wa-l-afʿāl* (Beirut: Mu'assasat al-Risāla, 2008), 3:106; and *ḥadīths* in Muḥsin Fayḍ Kāshānī, *ʿIlm al-yaqīn fī uṣūl al-dīn* (Qom: Intishārāt Bīdār, 1997), 1:257.

95 See Siyeon Lee, 'Children's Right to Access Information', in *The United Nations Convention on the Rights of the Child: An Analysis of Treaty Provisions and Implications of U.S. Ratification*, ed. Jonathan Todres, Mark E. Wojcik and Cris R. Revaz (Leiden: Brill, 2006), 177–88; Karen Milligan, Marjory Phillips and Ashley S. Morgan, 'Tailoring Social Competence Interventions for Children with Learning Disabilities', *Journal of Child and Family Studies* 25, no. 3 (2016): 856–58.

restricting their freedoms unjustifiably.[96] They are only justified in restricting the freedom of expression absolutely when instituting and enforcing legislation pertaining to the harm principle (which is that their respective followers and subjects do not have the right to express thoughts harming or misrepresenting an individual and/or a collectivity).[97] According to the existential framework, this is because the act of harming or misrepresenting an individual and/or a collectivity contravenes the existential property of growth.

Conclusion

All existent entities are evolving due to their being imbued with the existential telos of growth. The freedoms of thought and expression are an integral part of the human growth process. All aspects of the Sharīʿa in its broadest sense, which includes the Qur'an, Sunna, theology, moral teachings, regulations and rights, are open to critique unrestrictedly. This is because the freedom of thought is a prerequisite for the wilful surrender of the human soul to God, which in turn is a necessary requirement for salvation in Islam.

An implication of the principiality of the existential property and telos of growth is that all aspects of the Sharīʿa, including its theology and normativity, have to be liberating and growth promoting. This is because the Sharīʿa, like every other entity, system, idea and norm, is operating within the confines of the existential property and telos of growth, and not vice versa. Thus, the purpose of Sharīʿa normativity is to assist in the actualisation of the human potential by providing optimal regulations in line with existential aptitudes. Accordingly, Sharīʿa normativity may lose its optimality as and when the existential aptitudes of individuals and collectivities grow, and existential contexts change. Therefore, Sharīʿa normativity is fallible essentially, which means the potential for revision is part of its essence; hence its optimality must be scrutinised constantly.

---

96 For instance, see Brenner A. Allen, 'A Cause of Action against Private Contractors and the U.S. Government for Freedom of Speech Violations in Iraq', *North Carolina Journal of International Law* 31, no. 2 (2005): 543–56; Jørgen Møller and Svend-Erik Skaaning, 'Autocracies, Democracies, and the Violation of Civil Liberties', *Democratization* 20, no. 1 (2013): 86–97.

97 See Rebecca L. Brown, 'The Harm Principle and Free Speech', *Southern California Law Review* 89, no. 5 (2015): 954–56; Bakircioglu, 'Freedom of Expression and Hate Speech', 4–6; Heyman, 'Righting the Balance', 1323–64.

The faculty of reason has primacy in judging the efficacy of regulations, rights and freedoms due to its ability to evaluate their optimality in facilitating the growth of the individual and collectivity. It is also able to reformulate them if need be. Hence, it is the faculty of reason that both ascertains the worth of the regulations of the Qur'an and Sunna in their own existential contexts and abrogates them in contexts differing from the revelatory ones. In this respect, the faculty of reason demands unrestricted freedom to critique the Sharīʿa qua 'a body of regulations', and as such, it does not admit to any sacred space immune from inquiry.

The freedom to think and critique can only be curtailed in extreme circumstances; however, all such restrictions are to be deemed as momentary, that is, until the appropriate degree of research has been carried out and/or suitable platforms are created to facilitate the freedoms of thought and expression. There are two ways by which the restriction of the freedoms of thought and expression may be effected justifiably: the first is to exhort individuals to wilfully abstain from thought and its expression vis-à-vis certain domains due to the potential harm posed to themselves and others by engaging in such thought, and the other is instituting and enforcing legislation pertaining to the harm principle. Today, the censorship laws of various nation-states are instances of the latter. They seek to curtail the freedom of thought and are formulated by the faculty of reason in accordance with the existential limitations and aptitudes of the individuals of a collectivity of a particular existential context. Other instances include legislation prohibiting hate speech and incitement to violence, and national and local measures preventing minors and individuals with learning disabilities from accessing certain materials; however, all such regulations are subject to change in accordance with the growth of the existential aptitudes of individuals and their collectivities.

ALI-REZA BHOJANI AND MORGAN CLARKE[1]

Free Speech as Ethical Speech in Islam: An Essay in Ethnographic Moral Theology

The relationship between Islam and freedom of speech is a topic of intense concern in the world today, not least due to the furious and ongoing controversy over the notorious Danish cartoons published in 2005, which has in many ways replayed that over the publication of Salman Rushdie's *Satanic Verses* in the late 1980s. These controversies, and the violence that they have inspired,[2] play into, and play with, a narrative of a 'clash of civilisations', a fundamental divide between Muslim notions of what can and cannot be said, on the one hand, and (primarily Western) liberal secular ones, on the other. The intensity and polarisation of these debates is paralysing. Further, they have monopolised discussion over Islam and free speech, channelling it towards questions of blasphemy, insult and intolerance. And yet, freedom of speech transcends the issue of blasphemy, and is as much an issue within Muslim communities as between them and non-Muslim ones. In this paper, we thus seek to develop the conversation about the ethics of speech in Islam in alternative directions. As will become clear, the distinctive directions that we take flow from what is a wider interdisciplinary research collaboration: one of us (Bhojani) is primarily trained in the field of *uṣūl al-fiqh*, the other (Clarke) in anthropology.

The theme that we wish to pursue is the power that speech has to shape the ideas and character of others, for better or for worse – that is, its 'ethical' or pedagogical effects. This notion of ethical speech has been a prominent strand of recent work in the anthropology of Islam. For Saba Mahmood and Charles Hirschkind, when Muslims listen to sermons, lessons and other religious discourse, they do so in the hope of making better Muslims of themselves, of changing their character and inclinations in more pious directions. Religious

1 We would like to thank the Khoja Ithna'asheri Council of European Jamaat for facilitating our research, as well as all the *jamāʿat*s and individuals from the UK Twelver Shīʿī Khoja community who so kindly gave us their time and support. We would also like to thank the organisers and participants of the conference at the Al-Mahdi Institute where this paper was first presented.

2 That violence tragically now includes the attempted murder of Salman Rushdie himself in 2022.

teaching is not just a matter of communicating the rules of right action; it is also a matter of inculcating the virtuous dispositions that will ensure that right action takes place. As Talal Asad has pointed out in a discussion of public politics in the Muslim Middle East (Saudi Arabia specifically), where critical speech is better framed as 'advice' (*naṣīḥa*) rather than criticism, the exercise of such pedagogical speech can be seen as a duty as much as a right, bound up in the wider duty to 'command right and forbid wrong' (*al-amr bi-l-maʿrūf wa-l-nahy ʿan al-munkar*). It can also be a risky undertaking.[3]

Our interest in this theme is not simply a theoretical one. Rather, we were brought to it through our experiences of fieldwork amongst a Muslim community in the UK, as part of a project to document attitudes towards and practice of the rules of *fiqh*. The community with which we have worked, the Twelver Shīʿī Khoja (described further below), enjoys, like many other Muslim communities, a rich variety of religious programming: sermons, seminars and lessons, all seeking to contribute to the moral and pious improvement of their audiences. But the content of such ethical speech, while hugely varied, is also the subject of concern and debate. The contributions of some speakers have been deemed in some quarters too challenging, dangerous even, to the religious well-being of the community. Controversially, some have even been barred from speaking altogether. Freedom of speech was thus an issue present in the background throughout our fieldwork, albeit framed in a particular way: who can speak from the pulpit (*minbar*, or *mimbar* in the vernacular of the community)? This is not simply a struggle for control over the community's platforms. We spoke to some teachers and preachers who censored themselves, for fear that some of their convictions might be too divisive to broadcast.

These are the everyday concerns of a real Muslim community. Here we take seriously the questions that they raise for discussions of free speech in Islam, and for *fiqh* in particular. We thus frame our approach to the *fiqh* of public

---

3 Saba Mahmood, *Politics of Piety: The Islamic Revival and the Feminist Subject* (Princeton: Princeton University Press, 2005); Charles Hirschkind, *The Ethical Soundscape: Cassette Sermons and Islamic Counterpublics* (New York: Columbia University Press, 2006); Talal Asad, 'The Limits of Religious Criticism in the Middle East: Notes on Islamic Public Argument', in *Genealogies of Religion: Discipline and Reasons of Power in Christianity and Islam* (Baltimore: Johns Hopkins University Press, 1993), 200–238. Contrast Asad and Mahmood's discussions of the Danish cartoon controversy, which pursue the now more familiar themes of blasphemy and insult. See Talal Asad, Wendy Brown, Judith Butler and Saba Mahmood, *Is Critique Secular? Blasphemy, Injury, and Free Speech* (New York: Fordham University Press, 2013).

speech not in terms of the law of blasphemy, say, but in terms of the tension between two different duties: to avoid harm, on the one hand, and to share knowledge, on the other. At this point, we can only offer the briefest of sketches as to what that might entail in *fiqhī* terms – we intend more a provocation to think differently than a definitive analysis. We further hope that this might have something to offer to the wider debate as well. The debates over blasphemy and the Danish cartoons assume radical, almost absolute differences between secular liberalism and Islam. While scholars like Asad and Mahmood seek to counter the prejudicial depictions of Islam in much liberal discourse, they have done so by arguing for the need to recognise Islam as a coherent but *non-liberal* tradition, making connections with the work of philosophers like Alasdair MacIntyre, himself deeply critical of post-Enlightenment moral thought and a proponent of the sort of 'virtue ethics' that Asad and Mahmood discuss.[4] While we too want to move beyond prevailing stereotypes, we also want to keep open the possibility of dialogue between contemporary Islamic and liberal secular thought. Resituating the debate away from the polarised debates over blasphemy, insult and intolerance – important though they are – and towards more obviously shared concerns over the balance of obligations to share or withhold knowledge might constitute grounds for such fresh dialogue.

This also, we hope, marks a methodological contribution. Our approach to the *fiqh* of speech is inspired by our observations and experience of the everyday life of a Muslim religious community rather than the preoccupations of the media. It also offers something other than the sort of 'armchair' theorising that might seek to mine and expand archaic historical topics in *fiqh* that could in some way relate to contemporary questions of free speech. Instead, this constitutes an exercise in 'ethnographic theology', or in this case, ethnographic moral theology: that is, allowing the observed realities of everyday life and religious practice to direct discussions in the religious sciences.[5] While ethnographic theology has become a prominent approach within Christian theology, its possibilities have not yet been exploited within the Islamic tradition.[6] We discuss this further below.

---

4 Alasdair MacIntyre, *After Virtue: A Study in Moral Theory* (London: Duckworth, [1981] 2006).

5 Moral theology being a common term for Christian practical ethics.

6 On ethnographic theology, see e.g. Christian Scharen and Anna Marie Vigen, eds, *Ethnography as Christian Theology and Ethics* (London and New York: Continuum, 2011). For an influential call for ethnographically situated moral theology in the Christian tradition, see Michael Banner, *The Ethics of Everyday Life: Moral Theology, Social An-*

1. The Ethics of Speech within a Muslim Community

The fieldwork with which we are concerned took place with the kind assistance of the Twelver Shīʿī Khoja in 2018–19. The Khoja are a global diaspora with roots in South Asia (Sind and Gujerat), which expanded through trade across the Indian Ocean and retains important and enduring ties to East Africa. The majority of the Khoja worldwide are Ismāʿīlī, but a significant number are Twelver Shīʿī.[7] Among this diaspora, the UK Twelver Shīʿī community is significant, in size and influence, and composed of a number of autonomous local associations (*jamāʿats*) in various towns and cities, where English is the dominant vernacular. The Twelver Khoja are relatively prosperous and highly educated, and have become a well-respected and influential element of both the global Twelver Shīʿī and local British Muslim landscape, while preserving a sense of themselves as a distinct and close-knit religious community.

We have spent many days at local associations, attending religious services and other events, alongside our interviews with community members on their understanding and practice of Sharīʿa. The sheer volume of ethical speech with which the community is presented, in terms of sermons and religious instruction, for youth, seniors, men and women, is impressive, as is its diversity. Alongside the careful and loving upholding of traditional ideas and practices, there is also a sense of lively intellectual debate. Modern life as a migrant, minority community poses many questions of the tradition, and there are many who hold non-traditional views in response.

We spoke at length with one such person, a woman whose wisdom and learning, as well as her energy and leadership, are made much use of in the community, and whose reputation and achievements as an educator are global in scope. She confessed herself impatient at best with the attitudes and teachings of some religious scholars. She had been brought up otherwise.

> I was brought up as a child ... to say that even whilst you had your periods you would pray. My father said there's nobody, anywhere, written anywhere, that says you wouldn't. So I'd come to the greater community and my God, it's written in light you know, you can't sit on the prayer

thropology, and the Imagination of the Human (Oxford: Oxford University Press, 2014).

7 See e.g. Iqbal Akhtar, *The Khoja of Tanzania: Discontinuities of a Postcolonial Religious Identity* (Leiden: Brill, 2016). From here on, where we refer simply to 'Khoja', we mean the Twelver Shīʿī Khoja.

> mat [during your period].

In her own practice, she chose to ignore the traditional understanding on this issue.

> Ignored it completely. That's my lifelong practice and I tell my children that. Show me a place where it's written and tell me that it's authentic and I will consider it, and nobody yet has come up with telling me that they've found somewhere. I mean how can I not connect to my God for whatever times in the month and say, excuse me I can't pray to you because ... Anyway, that's just an example of the way I think.

However, this is not something that she can say freely in her role as religious teacher.

> I cannot, I would not express [it]. I speak from the pulpit. I wouldn't because I would not want to break the fabric of the society or tear it. But I will gradually introduce it for my students, with my friends, with whoever it is, I will tell them this is the way I feel.

Here, she speaks of limiting herself in what she teaches from the pulpit out of concern for social harmony – although it was also clear that she has come under a great deal of pressure from others to do so as well. The potential intensity of such pressure should not be underestimated. We were discussing attitudes towards Sharīʿa with the leader of one local association when he told us of an incident that had occurred the previous year, before he became the association's president. A speaker came for a discussion circle held by a religious youth group. It was, he said, 'an amazing discussion'. The speaker questioned the audience's beliefs, the way culture has become mixed up with religion. He said that he sometimes does not cry on the day of ʿĀshūrā' – the peak of the mourning period for the martyrs of the battle of Karbala, a central pillar of the Shīʿī imaginary and religious calendar. This, which speaks presumably to a sort of modernist rationalism, was seen as very controversial by some within the community. One child told his father about it – and the father happened to be a member of the management committee of the local association and brought it up the next day. 'How dare he?' he said. This sort of discussion should be held in a seminary research class (*dars al-khārij*), not with children. A number of members of the committee said, 'Let's ban him,' and – to the discomfort of some – they dug into the speaker's online social media content trying to find further justification for doing so.

This ready recourse to banning people from speaking is not just part of the low-level frictions of everyday community life. There are much more high-profile incidents of the kind. One, dating back to the 1990s, involved a distinguished member of the academic Islamic studies community, now based in the United States, Abdulaziz Sachedina. Professor Sachedina is a Khoja, born in East Africa, and a vibrant progressive intellectual and scholarly voice. While his academic career in North America burgeoned, his sharing of his views at Khoja community religious meetings became perceived as worryingly unorthodox by some within the community. A dossier of his teachings, as expressed from the *mimbar* and from within his academic publications, was sent to the scholarly authority whom the Khoja Twelver institutions currently take to be the most authoritative, Ayatollah Ali Sistani, the leading figure in the prestigious seminaries of Najaf, Iraq. After some deliberations and a meeting between Sachedina and Sistani, Sachedina was effectively banned from speaking within community institutions and has not done so since.[8]

A more recent such affair is still very much alive, and an acutely sensitive point of tension, so we avoid naming those concerned. Members of the community have long supported the development of local institutions of scholarly instruction, sometimes talked of as a sort of local seminary, or *ḥawza*. Given the particular challenges of Muslim life in the UK, such local sites of scholarship have become a focus for progressive thought and jurisprudence. A leading such voice has now also become the subject of a campaign to silence him. This campaign again included a letter to the office of Sistani, in 2019, which has been posted online together with the reply.[9]

The letter, which is framed in general rather than particular terms, starts by stating concern over those who 'spread amongst our youths issues especially about the fundamental beliefs of the faith (Usool-e-Deen) and the practical

8 For Sachedina's own account of the affair (which we refer to below), see Ali Teymoori, 'What Happened at the Meeting of Ayatollah Sistani and Sachedina', Ijtihad Network, 22 April 2018, http://ijtihadnet.com/happend-meeting-ayatollah-sistani-sachedina/. For the contrasting account of Sayyid Muhammad Rizvi, who was the one who compiled and submitted the dossier to Sistani and participated in the meeting between him and Sachedina in Najaf, see 'Dr Abdulaziz Sachedina & Meeting with Ay. Sistani', al-Ma'ārif, https://al-m.ca/sachedina-meeting-with-ay-sistani/.

9 'Question to the Office of His Eminence Sayyid Ali Husayni Sistani and its Response ...', Imam Ali Foundation – London, 2 February 2019, www.najaf.org/english/1120.

branches of faith' (i.e. *furūʿ al-dīn*, the practical duties regulated by *fiqh*). After a series of examples (concerning salvation for non-Muslims, the rules of inheritance for women, etc.), they end by asking the Ayatollah's office 'to guide our youths, male and female ... on how to deal with such people'. The Ayatollah's reply (as translated by the petitioners) starts by expounding upon the pedagogical role of such speech that we have highlighted above:

> The duty of the Muslim preacher (muballigh) is to invite people towards Usool-e-Deen and to spread its well established teachings as represented in the clear verses of the holy Book and the beautiful sayings of the Holy Prophet Mustafa (SA) and the Holy Guides (AS); and to enjoin people and to guide them so they can grow in faith in God and in preparation for the day of judgement, and to strive to spiritually develop their souls and to purge them from evil traits and moral vices, and to adorn them with moral virtues and noble traits; and to better their relations and interactions with others even with those who differ with them in faith and belief.

And he goes on to say:

> It is inappropriate for the religious preacher (muballigh) to use the mimbar to spread his personal opinions which create divisions and differences among the religious people. So, whoever adopts this style of teaching and lecturing, it does not behoove [*sic*] the believers (may Allah increase their honour) to be inclined towards them and to entrust them with the religious training of their children; rather it is their duty to refer to others who are reliable from among the people of knowledge, piety and righteousness.

With this reply, the opponents of the scholar and teacher in question felt that their position had been vindicated, and he was effectively barred from speaking at religious events within community institutions, although he still receives invitations to teach and preach elsewhere around the world, and his sermons and teachings are widely available on YouTube.

2. The Pulpit, the Academy and 'the General Public'

Internal community politics are not our concern here. Let us instead concentrate on the main analytical points that arise. First, pedagogical speech is a central part of religious community life. Its importance can be testified to by the increasingly regular advice and guidance issued by, for instance, Sistani's offices to community speakers and orators,[10] as well as the efforts to police it through forms of exclusion that we have just described. Nevertheless, given the realities of life in the contemporary West, traditional certainties are under question. Amongst the issues at stake is how, where and when such questioning can be expressed. Preaching from the pulpit is seen as especially sensitive, as the paradigmatic location of ethical speech and authority. (As the female preacher quoted above put it, 'When you sit on the pulpit they think you know everything, which you don't.') Other locations such as 'the *ḥawza*', the learned seminary, may, it is said, be more suitable for the airing of radical thought. Critical debate is indeed a deeply embedded element of *ḥawza* culture, and the Twelver Shīʿī legal tradition maintains a central place for the role of human reason.[11] But how, where and when critical reason impinges on the life of ordinary, non-specialist Muslims – and 'the youth' in particular – is a distinct and somewhat fraught issue.

We referred earlier to Asad's thoughts on the differences between the attitudes to public critical speech in the Islamic tradition and Western liberal modernity. Fairly or otherwise, Asad takes the thought of Immanuel Kant – and in particular his famous essay of 1784 on 'What Is Enlightenment?' – as paradigmatic of the latter.[12] What is striking to us here is that, in that essay, Kant makes a similar point to that circulating in our community about how different audiences and roles might bear on these issues. Kant makes his distinction as one between the public and private use of reason. Its public use, which should be free, is 'that use which anyone may make of it *as a man* [*sic*]

10 See e.g. 'The Recommendations of the Supreme Religious Authority to the Speakers and Orators on the Occasion of the Coming Month of Muharram 1441' [in Arabic], Imam Ali Foundation – London, 8 August 2019, www.najaf.org/arabic/1163 (for the English translation, see www.najaf.org/english/1164).

11 See e.g. Ali-Reza Bhojani, *Moral Rationalism and Sharīʿa: Independent Rationality in Modern Shīʿī Uṣūl al-Fiqh* (Abingdon: Routledge, 2015).

12 Asad, 'The Limits of Religious Criticism'; Immanuel Kant, 'Answering the Question: What Is Enlightenment?', in *Political Writings*, ed. H. S. Reiss, trans. H. B. Nisbet, 2nd ed. (Cambridge: Cambridge University Press, 1991).

of learning addressing the entire *reading public*'. Its private use, which may be restricted, is 'that which a person may make in a particular *civil* post or office with which he is entrusted'.[13] Interestingly for us, his most fully fleshed out example is that of the religious teacher:

> [A] clergyman is bound to instruct his[14] pupils and his congregation in accordance with the doctrines of the church he serves, for he is employed by it on that condition. But as a scholar, he is completely free as well as obliged to impart to the public all his carefully considered, well-intentioned thoughts on the mistaken aspects of those doctrines, and to offer suggestions for a better arrangement of religious and ecclesiastical affairs. And there is nothing in this which need trouble his conscience. For what he teaches in pursuit of his duties as an active servant of the church is presented by him as something which he is not empowered to teach at his own discretion, but which he is employed to expound in a prescribed manner and in someone else's name.[15]

Here, then, we also have a distinction between what can be said by a religious expert on the pulpit and away from it. There are thus interesting similarities to, as well as differences from, the preoccupations of the Muslim community described above. The notion that the religious teacher's speech before the community is private, or domestic, in that it is oriented towards and governed by their needs, and thus not wholly free, makes a certain kind of sense in our ethnographic setting where the sense of a bounded community is strong. However, Kant's particular points about the restrictions placed upon a clergyman make more sense in a Christian context, where the religious professional is appointed by a church,[16] than in an Islamic one, where their difference from non-religious specialists is nominally simply a matter of their greater knowledge.

13 Kant, 'What Is Enlightenment?', 55 (emphasis in original).

14 Kant's gendered assumptions are not so true of our Muslim community, where there are a good number of women preachers and teachers, although they do remain the minority.

15 Kant, 'What Is Enlightenment?', 56.

16 In Kant's Prussia, clergymen were, however, also civil servants, paid by the state (just as professors like Kant were). See John Christian Laursen, 'The Subversive Kant: The Vocabulary of "Public" and "Publicity"', in *What Is Enlightenment? Eighteenth-Century Answers and Twentieth-Century Questions*, ed. James Schmidt (Berkeley: University of California Press, 1996), 253–69.

Admittedly, and especially in Shīʿī society, the 'turbaned' (*muʿammam*) class do form a distinct body of religious specialists. And the various local associations of the Khoja community do appoint and employ some to serve their local needs: leading prayers, providing edifying sermons and lessons, helping people with their dilemmas. And the contracts of some may not be renewed, for one reason or another. But the provision of ethical speech to the community and the sense of a calling to do so is not normatively restricted to such paid appointees. In normative terms, the duty to correct and improve the morality of others and of society at large is incumbent upon all Muslims, 'turbaned' or otherwise. Nor does such public speech fall formally under a unified institution of religious authority, whatever the practical realities of community institutional life. As Sachedina said of the (successful) attempts to bar him from speaking within the community, 'Islam is not Catholicism[17] where there is no room for another interpretation or dissension in the authoritative system of the "church".'

What, then, of the other half of Kant's distinction, the 'public' speech where one is free, as 'a man [or woman!] of learning', to express one's 'well-intentioned', but possibly critical views? In our Muslim community, this is thought more appropriate to the scholarly setting of the seminary. The audience Kant has in mind seems larger – 'the entire reading public', although this was still no doubt a restricted portion of the society of his day. That this was still a potentially subversive idea can be seen from the trouble it would later cause Kant himself, when he had to withdraw his 1793 work on *Religion within the Limits of Reason Alone* having fallen foul of the new king's edict on religion, which guaranteed freedom of conscience 'so long as [the citizen] keeps any peculiar opinion to himself and carefully guards himself from spreading it or persuading others'. Kant was forced to concede that his book was 'not at all suitable for the public' – here meaning precisely not 'scholars of the faculty'.[18] Today's liberal norms tend more towards Kant's original position: public speech should be broadly free.

Here we might compare Ayatollah Sistani's response to the latest controversy cited above. Sistani writes that, 'it is not right for the one who addresses *the general public* to present to them specialist issues wherein the audience has no grasp of the prerequisites of the issue as per the required academic

17 Of course, Kant's Prussia was not Catholic either – his immediate context was a Lutheran Protestant one, but the broader point stands.

18 Laursen, 'The Subversive Kant'.

standards.'[19] What has been translated by those disseminating the letter as 'the general public' (*'āmmat al-nās*, in Sistani's Arabic) might equally be translated as 'the generality of people', or even 'the masses'. That is, this is not so much a comment on different domains of speech, public versus private, as in Kant's argument, as on the capabilities for understanding of different sorts of audience – although it could then map onto the notion that those teaching and training in the seminary may be relatively well equipped, as opposed to those who learn their religion from 'the pulpit'.[20] This is one instance of a wider classical vision of a hierarchy of knowledge and understanding that distinguishes between the learned (*'ālim*) and 'the ignorant' (*jāhil*), or the elite (*khāṣṣa*) and the commoners (*'āmma*).[21] An intellectual separation between learned and ignorant may seem magnified for 'traditionalist' Khoja by the community's historical geographic, ethnic and linguistic distance from the great scholarly centres of the Middle East. This may indeed have made sense historically, when literacy was highly restricted, and the pulpit was indeed the primary focus for the dissemination of religious knowledge to the non-learned. But its logic seems much less appropriate to at least some within today's Muslim communities in the UK, and certainly for the Khoja communities in question, made up of highly educated professionals – doctors, dentists, accountants, IT specialists and businesspeople – with access to an extensive apparatus of scholarly education and resources, much in the vernacular, as well as international travel. Furthermore, with the advent of digital media, the circulation of speech has itself become radically freer. 'The seminary' (let alone the pulpit) is no longer a bounded location. Rather, it – and religious discourse more generally – is globally and immediately accessible via the Internet.

19 'Question to the Office of His Eminence Sayyid Ali Husayni Sistani'.

20 There seems no other reason in *fiqhī* terms to mark out 'the pulpit' as a privileged or distinct domain of speech.

21 The very structure of revelation in Islam can be seen to imply a vision of social hierarchy in terms of relative capacity to access the revealed Truth of the divine order. See Shahab Ahmed, *What Is Islam? The Importance of Being Islamic* (Princeton: Princeton University Press, 2015), 368–87. In more explicit form, such a hierarchy is apparent in reports attributed to the Prophet along the lines of, 'Surely we, the community of prophets, speak with people in accordance with their intelligences': Muḥammad Bāqir al-Majlisī, *Biḥār al-anwār* (Beirut: Dār Iḥyā' al-Turāth al-'Arabī, 1982), 1:106 (*ḥadīth* 4).

3. A Balance of Obligations

If we are right in thinking that – in *fiqhī* terms – any particularity here to the pulpit, as opposed to the seminary, stems from an assumption about the nature of its audience (unlearned) rather than, for instance, a sense of its especial sanctity,[22] then the ethics of speech becomes a contingent issue: one as to whether or not the listener may be misled, and thus possibly corrupted – a question of harm. It was this concern that led the female preacher that we quoted above to censor herself when speaking from the pulpit. Let us turn, then, to this tension between saying what you think, as a scholar and teacher, and the possibility of that causing harm. For heuristic purposes, as is common in *fiqhī* debate, this could be reduced to one between conflicting duties. *Uṣūl al-fiqh* (i.e. legal theory), then, offers general principles for the resolution of such conflicts.

One needs to start by characterising, even if schematically, the nature of these conflicting duties. On the one hand, there is a duty upon scholars to manifest their knowledge (*iẓhār al-ʿilm*), which correlates with a prohibition on concealing knowledge *(kitmān al-ʿilm)*, something condemned in scripture in the harshest of terms. It is reported that the Prophet has stated that, 'Whosoever conceals knowledge will be bridled by Allah on the Day of Resurrection with bridles of fire.'[23] Similarly, attributed to Imām ʿAlī is the statement that, 'If innovation appears within my community, then the scholar should make manifest his knowledge; whosoever does not do so, then upon him is the curse [*laʿna*] of Allah.'[24] Within the Qur'an we find similar condemnation: 'Indeed those who conceal what We have sent down of manifest proofs and guidance, after We have clarified it in the Book for mankind – they shall be cursed by Allah and cursed by the cursers' (2:159); and 'Indeed those who conceal what Allah has sent down of the Book and sell it for a paltry gain – they do not take in, into their bellies, [anything] except fire, and Allah shall not speak to them on the Day of Resurrection, nor shall He purify them, and there is a painful punishment for them' (2:174).

22 Within a long message of recommendations to 'preachers and orators' in the lead up to the Muharram ceremonies of 2019, Sistani is quoted as comparing the task and care required of preachers and orators to the experience of one when talking to his 'family members and children': 'The Recommendations of the Supreme Religious Authority' (see especially 'the eighth wisdom').

23 Majlisī, *Biḥār al-anwār*, 2:78 (*ḥadīth* 66).

24 Muḥammad ibn Yaʿqūb al-Kulaynī, *Uṣūl al-kāfi* (Beirut: Manshūrāt al-Fajr, 2007), 1:32 (*ḥadīth* 2).

On the other hand, the underlying impetus to censor scholarly reasoned criticism that we encountered in our ethnographic cases may be considered in terms of the duty to ward off possible harm (*daf' al-ḍarar al-muḥtamal*). Here, however, scriptural references such as 'And do not cast yourselves with your own hands into destruction ...' (2:195) do not ground the duty in themselves. Rather, such texts are understood to be directive (*irshādī*), towards that which sound reason understands irrespective of scripture. The obligation to ward off possible harm is thus considered to be among the non-scripturally dependent judgements of reason (*al-mustaqillāt al-'aqliyya*).[25] There is possible harm in exposing people to views, ideas and reasoned criticism that they may not understand. Preventing possible harm is a rational duty, and thus there may be a duty to curtail, even censor, critical scholarly thought in the public domain.[26]

These two duties, the duty not to conceal (or the duty to make manifest) one's knowledge and the duty to prevent possible harm, thus potentially stand in tension. This tension does not arise from any conflict at the level of the evidence (*ta'āruḍ al-adilla*) for each of the respective duties. There are times where making manifest one's knowledge is not deemed cause of possible harm; and the duty to ward off possible harm is far broader than issues related to the disclosure or non-disclosure of knowledge. The tension is purely at the level of implementation: should one conceal one's knowledge (breaching the prohibition), if and when it may lead to harm (respecting the obligation)? We are faced with two conflicting duties, where the conflict arises out of the agent's inability to fulfil them both. One either respects the prohibition of not concealing knowledge or one respects the obligation to ward off possible harm. This type of conflict, occurring at the level of implementation, is known in *uṣūl al-fiqh* as *tazāḥum*.[27]

25 On the duty to ward off possible harm, see Muḥammad Kāẓim al-Muṣṭafawī, *al-Qawā'id* (Qom: Mu'assasat al-Nashr al-Islāmī), 306–9; on non-scriptural dependent judgements of reason, see Bhojani, *Moral Rationalism.*

26 An alternative lens to consider the tension at play would be through considering the qualifications of the duty to 'command right and forbid wrong' (*al-amr bi-l-ma'rūf wa-l-nahy 'an al-munkar*). It is well established amongst modern Shī'ī jurists that this duty is qualified by an absence of detriment (*mafsada*) or harm (*ḍarar*). This may lead to a different resolution of the tension from the one that we explore, such that if one's ethical speech is known to, or likely to, cause harm, the duty is simply lifted. See e.g. Muḥammad Ḥasan al-Najafī, *Jawāhir al-kalām fī sharḥ sharā'i' al-Islām* (Beirut: Dār Mu'arrikh al-'Arabī, 1998), 7:682.

27 On distinguishing between conflicts at the level of evidence, conflicts at the level of

In a case of *tazāḥum* the active duty is deemed to be the one whose criteria are more important (*ahamm*), and thus preferred. The preferability of a more important duty (*ahamm*), over another less important (*muhimm*) duty, may be due to its being necessary (*ilzāmī*) and the other non-necessary (*ghayr ilzāmī*). Put differently, one may be obligatory and the other recommended. When both duties are obligatory, one of the two may still be deemed more important to the legislator. A typical example is to prefer the more important duty of saving a life over completing performance of an obligatory prayer. Alternatively, an obligatory act may be preferred over another obligatory act when it can only be performed at a specific time, whilst the other is afforded a range of a time within which it can be discharged. An obligatory act may also be preferred over another when it has only a single mode of discharge, whilst the conflicting duty is capable of being discharged in numerous ways.[28]

This Shīʿī *uṣūlī* analysis of how to resolve conflicting duties at the level of implementation provides a useful heuristic to consider possible normative responses to the tensions arising out of our ethnographic case. It also seems more widely recognisable. Contemporary liberal thought surely also perceives a tension between the imperative that thought be expressed freely and the possibility that some public discourse might cause some forms of harm,[29] although, as Asad has pointed out, the public exercise of reason is more often thought of in liberal terms as a *right*, rather than a duty.[30] Leaving aside whether the duties are grounded in Islamic sources or theorised in non-Muslim terms, it seems to us both instinctively that, of the two, it is the duty to manifest one's knowledge that should be considered the more important. That we are both academics may have a bearing on this of course (and we have taken the perspective of the scholar-speaker as our entry-point, rather than that of those with responsibility for regulating public speech, or those listening to it). And yet, to return to the modes of *uṣūlī* legal theory, although the scale and nature of the possible harm that might ensue may certainly be relevant in particular

implementation and the related but distinct category of simultaneity of commands and prohibitions, see Muḥammad Riḍā al-Muẓaffar, *Uṣūl al-fiqh* (Qom: Intishārāt Ismāʿiliyyān, 1959), 1:281–86.

28 On these specific points, see ibid., 265–66.

29 Worth noting too is that some audiences, notably children, are thought of as more vulnerable in this respect than others. It is interesting, in relation to the preceding discussion, that some have recently sought to extend this vulnerability to the university, the secular equivalent of the seminary, via the notion of preserving a 'safe space'.

30 Asad, 'The Limits of Religious Criticism', 215.

circumstances, ultimately we are talking about *possible* harm. Accordingly, in terms of general principle, this contingent possibility cannot be deemed a priori more important than the definite and active duty not to conceal one's knowledge. Furthermore, the duty to ward off possible harm may be fulfilled by means other than the restriction or even censure of scholarly expression. Raising the level of wider public education, offering opportunities for clarification, dialogue and doubt can all serve to ward off the possible harm of misunderstandings emerging from individual scholarly reasoned criticism. In fact, curtailing scholarly reasoned criticism itself leads to obvious societal harm by impeding the development of ideas, as well as of education and the capacity for critical thought in wider society, as among scholars themselves. Accordingly, amidst the ever-increasing potential cases of such conflicts, with scholarly expression rarely ever securely private, it seems that, in *fiqhī* terms at least, the admittedly reasonable urge to protect communities, and society more widely, from possible harm through restricting scholarly expression ought to be trumped by the need to preserve the more important duty of free reasoned scholarly expression.

Conclusion

In considering the question of free speech in Islam, we have allowed ourselves to be guided by the practical, everyday concerns of a Muslim community. Those took us in a somewhat different direction from that which has dominated public debate on these questions – away from questions of blasphemy and intolerance between religious communities and secular society, and towards the balance of obligations upon those with a vocation to engage intellectually with their religious tradition and to guide others in their own such engagement. In keeping with the agenda of the workshop and this publication, we have hoped thereby to suggest new possibilities for *fiqhī* research in this area – opening up avenues for conversation, rather than providing definitive answers.

That conversation could extend more widely. This balance of obligations would seem clearly recognisable in both Christian and secular liberal terms as well, for instance. The tension between scholarly freedoms and the risk of potential societal harm that reasoned scholarly expression might lead to is one confronting society at large, a tension that has become especially acute given how easily such scholarly expression can be misunderstood or taken out of context under the loss of intimacy and collapsing of public–private boundaries that digital social media have entailed. Although this paper could only briefly gesture towards the possibilities, the rich jurisprudential traditions of Islam offer their own resources for grappling with these questions. As we hope to have shown, the value of these resources lies not just in the way that *fiqh* aims to offer concrete responses to moral questions, as suggested by Christian theologian Joshua Ralston's recent call for Christian fatwas, for example.[31] It is also that, in *uṣūl al-fiqh*, the tradition offers a sophisticated body of meta-ethical and methodological resources for doing so in rigorous ways.

Finally, that we are exploring these resources in the light of our ethnographic data makes this an essay in *ethnographic* moral theology, even if – in the case of our particular intellectual partnership – any religiously normative implications have to be more the concern of the *fiqh* specialist than the anthropologist. Of course, it is not that Islamic scholars have historically been necessarily distant from the practical concerns of everyday Muslim life. *Fiqh* has itself very often developed in response to those concerns.[32] In the contemporary moment, the notion that *fiqh* and *uṣūl al-fiqh* need to be in close contact with social reality (*al-wāqiʿ*) has become increasingly widespread. However, this impetus to increase the explicit engagement of jurisprudential thinking with social reality is arguably largely taking the shape of engagement with other experts, in various fields of secular knowledge, rather than a more direct engagement with the everyday reality of Muslims themselves, such as we attempt here.[33] This move towards a more ethnographic approach to shaping expert engagement with the Islamic tradition – an Islamic 'ethnographic theology' – deserves more sustained reflection, something we aim to undertake elsewhere.

31 Joshua Ralston, *Law and the Rule of God: A Christian Engagement with Sharīʿa* (Cambridge: Cambridge University Press, 2020).

32 As argued by e.g. Wael Hallaq, 'From *Fatwās* to *Furūʿ*: Growth and Change in Islamic Substantive Law', *Islam Law and Society* 1, no. 1 (1994): 29–65.

33 See e.g. Al-Mahdi Institute's own International Centre for Collective Ijtihad (www.collectiveijtihad.org/).

REBECCA RUTH GOULD[1]

Dangerous Definitions: Free Speech Implications of Legal Definitions of Racism, Antisemitism and Islamophobia within the UK

In recent years, and particularly in the UK, the effort to combat racism has taken what might be called a definitional turn. While a large body of work has already emerged on the topic of the various definitions for Islamophobia and antisemitism that have been proposed, this definitional turn has only rarely been probed from the vantage point of its free speech implications. In this paper, which is part of a wider inquiry into the conceptualisation of free speech in Muslim and non-Muslim societies, I examine what the definitional turn in relation to Islamophobia might mean for the future of free speech within liberal democracies.[2]

This paper reviews recent calls within the UK for government-backed definitions of antisemitism and Islamophobia, while considering the consequences of such proposals, as well as the convergence of the discussion around defining antisemitism with defining anti-Muslim racism. I begin by showing how, considered in the context of contemporary efforts to regulate hate speech, the formulation and implementation of a government-sponsored definition has generated unforeseen harms for the Jewish community. Potentially, I argue, policing free speech might have similarly detrimental consequences for Muslim communities. Along the way, I briefly examine the negative impact of the International Holocaust Remembrance Alliance (IHRA) definition on Palestinian solidarity and its contribution to Islamophobia within the UK.

1 I would like to express my gratitude to the participants of the 9th AMI Contemporary Fiqhī Issues Workshop (Al-Mahdi Institute, July 2021) for their critical engagement with the ideas explored here.

2 Other contexts in which I explore these ideas include Rebecca Ruth Gould, *Erasing Palestine: Free Speech and Palestinian Freedom* (London and New York: Verso Books, forthcoming); Rebecca Ruth Gould, 'Is the "Hate" in Hate Speech the "Hate" in Hate Crime? Waldron and Dworkin on Political Legitimacy', *Jurisprudence* 10, no. 2 (2018): 171–87; and Rebecca Ruth Gould, 'The Limits of Liberal Inclusivity: How Defining Islamophobia Normalises Anti-Muslim Racism', *Journal of Law & Religion* 35, no. 2 (2020): 250–69. Some passages from the last-named work were adapted for this paper.

I then turn to the paper's primary focus on the definition of Islamophobia which in 2018 was proposed for adoption by the UK government and a range of civil society organisations, and compare and contrast that definition with approaches to anti-Muslim racism.

On 23 April 2018, the All-Party Parliamentary Group (APPG) on British Muslims issued a call for evidence 'to facilitate the adoption of a working definition of Islamophobia that can be widely accepted by Muslim communities, political parties, and the Government'.[3] In between this call and the release of the report, the mandate switched from a call for a 'working definition' into a call for a 'legally binding' one.[4] In both the UK and the US, political mobilisation for such a definition is growing, particularly among Muslim advocacy organisations. Although no government agency has adopted any such definition, UK political parties have.[5] Many formulas for defining Islamophobia have been proposed. These include 'the presumption that Islam is inherently violent, alien, and inassimilable'[6] and that it is 'an ideology similar in theory, function and purpose to racism ... that sustains and perpetuates negatively evaluated meaning about Muslims and Islam'.[7] Most recently, *Islamophobia Defined*, the report that resulted from the APPG's Islamophobia inquiry, proposes the following definition: 'Islamophobia is rooted in racism and is a type of racism that targets expressions of Muslimness or perceived Muslimness.'[8] Finally, another approach, closer to my own yet less frequently engaged by mainstream media, identifies 'the state, and more specifically the sprawling official "counter-terrorism" apparatus' as 'absolutely central to the production of contemporary Islamophobia – the backbone of anti-Muslim racism'.[9] This

3 This call was circulated on the APPG's Twitter account (@APPGBritMuslims) and is archived at https://twitter.com/APPGBritMuslims/status/988454757084909568.

4 All-Party Parliamentary Group on British Muslims [APPG], *Islamophobia Defined: The Inquiry into a Working Definition of Islamophobia* (2018), 27.

5 The APPG definition of Islamophobia was adopted by the UK Labour Party, the Liberal Democrats, Plaid Cymru and all Scottish political parties in 2019. For the Scottish positions, see www.holyrood.com/news/view,all-of-scotlands-political-parties-adopt-formal-definition-of-islamophobia_10221.htm.

6 Khaled A. Beydoun, 'Islamophobia: Toward a Legal Definition and Framework', *Columbia Law Review Online* 116 (2016): 111.

7 Chris Allen, *Islamophobia* (Farnham: Ashgate, 2010), 190.

8 APPG, *Islamophobia Defined*, 11.

9 Narzanin Massoumi, Tom Mills and David Miller, 'Islamophobia, Social Movements and the State: For a Movement-Centred Approach', in *What Is Islamophobia? Racism, Social Movements and the State*, ed. Narzanin Massoumi, Tom Mills and David Miller

reading, which emerges from Critical Muslim Studies, holds that 'Islamophobia can perhaps be defined as the disciplining of Muslims by reference to an antagonistic Western horizon'.[10]

In the face of such momentum, well-intentioned efforts to develop a legally binding definition suitable for governmental adoption may have the negative effect of bringing Muslims further under governmental surveillance. Past government efforts to regulate speech targeting other minorities and religions indicate that a governmental decision to back a definition of Islamophobia with the coercive force of the law will do more harm than good, to Muslims specifically, and for society generally. Finally, and most crucially, I argue that the adoption of such definitions on behalf of any religion or minority group for the purpose of censorship threatens to undermine a state's democratic legitimacy.[11]

In order to grasp the intersection of anti-Muslim racism and the policing of controversial speech, we must consider the relationship between government-led efforts to *protect* vulnerable minorities and government-led efforts to *police* them. The latter involves viewing them as inherently suspect, and placing Islamic discourse under disproportionate scrutiny. I examine how these two agendas, incompatible though they appear on the surface, actually reinforce each other. Beyond considering the mutual reciprocity of efforts to ban Islamophobia and to intensify government surveillance of Muslim communities, I also consider their convergence in post-9/11 liberal democracies such as the UK.

None of the proposals for a governmental definition of Islamophobia that have been aired to date have taken account of the lessons that should have been learned from the governmental adoption of the so-called IHRA definition of antisemitism in 2016. Yet the problems with such definitions and with their application become more apparent with every censorious exclusion of leftist Jews and anti-Zionist critics of Israel from the public sphere. My past work documenting the harms of censoring Israel-critical speech following the UK government's adoption of the IHRA definition has led me to regard the campaign for a government-backed definition with reservations.[12] The example

(London: Pluto, 2017), 8.

10 S. Sayyid, 'Out of the Devil's Dictionary', in *Thinking through Islamophobia: Global Perspectives*, ed. S. Sayyid and AbdoolKarim Vakil (London: Hurst & Company, 2010), 15.

11 Here I further develop arguments first articulated in Gould, 'Is the "Hate" in Hate Speech the "Hate" in Hate Crime?'.

12 Rebecca Ruth Gould, 'Legal Form and Legal Legitimacy: The IHRA Definition of Antisemitism as a Case Study in Censored Speech', *Law, Culture and the Humanities* 18, no. 1 (2018): 153–86.

of the IHRA adoption shows how government-sponsored censorship tends to undermine the fight against racism, while marginalising dissidents and further entrenching the boundaries of permissible speech.

Among the most pressing, yet most obscured, issues in the debate around defining Islamophobia for legal purposes is how the government's 'sifting of Muslims' transpires amid 'a highly securitised discourse around Islam'.[13] Proposals underway to adopt a government-supported definition of Islamophobia in order to facilitate the criminalisation of anti-Muslim speech risk normalising this securitised discourse under the guise of protecting Muslims.

There are many reasons to support efforts to define Islamophobia for the purpose of *critiquing* – in contrast to banning – public discourse, provided that we resist falling into 'the trap of regarding Islam monolithically'.[14] More dangerous and less helpful are efforts to give any such definition government backing, or otherwise aligning an adopted definition with the coercive force of the law. In using a definition of Islamophobia to facilitate the censorship of Islamophobic speech, the state ascribes to itself the mantle of defining Islam while evading the most injurious and impactful type of Islamophobia: that fostered by the government itself, through a range of securitising policies. Most notoriously among these in the UK context is the Prevent legislation, introduced in 2006 as part of a wider counter-terrorism strategy and updated in 2015 in Section 26 of the Counter-Terrorism and Security Act.

While definitions can help to identify harms, when used to silence controversial speech, government-backed definitions may also undermine democratic governance. To the extent that a state aims to be democratic, it must uncompromisingly uphold the citizen's free speech prerogative rather than engage in the invidious task of defining Islam. Since pluralistic democracy cannot legitimately police the boundaries of Islam, it therefore also ought not to give its backing to any definition of Islamophobia that presupposes a definition of Islam. Instead, it should actively oppose anti-Muslim racism, and refrain from targeting Muslims as racial, cultural and religious others.

---

13 'If We Want to Stop Islamophobia, We Have to Challenge the Laws That Enable It', CAGE, 22 November 2018, www.cage.ngo/if-we-want-to-stop-islamophobia-we-have-to-challenge-the-laws-that-enable-it.

14 Mohammad H. Tamdgidi, 'Beyond Islamophobia and Islamophilia as Western Epistemic Racisms: Revisiting Runnymede Trust's Definition in a World-History Context', *Islamophobia Studies Journal* 1, no. 1 (2012): 76.

1. Defining and Countering Hateful Speech

On 12 December 2016, the UK became one of the first governments in the world to formally adopt a controversial definition of antisemitism proposed by the International Holocaust Remembrance Alliance (IHRA), an intergovernmental body founded in 1998 to 'strengthen, advance, and promote Holocaust education, remembrance, and research worldwide'.[15] Neither the definition nor the process of its adoption was subjected to parliamentary scrutiny. Along with the definition's contentious content, these procedural failures have contributed to numerous ongoing violations of freedom of expression. The cancellation of events seen as potentially offensive to supporters of Israel, inquiries into controversial social media postings, and censorship of academic publications critical of Israel are just some of the more measurable ways in which the debate around Israeli policies has been constrained by the definition.[16] Amid these censorious acts, few voices have spoken out in defence of freedom of expression. Most institutions and most individuals in positions of authority have not hesitated to compromise on free speech when under pressure to conform to the government's (convoluted) policy.

Among the problematic aspects of the IHRA definition is its presumptive stigmatisation of views on Israel that are not necessarily motivated by racial animus. Marked by a clear political slant, the IHRA definition in effect excludes many Jewish points of view, especially those that are distant from or hostile to Zionism. While many critiques of this definition have been aired in recent years, its implications for the comparative study of group-specific definitions of racism have not been fully probed.[17] The tensions that have emerged in connection with the IHRA definition are likely to appear in connection with any group-specific definition of racism. Such definitions are useful only when they address the systematic structures and social norms within which such bigotry

15 This description is taken from the IHRA website: www.holocaustremembrance.com/.

16 A recent example of the latter is the controversy around an article critical of Israel published by Glasgow University's postgraduate student journal, *eSharp*. Under pressure from Israel advocates, the editors decided to preface the article with a disavowal after its publication, which can be found here: www.gla.ac.uk/media/Media_792691_smxx.pdf.

17 This is, however, precisely the focus of a forthcoming volume edited by David Feldman and Marc Volovici, entitled *Antisemitism, Islamophobia, and the Politics of Definition* (Palgrave, in progress). See in particular the chapters by Tariq Modood ('Islamophobia, Antisemitism and the Struggle for Recognition: The Politics of Definitions') and Rebecca Ruth Gould ('Does Defining Racism Help Overcome It?').

is normalised. Dismantling the processes through which racial and religious hatred is constituted will neutralise the power of prejudice more effectively than any act of banning can achieve.

Having examined the politics of definitions from the point of view of their implications for democratic governance, I will now develop an immanent critique of recent efforts to define Islamophobia that is informed by the history of Muslim integration into Muslim-minority societies. Any legal definition begins by considering the role of the state in defining its object. Muslim scholars such as Abdullahi Ahmad An-Naʿim have argued that the very idea of an Islamic state is a contradiction in terms, because a genuinely Islamic understanding of the state cannot be assimilated into modern bureaucratic structures.[18] Legal scholar Wael Hallaq has developed this argument further. Hallaq criticises the projection of the nation-state onto classical Islamic political formations. In Hallaq's view, 'any conception of a modern Islamic state is inherently self-contradictory'.[19]

An-Naʿim's argument has helped scholars challenge the Islamic postures adopted by regimes such as Saudi Arabia and Iran, which commit human rights violations while claiming to represent a rigorous version of Islam. Hallaq's argument concerning the impossibility of achieving Islamic governance is explicitly made with reference to modern theories of the state. In Hallaq's view, 'modern forms of globalization and the position of the state in the ever-increasing intensity of these forms are sufficient to render any brand of Islamic governance either impossible or, if possible, incapable of survival in the long run'.[20] While the relevance of these arguments for Islamic political theory is widely recognised, less attention has been given to how the impossibility of Islamic governance pertains to the internal logic of secular European states seeking to represent the political prerogatives of their Muslim citizens.

Hallaq maintains that 'for Muslims today to seek the adoption of the modern state system of separation of powers is to bargain for a deal inferior to the one they secured for themselves over the centuries of their history'.[21] In contrast to the Sharīʿa in its historical meaning, which 'was not designed to – serve

18 Abdullahi Ahmad An-Naʿim, *Islam and the Secular State: Negotiating the Future of Sharīʿa* (Cambridge, MA: Harvard University Press, 2012).

19 Wael Hallaq, *The Impossible State: Islam, Politics, and Modernity's Moral Predicament* (New York: Columbia University Press, 2013), xi.

20 Ibid., xiii.

21 Ibid., 72.

the ruler or any form of political power', the modern state can only serve itself.[22] Hallaq recognises contemporary nation-based sovereignty as a state's primary mechanism of self-preservation, and by implication, as the means through which the state surveils its citizens. It follows that neo-liberal states will be tempted to violate the citizen's right to freedom of expression when it gives legal effect to group-specific definitions of racism. This will be the case regardless of the intentions behind those definitions.

Democratic legitimacy requires that all citizens are represented in law-making. It entails, above all, consent, however mediated. For a government act to be legitimate, there must be a plausible basis for assuming that the procedure from which the action arises was consented to by those most directly affected by it, and that they have had and will have opportunities to meaningfully contest the laws they are expected to obey. A proposed governmental definition of Islamophobia would need to be able to reasonably claim to represent *all* Muslims – as well as anyone who might be identified as Muslim – within this definition. The constitution of the modern pluralist state makes such representation impossible. In consequence, any governmental definition of Islam (or of Islamophobia) would be illegitimate because the criteria imposed by representation and consent in order to attain legitimacy are impossible to satisfy in a pluralistic state.

In *Islamophobia Defined*, the APPG on British Muslims advocated for a government-backed definition on the grounds that 'adopting a definition of Islamophobia not only identifies a widespread phenomenon, but sends a positive message to all those communities and individuals who suffer from it'.[23] Given the report's call for a 'legally binding definition', it appears that the benefits of 'identifying a widespread phenomenon' and 'sending a positive message' were deemed to outweigh the dangers noted here.[24] Yet the report does not consider how, in defining a group as vulnerable, and in enshrining that group's characteristics in law, the state contributes to that group's vulnerability by placing it under more extensive surveillance.

Not all Muslim groups in the UK have welcomed their reification by the state through a governmental definition. Among the most outspoken and articulate of these groups is CAGE, an organisation that describes itself as 'an independent advocacy organisation working to empower communities impacted by the

22 Ibid.

23 APPG, *Islamophobia Defined*, 32.

24 The call for a 'legally binding definition' is repeated in ibid., 17, 30, 32, 35, 42, 43.

War on Terror'.[25] In responding to the APPG's call for evidence, CAGE argued that the government's use of counterinsurgency methods and tactics to treat the 'wider [Muslim] population as an enabler and supporter of insurgency and terrorism' illustrates how 'institutionalised Islamophobia is linked to the erosion of the rule of law'.[26] Overall, CAGE's substantive and detailed response to the call for evidence effectively exposes a 'strong stench of Islamophobia' within British government policies relative to Muslims.[27]

In its response to the APPG report, CAGE noted how the 'War on Terror' has ushered in 'a raft of counter-terrorism legislation ... and policies such as PREVENT, which reinforce securitised narratives about Islam, and compel public sector workers to implement a discriminatory approach to Muslims, which has seen children as young as four criminalised'.[28] From the viewpoint of CAGE, governmental definitions of Islamophobia are best treated with scepticism so long as the more basic structural phobias introduced by the War on Terror remain unaddressed. As Asim Qureshi, research director of CAGE, stated in response to the APPG on British Muslims Islamophobia report: 'If the definition of Islamophobia cannot hold those in power to account for their role in manufacturing Islamophobia, then it is inadequate.'[29] Unsurprisingly, although CAGE did submit written evidence to the APPG Islamophobia inquiry, its evidence was not engaged with or referenced in the report itself.

Any assessment of a democracy's success in protecting minority groups – and thereby in upholding its pluralist mandate – must consider how the state's involvement affects those on the margins of the protected group as well as those within that group's mainstream. We should also ask whether all members of the protected group can reasonably be understood to have consented to be defined in the way presupposed by the definition. Race and gender-based discrimination are readily identifiable on grounds that are relatively (if not absolutely) easy to specify. Hateful discourse that targets more amorphously constituted groups, for which membership is determined by a system of beliefs,

25 'About Us', CAGE, www.cage.ngo/cage-about-us.

26 'CAGE Response to a Call for Evidence on a Working Definition of "Islamophobia/Anti-Muslim Hatred"', CAGE, 26 June 2018, 9, www.cage.ngo/cage-submission-to-call-for-working-definition-of-islamophobia-anti-muslim-hatred.

27 Ibid.

28 'If We Want to Stop Islamophobia'.

29 'Discussions around the Definitions of Islamophobia Skirt the Real Issues We Need to Address', CAGE, 29 November 2018, www.cage.ngo/discussions-around-the-definitions-of-islamophobia-skirt-the-real-issues-we-need-to-address.

pose greater challenges to the state's aspiration to democratic legitimacy. A pluralistic democracy must oppose racism without censoring purely discursive speech. Tariq Modood's threefold typology of approaches to controversial speech – unlawful discrimination, to be censured but not censored and reasonable criticism – may be of use here.[30]

Although they differ both as regards their internal logic and substantive content, both the APPG definition of Islamophobia and the IHRA definition of antisemitism share in common a classification that is both exceedingly broad (in that they extend to ideational characteristics, belief systems and political alliances) and exceedingly narrow (in that they exclude members of the community whose views may not match up with the definition). Democratic legitimacy is undermined in both respects.

Definitions erect borders around concepts that otherwise overlap. While the borders they create impart cognitive coherence, the identities they capture undergo simplification when they are constrained to fit narrow definitions. Religions in particular confound most reasonable attempts at definition. This point is borne out through the examples of efforts to define the three major Abrahamic religions: Judaism, Christianity and Islam. Each admits of such diversity in doctrinal and other realms, that any efforts at definition are bound to be contested, by gatekeepers as well as by dissenters. Historically, monotheistic religions have often embraced exclusive definitions, but pluralist states are compromised by such border policing of identities. While *aspects* of each of these religions can be captured within the pluralist state, the selection process – which considers some characteristics more relevant than others, and defines groups according to these values – is necessarily hierarchical, political and affected by bias.

From a pluralistic and democratic perspective, religions can be *thickly characterised*; they cannot be comprehensively defined. To the extent that we define religions by contrasting them with what they are not, we are engaging in theology, not legal or political reason. No extrinsic verbal formulation – whether a simple sentence or a book-length report – can definitively capture what it means to identify as Jewish, Christian or Muslim (or to belong to any other religion). In each case, the range of valid meanings exceeds the scope of any definition. We might more usefully aim for what Clifford Geertz has described as 'thick description' in the context of ethnographic fieldwork than aspire to generate finalising definition for legal ends.[31]

---

30 See Modood, 'Islamophobia, Antisemitism and the Struggle for Recognition'.

31 The potential of Geertz's proposal for defining racism is further explored in Gould,

From the premise that a pluralist democracy cannot definitively define religions, it follows that attempting to define bigotry against a specific religion for legal purposes may cause more harm than good. Bigotry against members of a religion should be prosecuted as a hate crime when it involves criminal violence or destruction to a person or property based on the characteristics associated with members of a religion; there is also scope for criminalising anti-religious bigotry in the context of anti-discrimination legislation. To the extent that they pertain to material harms, neither hate crime nor anti-discrimination legislation necessarily or inevitably infringe on free speech. But when bigotry is expressed discursively, because it is grounded in racist stereotypes and relies on fictions concerning the object of contempt, justifications for its censorship are inherently subjective. The specific content of bigotry's fabrication is incidental to its definition; if it conforms to an identifiable pattern that is grounded in stereotypes and devoid of evidence, it is reasonable to describe that attitude as bigoted, regardless of the object of its animus, or the bigotry's content. Such an approach counters a tendency to identify the source of bigotry in the victim by recognising the origin of the prejudice in the bigot. Certain forms of identity politics, for example, fall into the trap of reifying the bigotries to which minorities are subject, rather than exposing their disconnect from reality. By permitting hateful speech that is not directly linked to conduct, a pluralistic democracy can reveal how bigoted discourse is disconnected from reality, and thereby sever any perceived link with the ostensible target of animus.

The above pertains to bigotry against people perceived to belong to certain races. But what of hostility towards religions, and towards members of these religions? We can arrive at a plausible definition of such hostility only through a workable and widely accepted definition of what Islam (or Judaism or Christianity) is. Here the problems begin. For a pluralistic democracy cannot define a religion. Every religion must define itself on its own terms; this must be done internally rather than defined by a state, whether or not it is a democracy. Yet any definition of Islamophobia presupposes a definition of Islam. While believers may define these concepts in the ways that make the most sense to them, the moment the state becomes involved in mandating or even preferring certain definitions over others is the moment when a government-backed definition of Islamophobia begins to pose a threat, not only to free speech, but also to freedom for Muslims within that state to define themselves as they choose. Here

'Does Defining Racism Help Overcome It?'.

we see how free speech violations threaten pluralistic legitimacy and vice versa. Such manoeuvrings limit the autonomy of individual Muslims, particularly in Muslim-minority societies such as the UK, to define Islam for themselves and on their own terms. They also compel such individuals to align with specific Muslim groups and specific versions of Islam. While it may be claimed that every Muslim community requires a minimalist definition of Islamophobia, history offers many examples of scenarios in which it is not advisable for such definitions to receive backing from the state.

2. Regulating Islam

In order to illustrate how a definition of Islamophobia could be harmful to Muslims, I will examine the recent history of governmental efforts to counter Islamophobia within the UK. The APPG on British Muslims was formed in July 2017, with the aim of informing 'Parliament and parliamentarians of ... the aspirations and challenges of British Muslim communities' and of investigating 'the forms, manifestations and extent of prejudice, discrimination and hatred against Muslims in the UK'.[32] Although the APPG is not solely focused on defining Islamophobia, this has become its primary mandate. This group has been haunted by definitional ambiguity and political infighting from its inception. Following public pressure, six MPs affiliated with the APPG abruptly cancelled their plans to attend an Islamophobia awareness event sponsored by Muslim Engagement & Development (MEND) on the grounds that the group did not 'have the best of reputations'.[33]

The basis for the MPs' recusal remains obscure and therefore difficult to assess. News reports suggest that it was linked to a report by the neoconservative Henry Jackson Society (HJS). According to the report, which is unsurprisingly hostile towards its subject, 'Mend and its employees and volunteers have on numerous occasions attacked *liberal* Muslim groups and *Muslims engaged in*

32 'Register of All-Party Parliamentary Groups [as at 28 September 2017]', Parliament.uk, https://publications.parliament.uk/pa/cm/cmallparty/170928/british-muslims.htm.

33 Quoted in Iram Ramzan and Andrew Gilligan, 'MPs Ditch Meeting with Muslim Group Mend over Islamist Claims', *Times*, 29 October 2017, www.thetimes.co.uk/article/mps-ditch-meeting-with-muslim-group-mend-over-islamist-claims-rgxqnoso5. For a detailed account, see Chris Allen, '"A Momentous Occasion": An Independent Report to the All Party Parliamentary Group on Islamophobia', 15 July 2011, https://issuu.com/drchrisallen/docs/chrisallen-appg_narrative_report-july_2011/13.

counter-extremism, and on occasion, Mend volunteers have expressed *intolerance* towards other Muslim denominations.'[34] The phrases highlighted here reveal a pronounced tendency to police the boundaries of Islam, such that only 'liberal' Muslim groups which reject 'intolerance' and support 'counter-extremism' are deemed worthy of inclusion within British society. Pluralistic democratic legitimacy requires a much more inclusive approach than that proposed by the HJS and apparently internalised by the APPG on British Muslims. A pluralistic democracy will inevitably include among its members individuals who are neither liberal nor tolerant, yet whose speech is as deserving of protection as anyone else.

The internal differences given in the HJS report as a reason for the government to distance itself from MEND illustrates why a democratic state should refrain from endorsing any definition of Islamophobia that would legitimate one specific Muslim group while delegitimising others. Within a pluralist democracy, the authority to address internal differences within Islam is best left to Muslims themselves. A secular government that intervenes in such affairs, by refusing to align with certain groups on reputational grounds, and in response to media pressure, is, according to this standard, made less democratic by virtue of such intervention. The government's adoption of the IHRA definition of antisemitism provides ample evidence for how government involvement in defining prejudice against a religious community can work to that community's detriment. Many Jewish organisations and individuals have voiced their opposition to the IHRA definition, even as their objections have gone ignored, by the conservative-leaning Board of Jewish Deputies which spearheaded the IHRA adoption and, following their lead, the government itself.[35] Elevating one group over another, definitions like that of the IHRA are inherently conservative in that they offer simplistic solutions to complex realities.

A definitional framework leads us to focus on Islam as a religion, when it would be more productive to focus on anti-Muslim racism (in the case of discrimination) and on violence directed against Muslims (in the case of hate crimes) and on neutralising the discursive and material power of such expressions of bigotry. Definitional frameworks situate legal systems within a victim-blaming epistemology, turning offenses against religious communi-

34 Tom Wilson, *MEND: 'Islamists Masquerading as Civil Libertarians'* (London: Henry Jackson Society, 2017), 81 (emphasis added).

35 At least three UK Jewish groups have been outspoken in their opposition to the IHRA definition: Free Speech on Israel, the Jewish Socialists Group and Jewdas.

ties into occasions for scrutinising the targeted community, in the name of their protection. When engaged in by sympathetic politicians, the scrutiny may appear favourable and intended to reinforce Islam's positive qualities. It would be a mistake, however, to take comfort in the simulated benevolence of the neo-liberal state. Even Conservative Prime Minister David Cameron had positive words for Islam in his paternalistic 'Extremism' speech that set the stage for future government policy on British Muslims, including Prevent.[36] As I have argued here, regardless of how such a rapprochement might appear to support Muslim integration into European societies, it can be harmful to Muslim minorities in the long run, particularly when the same agencies mandated to protect to Islam disproportionately surveil Muslims, even while categorising Islam as a religion they must protect.

3. Conflating Terrorism and Hateful Speech

The strongest argument against a governmental definition of Islamophobia lies with the government itself. UK government policy and legislation in relation to Muslims conflates religious incitement with the propagation of hate speech. The Racial and Religious Hatred Act of 2006 (henceforth RRHA), drawn up shortly after the London bombings of July 2005, exemplifies this conflation. 'A person who publishes or distributes written material which is threatening is guilty of an offence if he intends thereby to stir up religious hatred,'[37] the legislation reads. With such a formulation, the legislation defines 'religious hatred' as a form of expression that is subject to criminal sanctions. Among the side effects of this conflation is a focus on (Islamist) terrorism – the backdrop against which the RRHA was created – as an ideology, rather than as a mode of violence, and an assumption that the best way of combating it is to wage ideological warfare on certain varieties of Islam. Human rights advocates have criticised this ideological turn, with Conor Gearty noting that the 'evolution of the term "terrorism" from describing a kind of violence to a morally loaded condemnation of the actions of subversive groups regardless of the context of their actions – or even sometimes their non-violent nature ... is a movement

36 David Cameron, 'Extremism: PM Speech', 20 July 2015, www.gov.uk/government/speeches/extremism-pm-speech.

37 'Hatred against Persons on Religious Grounds', www.legislation.gov.uk/ukpga/2006/1/schedule/data.xht?view=snippet&wrap=true.

in language that operates wholly in favour of state authorities'.[38] Government efforts to broaden the meaning of terrorism are related to the drive to broaden the meaning of Islamophobia. In both cases, broadening the definition extends the remit of the state and enhances its coercive powers.

While the association between terrorism and Islam is widespread among the public and is also propagated by media coverage, most problematically from the point of view of democratic legitimacy, it is also entailed in the RRHA. Without naming Islam, the legislation criminalises the propagation of religious hatred on the grounds of its association with incitement to violence. This association recalls the guidelines drafted by the government to assist in the implementation of Prevent. One formula that features in such guidance runs as follows: 'non-violent extremism ... can create an atmosphere conducive to terrorism and can popularise views which terrorists then exploit.'[39] Another Prevent guidance document notes this change in policy, while repeating the same formula: 'the Prevent strategy was explicitly changed in 2011 to deal with all forms of terrorism and with non-violent extremism, which can create an atmosphere conducive to terrorism and can popularise views which terrorists then exploit.'[40] In both the RRHA and the Prevent guidelines, the definition of dangerous discourse is purposively extended to encompass views which are not *prima facie* supportive of violence. So long as they fall under the rubric of 'extremist', such views, according to this government policy, should be suppressed. Of course, views are not 'extremist' in the abstract; they necessarily have substantive content. In the understanding of the government as well as in the popular imagination, the substantive content of extremism overlaps with Islam.

Aware perhaps that 'extremism' may seem vague, the government has (predictably) offered a definition. According to the Prevent duty guidance, extremism is 'vocal or active opposition to fundamental British values, including democracy, the rule of law, individual liberty and mutual respect and tolerance of different faiths and beliefs'.[41] Echoing Cameron's 2015 speech, this definition blurs analytically distinct boundaries while nationalising ideological warfare as the defence

38 Conor Gearty, 'Human Rights in an Age of Counter-Terrorism', in *'War on Terror': The Oxford Amnesty Lectures*, ed. Chris Miller (Manchester: Manchester University Press, 2013), 85.

39 'Prevent Duty Guidance', 6, www.legislation.gov.uk/ukdsi/2015/9780111133309/pdfs/ukdsiod_9780111133309_en.pdf.

40 This specific formulation is scrutinised in Conor Gearty, *On Fantasy Island: Britain, Europe, and Human Rights* (Oxford: Oxford University Press, 2016), 206.

41 'Prevent Duty Guidance', 6.

of 'British values'. Elided from this equation are the ways in which British values also encompass racism, contempt for the poor, colonialism, homophobia and sexism. Generations of scholarship support such characterisations, even though these flaws are not uniquely British. Is the scholarship on British colonialism, austerity, homophobia and misogyny 'extremist'? Why assume without demonstration that 'British values' are epitomised by 'mutual respect and tolerance of different faiths and beliefs'? Worst of all, why embed such loaded language in legislation? The government's definition of extremism leaves these questions unresolved, resulting in the appearance of a state that aims above all to protect the status quo, even at the cost of denying equality to all citizens.

Further contributing to an impression of double standards in regards to Muslims, the section of the RRHA that protects freedom of expression focuses on the protection of anti-Muslim sentiment without extending comparable protections to the expression of non-violent Islamic belief. In terms that, considered in the context of the War on Terror, clearly evoke (and render immune from prosecution) criticism of Islam, the legislation stipulates that it should not be interpreted in ways that would restrict 'discussion, criticism or expressions of antipathy, dislike, ridicule, insult or abuse of particular religions or the beliefs or practices of their adherents'. By contrast, no provision within the RRHA protects Islam from being vilified through its association with violent incitement and hate speech. This would appear to be a textbook case of prejudice inscribed within the law, since the free expression of anti-Muslim sentiment is protected by this legislation, which has as its primary purpose the censorship of hateful speech that speaks in the name of religion, and which the government has already associated with Islamic discourse. No explanation is given for why hateful speech should be further criminalised on the grounds of its religious content, or why Islamic discourse is perceived as more dangerous than white supremacist bigotry.

It can be argued that, far from countering Islamophobic prejudice, such confusing provisions within the RRHA legitimate passive racism. Equally, it is at least arguable that the claims made in the Prevent guidance concerning 'British values' stem from nationalist prejudice regarding the superiority of British culture to other cultures that Nasar Meer and Tariq Modood have characterised as 'cultural racism' (though they may not agree with this specific application of the term).[42] The British government's formulation seems

42 Nasar Meer and Tariq Modood, 'Islamophobia as Cultural Racism? Martin Amis and the Racialization of Muslims', in *Thinking through Islamophobia*, 69–83.

to presuppose the inferiority of 'Islamic values' to 'British values', even while claiming to protect them. Would the opposite view – that 'Islamic values' are superior to 'British values' – be deemed 'extremist'? Surely, in a democratic pluralist society, this should be regarded as just one more legitimate point of view – among many. Why should a government that enshrines a double standard of suspicion against Islam into its legislation be trusted to protect this religion through a legal definition of Islamophobia? Would it not be more sensible to critically scrutinise the Islamophobic dimensions of a state's legislation rather than to entrust that state to criminalise views that are in fact reinforced and legitimated by its War on Terror?

HAIDAR HOBBALLAH

Intellectual Media: Jurisprudence and the Books of Misguidance

Translated by Fatima M. Zaraket and Dima El-Mouallem

1. Introduction

The issue of intellectual and cultural media is one of the most important and sensitive issues of our present age. Muslim jurists have addressed it under different titles, the most important of which is 'The Books of Misguidance' (*kutub al-ḍalāl*). They mostly focused on the permissibility of keeping such books, in addition to other matters. A 'book' for them is only the most prominent example of any communicative media activity. When I use the word 'books' in this paper, I mean the general concept of every misguided media, publication or other means of communication.

I do not wish to go into the history of this matter, which, for the Imāmīs, goes back to the books of Shaykh al-Mufīd and Shaykh al-Ṭūsī, among others. This matter was first raised under the name of 'The Books of Blasphemy' (*kutub al-kufr*). The scope of this category gradually expanded to include the books of misguidance, such as books that contain innovation, abrogation, distortion, derision, lampooning, sorcery (*siḥr*), ichnomancy (*qiyāfa*) and legerdemain (*sha'wadha*). Later, exceptions were made in favour of keeping such books for the purpose of responding to misguidance. These exceptions eventually expanded as jurists came to realise the usefulness of keeping such books in general.

In this day and age, this issue has come to hold an even greater importance with its scope of application becoming much larger in the face of a number of questions which this paper shall attempt to address. Some of these questions are the following:

- Essentially, what is misguidance? What is the concept around which the rulings of our discussion revolves? Is it the concept of blasphemy, misguidance, innovation, deviation, encouraging corruption or something else? How can we determine these concepts and what are their standards? Who determines these standards and how?

- Can a person keep books of misguidance in his own personal library, for instance? Can he lend them to others and facilitate their usage?

- Should the state or society keep or agree to keep the books of guidance in their midst or should they take certain measures? What are these measures? Can the state subsidise these books at the level of paper and printing costs, for example?

- Is this ruling limited to the books of misguidance or does it include all sorts of misguided media, such as audio-visual, newspapers, publications, periodicals, books, advertisements, lectures, speeches, not to mention plays, acting roles, photography and all other media and means of expression? Would it include intellectuals, preachers, merchants, storytellers, poets, actors, photographers, painters, programmers and those who work on the Internet?

- What is the ruling when it comes to an individual reading books of misguidance? How about society as a whole?

- Is it permissible to compose books of misguidance? Is it permissible to propagate misguided ideas in society?

- What is the ruling about propagating, distributing and promoting misguidance using different media? What is the responsibility of publishing and distribution houses and satellite channels? Is it permissible to publish an article of misguidance? Is it permissible if a response is appended to it? Is it permissible to host a guest with misguided and un-Islamic thoughts in the media to present his ideas? Is it permissible to host such a person in scholarly venues or should he be categorically boycotted? Is citing misguided sources in bibliographies, for instance, Islamically problematic? Is introducing people to such sources permissible? Is propagation and promotion permissible on the grounds that such thought is bound to be known sooner or later?

- Is it permissible to use books or topics of misguidance as teaching materials? Is it permissible to teach atheistic thought, for example, with or without refuting it? What is the position of ministries of education and higher education and school and university administration from raising such issues in curricula?

- Is freedom of thought guaranteed in Islam or is it categorically prohibited? Alternatively, is the issue more nuanced? And if yes, what are these nuances?

- Are there primary and secondary considerations that govern all these themes? What are the most important secondary considerations and their justifications?

- Does the problem with misguided thought concern this thought's very existence or is it limited to when it undermines the religious feeling in society? An equivalent example would be if fears surfaced in the West about undermining democracy.

- Does Islam forbid the support of misguidance, forbid silence about it or forbid its very existence?

- What are the jurisprudential propositions on this? What can we conclude from comparing Islamic jurisprudence and the West concerning these types of freedom?

These are just some of the questions that emerge in this regard. I should point out that this research only concerns freedom of intellectual and cultural media. We are not talking about political, religious and other freedoms. Rather, I am discussing pure media freedom that encompasses the intellectual sphere in its entirety. These are two distinct issues, yet they remain closely connected.

2. What Is Misguidance?

The most critical and important point here is the definition and limits of misguidance. The jurists often addressed this point by offering definitions that are more nebulous than the term itself. They assumed that the term was clear and proceeded to explain the ruling (*al-ḥukm*) while neglecting the subject (*al-mawḍūʿ*). Scant references are made to examples from the Torah and the Gospel in this regard. What is the kind of misguidance whose books are prohibited? What is the kind of misguidance whose propagation is prohibited? Does misguidance include the books of blasphemy and the books of other religions? Does it include the books of all or some sects? Does it include books that deride and lampoon religion, as the elaborated categories of some works suggest? Are books on sorcery, ichnomancy, legerdemain and the like books of misguidance? Is misguidance, rather, anything that contradicts the truth (*al-ḥaqq*) as al-Muḥaqqiq al-Narāqī holds?[1] What truth does he mean? Is he talking about the truth in all branches of knowledge or the truth in religious sciences or creed alone? What if two *mujtahid*s disagreed on something such that one affirmed that what the other was saying was false in a way that he was convinced that the latter jurist opposed the truth? Some even consider the books of truth as books of misguidance if they lead to the misguidance of the people. An example of this is the books of the mystics (*al-ʿurafāʾ*). Muṭahharī replaced the concept of books of misguidance by misguiding books (*kutub al-iḍlāl*).[2] Others connect the issue to the author's intention and not to the book and its effects.

According to general religious principles, there are things that may be automatically classified under the umbrella of misguidance, such as denying the existence of God. According to Islamic standards, some things classify as manifest misguidance such as denying God's unity or denying prophethood. According to more specific sectarian principles, denying the Imāmate constitutes misguidance for the Shīʿa and denying the Islam and uprightness (*ʿadāla*) of the major Companions constitutes misguidance for the Sunnīs. Nevertheless, these are limited cases that do not have a clear benchmark.

A question poses itself here: is there a rubric according to which we can classify books and ideas as falling within or without the domain of misguidance? If yes, what is this rubric? If we go back to the root of the word and view misguidance as an antonym of guidance and as a synonym of bewilderment, perplexity and deviation, this will result in new problems. This is because each jurist would consider the other jurists misguided and would classify their books as books of misguidance. Similarly, every group of people would view the others as misguided, whether at the level of theology, philosophy, tradition (*ḥadīth*), history, politics or other fields. This is because the term *ḍalāl* itself encompasses such a meaning; in Arabic, anyone who makes a mistake is someone who has lost his way (*aḍalla al-ṭarīq*). This understanding is tantamount to closing the gates of *ijtihād*, and it contradicts the consensus of the Umma. No one can accept such an understanding, nor do I believe that anyone adheres to it.

1 See Aḥmad al-Narāqī, *Mustanad al-Shīʿa* (Qom: Muʾassasat Āl al-Bayt li-Iḥyāʾ al-Turāth, 1994–99), 14:158.

2 Murtaḍā Muṭahharī, *Majmūʿa-yi āthār* (*al-Majmūʿa al-kāmila*) (Qom: Intishārāt-i Ṣadrā, n.d.), 30:566.

2.1 What Is Misguidance, Then?

I believe that we ought to omit this word out of our discussion because it is a cause for confusion. If some examples, such as denying the existence of God, definitively fall under this heading, this does not present us with a standard and a rubric that we can legally use. For this reason, we omitted the term from the title of this study and replaced it with the present title – 'Intellectual Media'. I think that concepts like misguidance and innovation and so on have been taken advantage of by certain religious and political history because they are nebulous and unclear in order to settle scores with religious, sectarian and intellectual minorities. This latter group particularly includes the Muʿtazila, the Shīʿa, the Sufis and the philosophers, who themselves accused others of misguidance and innovation. This only served to make these concepts and their limits more mystifying and ambiguous throughout history. The Ḥanbalīs and others wrote books and issued legal opinions prohibiting works of theology for being symbols of books of misguidance. Ibn Qudāma al-Maqdisī wrote his famous treatise, *Taḥrīm al-naẓar fī ʿilm al-kalām*, which ultimately led to burning philosophy books in public areas. These were famous and avowed incidents in Islamic history; some of them must be known to people who are familiar with the lives of Imām al-Ghazālī, the philosopher Ibn Rushd and others. Even in contemporary times, the books of figures like al-Sayyid Muḥammad Ḥusayn Faḍlallāh, 'Abd al-Karīm Soroush and 'Alī Sharīʿatī have been considered by some jurists as books of misguidance.

Many Muslim jurists took the decisive decision of prohibiting even a look at such works. Consider the following by al-Bahūtī where he says, 'It is impermissible by textual evidence to look into the books of the People of the Book ... the books of innovators and the books that contain a welter of truth and falsehood. Likewise, it is impermissible to transmit such works because all this carries the risk of corrupting sound doctrines.'[3] Following this same logic, al-Shāṭibī issued a legal opinion prohibiting the reading of some of the books of Abū Ṭālib al-Makkī considering the ecstatic utterances (*shaṭaḥāt*) that they contained, and Ibn Ḥajar prohibited people who are not steadfast in knowledge from looking into such books. Many open-minded jurists did just that, such as Muḥammad Rashīd Riḍā and others.

3 Manṣūr ibn Yūnus al-Bahūtī, *Kashshāf al-qināʿ*, ed. Muḥammad Ḥasan Ismāʿīl al-Shāfiʿī (Beirut: Dār al-Kutub al-ʿIlmiyya, 1997), 1:525–26.

In other words, the only thing we can do here is proceed right to the evidence and then deduce the subject's limits and domain. The category of misguidance is most likely created by the jurists themselves. This will become clear in the course of this paper.

3. General Proofs

There are primary proofs that have been instrumental for Islamic jurisprudence on this topic. We have to deduce these and other proofs to try and discern their scope. They are as follows.

3.1 The Qur'anic Basis

The jurists spoke about a number of verses, which are set out below.

— The Verse on Diversionary Talk: What Is the Relation?

The first verse is God's saying, 'Among the people is he who engages in vain talk that he may lead [people] astray from God's way without any knowledge, and he takes it in derision. For such there is a humiliating punishment' (31:6).

This Qur'anic verse was considered key here, especially considering its occasion of revelation. It was mentioned that Ibn al-Ḥārith sought to travel to the Sassanian Empire during the reign of the Prophet. His goal was to bring back books of mythology and promote them in Arabia, hoping to obstruct the Islamic message.[4]

The relation of this incident to the verse is that it considered the engagement in vain discourse a form of misguidance and a prohibited act that aims to mislead people. Anyone who does this is deserving of punishment, and any book, periodical or TV show that includes such content is subsumed under the verse.

However, if we examine the verse closely, either disregarding the occasions of revelation because of their doubtful historicity, or taking them into account, we will conclude the following. First, the verse prohibits promoting misguidance and diversionary content, but it does not prohibit keeping it to refute it,

4 See al-Faḍl ibn al-Ḥasan al-Ṭabrisī, *Majmaʿ al-bayān*, 2nd ed. (Beirut: Dār al-Maʿrifa, 1988), 8:76.

listening to it, reading it, buying it, and so on. Although the verse condemns a specific individual for promoting misguidance through *lahw al-ḥadīth* (vain speech), it does not contain any indication about the religious duties or obligations upon others in relation to him or his ideas. Second, the segment 'that he may lead [people] astray from God's way' imposes a further specification. There is a difference between the person who writes a book with the intention of leading people astray and another who writes a book with the intention of displaying a view that he believes is correct. A *mujtahid* may believe that a certain theological proposition is correct, but this belief of his may be incorrect. It is not right to say that the intention of such a person is to misguide people and lead them astray from the way of God. The agent's intention has an effect, namely, whether or not he is included in the punishment of God. Sometimes, his view may be excusable. Since the verse imposes humiliating punishment, it is doubtful that it signifies any and all forms of misguidance, up to and including excusable confusion. This behoves us to accept the certain part of the verse's signification, which is misguiding people without excuse. Otherwise, the ruling would include many jurists, theologians, Uṣūlīs, Akhbārīs and exegetes, especially ones who disagree among each other about major issues that have an influence on understanding religion in general.

Third, the part 'he takes it in derision' further clarifies the situation. The pronoun 'it' refers to the way of God. This would mean that the verse implies 'he who buys diversionary talk wants to misguide people and mock and demean the way of God'. The verse is then discussing an offensive context. As for those who present their ideas in a purely scholarly way, with the aim of proving or disproving something, they are not included in the verse. Four, if we closely consider 'without any knowledge' in order to better understand this part, we will find ourselves before two possibilities. The first possibility is that the meaning of knowledge is the same as what is understood today, which is contrasted by ignorance and lack of knowledge. In this case, the meaning would be as follows: among the people is he who buys diversionary talk that he may misguide [people] without knowing that he is doing so, that is, he does not realise that he is misguiding people. In the phrase 'without knowledge' (*bi-ghayr 'ilm*), the genitive clause (*jārr wa-majrūr*) is related to 'that he may misguide'. The meaning would be misguiding in ignorance or misguiding without knowing that he is misguiding.

Such a consequence seems incongruent with the accepted rational and religious principles of reward and punishment. If this person does not know that he is buying misguiding materials that misguide other people, how can he be punished? It is assumed that he is ignorant, and there is no obligation upon the ignorant. For this reason, and as some modern jurists have stated, this possibility may be eliminated.[5]

The second possibility was expressed by some modern jurists to the effect that the phrase 'without knowledge' means without awareness and out of rashness and personal desire. The person who does this out of lack of awareness and based on rashness and whims is the person intended in the verse.[6] This possibility explains the lack of knowledge as ignorance in the meaning of rashness.

The most probable interpretation of 'without knowledge' is likely 'without proof'. In this case, the meaning would be that a person is misguiding people and leading them away from the way of God without proof that supports his actions. In other words, the meaning is not that he misguides without knowing it for us to talk about the obligation of the ignorant and how detestable it is to punish him. Rather, the meaning is that he is misguiding others without knowledge of the thing that he is misguiding people towards or away from.

Although my own explanation eventually coincides with the second explanation of some contemporaries, it is different in its consequences and rationale. This understanding that combines my view and that of other contemporaries is supported by the use of this term in the Qur'an multiple times. God says, 'Indeed many mislead [others] by their whims, without any knowledge. Indeed your Lord knows best the transgressors' (6:119); 'They are certainly losers who slay their children foolishly without knowledge, and forbid what God has provided them, fabricating a lie against God. Certainly, they have gone astray and are not guided' (6:140); 'Eight mates: two of sheep, and two of goats. Say, "Is it the two males that He has forbidden or the two females, or what is contained in the wombs of the two females? Inform me with knowledge, should you be truthful." And two of camels and two of oxen. Say, "Is it the two males that He has forbidden or the two females, or what is contained in the wombs of the two females? Were you witnesses when God enjoined this upon you?" So who is a greater wrongdoer than him who fabricates a lie against God to mislead the people without any knowledge? Indeed God does not guide the wrongdoing lot' (6:143–44); and 'Among the people are those who dispute concerning God without any knowledge or guidance, or an enlightening Book, turning aside disdainfully to lead [others] astray from the way of God. For such there is dis-

5 Yūsuf al-Ṣāni'ī, *Muqārabāt fī al-tajdīd al-fiqhī*, ed. and trans. Ḥaydar Ḥubb Allāh (Beirut: Mu'assasat al-Intishār al-'Arabī, 2010), 68.

6 Ibid., 68–69.

grace in this world, and on the Day of Resurrection We will make him taste the punishment of the burning' (22:8–9; see also 22:3, 31:20). These verses show that what is meant by knowledge is proof, basis and objective information in contrast to whims, personal preferences, tendencies and interests.

Nevertheless, the main question here is whether this is a hypothetical example that God makes as a legislating master or whether it is informing us that those who misguide from the way of God do not actually know what they are saying, meaning that what they imagine as proof and knowledge is nothing but speculation and conjecture. It seems that the aim of the verse is to inform, but this information does not concern everyone who contradicts religion. Its purpose is to inform us that there are people like this, while remaining silent about others who also misguide people. This means that the verse does not include a misguiding person who is knowledgeable but confused about a certain issue, regardless of whether such a person actually exists. All the verse is saying is that there are some people who have no knowledge or understanding of things and who misguide from the way of God without having any scholarly proof to justify their position. If a person had such proofs, even if he was wrong, he would not be included in the verse. If you say to Zayd, 'If you hit 'Amr for stealing without knowing that he in fact stole, I will punish you,' this does not apply if Zayd had objective evidence to prove that 'Amr had stolen. At most, Zayd might have gotten confused about a minor detail, as sometimes happens with some intellectuals, *mujtahids*, judges and other figures.

This opens up the way for discussing a phenomenon important for understanding the context of the verses. Were the objections of the Arabs during the Prophetic age scholarly and objective or were they the result of egotism, obstinacy, malice and whims? In other words, was the Arabian misguidance at the time similar to the misguidance of intellectuals in this age of scholarly complications and qualitative doubts? Was their misguidance mostly a result of personal whims and not scholarly complications, whereas the misguidance of today includes both kinds? Were the opponents of the prophets intellectuals who had their own views or did they oppose the prophets out of obstinacy and personal interests although they knew the truth in themselves or their sacred books but suppressed it? Some Qur'anic texts refer both to knowledge and the suppression of it. This is the case of people who witness miracles with their own eyes. This is an important topic that paves the way for understanding many Qur'anic texts that berate the faithless, but this is a topic for another time. In summary, the part 'without any knowledge' in the verse does not include instances of misguidance and misguiding that result from the sheer complexity of honest scholarly endeavours.

Fifth, what is the meaning of 'God's way' in the verse? Some scholars mention that it refers to the Qur'an.[7] Taking the occasion of revelation into consideration, the misguidance concerned would be the kind that opposes the Qur'an and contradicts the way of the prophets.[8] We will not rely on the occasions of revelation because they are historically doubtful. However, if we note the many places in the Qur'an where the expression 'God's way' occurs, we will see that it means the way of monotheistic religion that was brought forth by the prophets. Every deviation from this path constitutes misguiding away from God's way.

Nevertheless, the question that arises is this: does it mean turning people away from the true religion and directing them to idolatry versus monotheism such that it may be said, 'We turned them away from Islam'? Does it include partially turning people away, such as turning someone away from committing to a particular legal ruling? Does the verse include the second case or not? In other words, is the way of God an inseparable whole? Is it a path that requires the entire set of obligations or is it the aggregate number of doctrines, obligations and other matters?

If we consider the occasions of revelation or the historical contexts of these texts, we should limit ourselves to the more restricted meaning because this is the kind of turning away and misguiding that was present back then. Even the Qur'anic context itself encourages such a proposition; the immediately subsequent verse which continues the topic states: 'When Our manifest signs are recited to them, you perceive denial on the faces of the faithless: they would almost pounce upon those who recite Our signs to them. Say, "Shall I inform you about something worse than that? The Fire which God has promised the faithless. And it is an evil destination"' (22:72). It may be inferred from this verse that it concerns a person who does not believe in the Qur'an and does not want to hear its recitation, and is eager to turn people away from the core of the prophetic, monotheistic project. Despite this, it might be said that there is no problem in generalising the text and making its most obvious manifestation the absolute turning away from the way of God.

7 See Muḥammad Ḥusayn al-Ṭabāṭabā'ī, *al-Mīzān* (Beirut: Mu'assasat al-A'lamī li-l-Maṭbū'āt, 1970), 16:208.

8 al-Ṣāni'ī, *Muqārabāt fī al-tajdīd al-fiqhī*, 68.

Sixth, the verse contains the concept of buying diversionary talk. Nevertheless, it is not improbable to generalise the concept to include any engagement of diversionary talk with the purpose of misguiding, even if this acquirement was not by way of buying and selling. It is not improbable for this act of buying to have a general meaning whose most important manifestation is buying with money, with the meaning of bartering or acquiring something. The purpose within the verse itself permits such a generalisation.

In conclusion, this verse announces a prohibitive, punitive ruling against anyone who seeks to use any diversionary, futile, false talk to misguide people away from the way of God and deride it out of whims and other motives. It seems that more general meanings are not included in the verse. This means that there is no point in including this verse in the discussion of the rulings on keeping the books of misguidance, regardless of the intention to misguide. The verse is equally unrelated to censoring the freedom of intellectual and cultural media, because it speaks of the agent but not of our position and duties towards him.

— The Verse on Avoiding False Speech

The second verse is 'So avoid the abomination of idols, and avoid false speech' (22:30). The verse was understood as prohibiting books of misguidance.[9] However, using this verse as proof of the prohibition of books of misguidance is problematic in more ways than one.

The first problem is that the apparent meaning of avoiding false speech is avoiding uttering it. If I say, 'Avoid false speech, lying, treachery and frivolity,' it should be understood that I am asking you not to do any of these things. I am not asking you to avoid listening to them, seeing them or transmitting them, nor am I asking you to forbid others from doing them. This is of certain significance to the text. According to custom, avoiding false speech does not mean the illicitness of listening to false speech in court. Such an interpretation is somewhat convoluted because avoiding a thing depends on the thing itself. Avoiding false speech is customarily understood as not engaging in it.

This is why some exegetes have said that false speech here means the *talbiya* [from the Arabic verb *labbā*, i.e. to obey the call or invitation of someone] of the pre-Islamic Arabs, which constitutes polytheism because they used to say,

9 See Muḥammad Ḥasan ibn Bāqir al-Najafī, *Jawāhir al-kalām fī sharḥ Sharā'i' al-Islām*, 7th ed. (Beirut: Dār Iḥyā' al-Turāth al-'Arabī, n.d.), 22:57.

'Here I am, O God, here I am. Here I am. You have no partners except one, and You own him and everything that he owns.'[10]

The second problem is that the context of the verses themselves helps my own interpretation. The verse is part of the context on the verses on the pilgrimage. If we consider the full verse as well as the subsequent verse that is grammatically linked to it, we will realise the following. God said, '... And whoever venerates the sacraments of God, that is better for him with his Lord. You are permitted [animals of] grazing livestock except for what will be recited to you. So avoid the abomination of idols, and avoid false speech, as persons having pure faith in God, not ascribing partners to Him. Whoever ascribes partners to God is as though he had fallen from a height to be devoured by vultures, or to be blown away by the wind far and wide (22:30–31).'

This means that in the context of a series of verses on the pilgrimage, this verse is commanding avoiding idols and false speech. The Arabs used to daub the blood of the sacrifice on the idols, uttering polytheistic *talbiya*s and such. This is why the following verse includes persons having pure faith in God as a circumstantial adverb (*ḥāl*) with the meaning 'avoid idols and false speech in the circumstance that you are people of pure faith in God who do not associate anything with Him'. This implies that the meaning is something that has to do with polytheism, which increases the possibility that the aim of this verse is to forbid polytheistic phenomena during the pilgrimage and reforming the pilgrimage religiously from an Islamic perspective.

Based on this, the exegete or jurist might be able to bypass this context and take the phrase 'avoid false speech' on its own as a general rule that has the pilgrimage as one of its examples. In this case, he would be forced to include singing, lying, false speech, misguided thought and misguided false speech within false speech. However, expanding the application of the term to a case where the person himself was not the one who uttered the false speech would be a textually unwarranted exaggeration. The verse forbids false speech and uttering misguidance. However, reading, keeping and allowing such speech is not forbidden. In addition, those who utter false speech while thinking that it is the truth are not included in this text and held accountable. If such

10 al-Faḍl ibn al-Ḥasan al-Ṭabrisī, *Jāmiʿ al-jawāmiʿ* (Qom: Muʾassasat al-Nashr al-Islāmī al-Tābiʿa li-Jamāʿat al-Mudarrisīn, 1997), 2:558; al-Ṭabrisī, *Majmaʿ al-bayān*, 7:148.

a person supposedly believed false speech to be true, he would not consider himself addressed by the verse. He would be excused in such a case as long as there are no intentional shortcomings.

The most the verse says, even if we generalise it, is that it is prohibited to utter misguidance by speaking it, endorsing it and encouraging it. As for publishing the misguidance of others, transmitting it, keeping it in books or allowing others to say it, without intending to support or endorse their – for argument's sake – 'misguidance', even then they are things utterly unrelated to the verse.

The third problem is that if we accept the alleged generalised exegesis of the verse, we would have to issue rulings that the proponents of this opinion themselves would not agree with. Generalising the avoidance necessitates the illicitness of hearing misguidance, lies and false speech, in addition to conversing with the faithless and the misguided and their ilk. When false speech is interpreted to mean falsehood in general, this necessitates that the opinion of one exegete or jurist should be false for another exegete or jurist and therefore should be avoided. Can anyone accept such a thing?

A fair commentator on this issue would say that the verse has nothing to do with our topic aside from the extent that I already pointed out, that is, the prohibition of uttering misguidance, choosing it, adhering to it, defending it and strengthening it. This is a prohibition that is not effectuated absolutely, but only after the person knows that this misguidance is indeed misguidance. This is one of the axioms of Islamic law that does not require Qur'anic proof. As for the position of others from misguidance and propagating it, it has nothing to do with the verse.

— The Verse on Fabricating Lies against Allah: A Critical Assessment of al-Muḥaqqiq al-Najafī

The third verse is 'Look, how they fabricate lies against God! That suffices for a flagrant sin' (4:50). Al-Muḥaqqiq al-Najafī based his position on this verse to suggest that the rest of the verses on fabricating lies against God are relevant to our discussion.[11]

However, al-Muḥaqqiq al-Najafī's attempt in this regard is singularly unclear. The verse is entirely irrelevant to our discussion; it concerns fabricating lies and sayings against God and misguiding people by them. What is the relation between this issue and the legal dimensions of intellectual and cultural media

11 al-Najafī, *Jawāhir al-kalām*, 22:57.

or the books of misguidance? The most that the verse entails is the prohibition of fabricating lies against God, attributing things to Him that He did not say, and misguiding others by fabricating things and attributing them to God using lies and falsehood. This is clear enough that it does not even need to be proven using this verse, and it has nothing to do with giving intellectual religious movements their right to practise and express *ijtihād* and allowing the media to discuss these and other matters.

— The Verse on Fabricating Divine Books: A Critical Approach

The fourth verse is 'So woe to those who write the Book with their hands and then say, "This is from Allah," that they may sell it for a paltry gain. So woe to them for what their hands have written, and woe to them for what they earn!' (2:79).

Najafī also relied on this verse without clear proof.[12] The most that this verse prohibits is fabricating books and falsely attributing them to God for money. The verse states that these people knew that they were fabricating lies against God and that they were doing it for a paltry sum. This means that the verse does not include those who mistakenly or unknowingly attribute things to God. Clearly, such a person is excused about his theological, legal or philosophical *ijtihād*.

— Cooperating in Sin: An Analytical Stance

The fifth verse is 'O you who have faith! Do not violate God's sacraments, neither the sacred month, nor the offering, nor the necklaces, nor those bound for the Sacred House who seek their Lord's grace and [His] pleasure. But when you emerge from the pilgrim sanctity you may hunt for game. Ill feeling for a people should not lead you, because they barred you from [entering] the Sacred Mosque, to transgress. Cooperate in piety and Godwariness, but do not cooperate in sin and aggression, and be wary of God. Indeed God is severe in retribution' (5:2).

This verse might be proof of the illicitness of cooperating or helping to print the books or publications of misguidance, distributing them, publishing them, disseminating them in the media, buying them, advertising them or introducing people to them. The illicitness also includes any activities that count as

12 Ibid., 56.

supporting these publications and ideas to prosper. All these things are illicit according to this interpretation.[13] I do not wish to delve into the rule on the illicitness of assisting in sin, which a number of scholars have rejected. What I would like to do is determine the minor (*ṣughrawī*) premise of the topic as well as its external referent (*miṣdāq*). In addition, I would like to analyse into the scope of the verse itself.

As for the verse's scope, the most it signifies is the illicitness of assisting in sin, but it does not indicate the necessity of forcefully standing up to ideas of misguidance. This means it does not offer any ruling on seizing or shutting down the centres, books, publications and media of misguidance. Not seizing these materials is not customarily seen as an act of assistance, because assistance itself is a positive concept. In addition, the verse does not specify any punishable offense, so it cannot be used to prove the licitness of limiting others' freedoms when they promote and produce misguidance. The verse is merely encouraging not assisting in misguidance, which is different from actively confronting it. Even peaceful, scholarly responses to misguidance have nothing to do with the verse unless they are proven to be instances of piety and Godwariness. As for the minor premise of the verse, it can be said that the prevalence of misguided and deviant thoughts has more than one form. This phenomenon has many manifestations on the ground, and I will point some of them out. This idea will become clearer by the end of our discussion, God willing.

The first manifestation is publishing, distributing or buying such materials, which actually necessitates the weakening of faith and general spirituality. Such a thing is clearly prohibited. The second manifestation is when these materials necessitate a weakening of faith, but when this weakening is bound to happen either way, regardless of whether I was the cause of it or someone else. In this case, I might choose to publish such materials myself in a way that mitigates the absolute weakening of faith. This means that what is at stake here includes two possibilities. The first possibility is that other people would publish these materials and weaken the faith to a certain extent. The second possibility is that I would publish them myself in a particular way that would weaken the faith to a much lesser degree. In this case, it is not rational to actually prohibit this if we are certain that we are doing a good and necessary thing. An example is establishing gyms although we know that some prohibited acts are bound

13 See Muḥammad Jawād al-Ḥusaynī al-ʿĀmilī, *Miftāḥ al-karāma fī sharḥ Qawāʾid al-ʿAllāma*, ed. Muḥammad Bāqir al-Khāliṣī (Qom: Muʾassasat al-Nashr al-Islāmī al-Tābiʿa li-Jamāʿat al-Mudarrisīn, 1998), 12:207.

to happen. However, we still do it to keep the youth from resorting to drugs instead. Such an act is not prohibited, and it might even be obligatory.

National or social cultural policies are necessarily attentive to this dimension. The total eclipse of opposing thought, even if it was misguided, and while knowing full well that I cannot fully prohibit it, might actually have more negative consequences than the alternative.

The jurists accept differentiating between the cases that I am mentioning here; they have always allowed mentioning the opponents' claims and refuting them, although this is a propagation of these ideas whether we like it or not. However, when such claims were followed up with refutations, their propagation was not considered assisting in sin. In other words, not every act of publishing, distributing and licensing such materials is prohibited. The prohibition becomes applicable on a case-by-case basis depending on every jurist's view of the interests and balances of everyday life.

The conclusion is that the verse proves the prohibition of some things at most. In addition, the verse concerns sin and aggression, meaning it is irrelevant to juristic, philosophical and theological differences unless these differences have a personal, egotistical or aggressive background. If someone wrote a philosophical book and looked into the unity of existence (*waḥdat al-wujūd*) from a strictly scholarly perspective, this verse does not indicate that it is prohibited to publish his work even if we personally did not agree with his conclusions. This is because his book is not an instance of sin and aggression, so publishing it would not constitute assisting in sin and aggression. The concepts of sin and aggression is different, according to custom, from truth and falsehood and right and wrong.

The result of examining the Qur'anic proofs is that the Qur'an itself does not address this topic at all. It does not address the legal dimensions of dealing with intellectual and cultural media. The verses that the jurists relied upon in this regard are peripheral to our discussion, and the Qur'anic text does not contain any clear legal rationale that directly or semi-directly addresses the issue of intellectual and cultural freedoms. The only things that the Qur'anic text does address are the following:

- It is prohibited to knowingly generate misguidance and falsehood or to defend misguidance without proof. Every activity that a person undertakes with the intention of knowingly supporting misguidance and deviation is illicit and Qur'anically rejected.

- It is impossible to generalise the Qur'anic framework of misguidance to include the differences in theological opinions, not to mention opinions about exegesis, *ḥadīth* and jurisprudence, unless these opinions contain an element of aggression or obstinance and knowingly support falsehood. Only in this case are such opinions prohibited.

- The Qur'an does not accord us a duty towards misguided thought except seeking to counter it and guide the people to the Truth and not assisting people with such thought if they are aggressive; you know that they are misguided, and you know that your assistance would actually strengthen them. As for forbidding such thought, shutting down the centres that promote it or seizing the materials that feature it, they are very difficult to deduce from the Qur'anic text. Where did the Qur'an stipulate seizing misguided intellectual works, shutting down misguided intellectual centres by force, burning and destroying books of misguidance or preventing misguided movements from expressing their opinions in society? The only thing the Qur'an did was to address the misguided, the obstinate, the fabricators of falsehood, the liars and the attributors of falseness to God and told them to stop what they are doing because a punishment would await them in the hereafter unless they had an excuse. The Qur'an gave us the general guideline, which is to be careful of misguidance, without referring to legal details at all.

I will later address the idea of commanding the right and forbidding the wrong and its relation to our discussion. It will become apparent that although religion, the Qur'an and reason commanded this obligation, it is irrelevant to forbidding or censoring misguided thought in the media.

3.2 The Prophetic Sunna

In addition, some jurists similarly relied on the texts of the Sunna. In this regard, a number of narrations are mentioned, which we must trace and examine. The most important of these narrations are the following.

The first narration is the report of ʿAbd al-Malik ibn Aʿyan. He said, 'I said to Abū ʿAbd Allāh (peace be upon him), "I am obsessed with this knowledge. If I wanted to do something, I would look at my forecast and if it was inauspicious, I would be deterred. If it was auspicious, I would proceed." He said to me, "Would you listen to me if I told you what to do?" I said, "Yes." He said, "Burn your books."'[14] (In *Da'awāt al-Rāwandī*, the Imām said, 'Would you do something for me?'[15]) Using this narration as proof is based on the assumption that it indicates the prohibition of keeping the books of misguidance and necessitates burning and destroying them. The narration is primarily understood to indicate the prohibition of any form of supporting and keeping such works. Since there is no difference between books of astrology and others, this ruling would apply to all kinds of books, publications, newsletters and programmes of misguidance no matter what they are.

However, using this narration as proof is problematic for more than one reason, the most important of which are as follows. First, it may be said, as Shaykh al-Anṣārī proposed, that the command to burn the books was not divine; rather, it was a piece of advice to address a problem that 'Abd al-Malik ibn A'yan was facing and that he said was troubling him. The command to burn the books was issued to rid 'Abd al-Malik of this trouble and obsession completely. However, this does not mean that it is an established legal ruling in this regard.[16]

This understanding of the narration is not improbable, but a question remains here. Why did the Imām tell 'Abd al-Malik to destroy his books, which involves wasting money, although he could have told him to sell it to someone who will certainly not be negatively affected? Opting for destroying money rather than preserving it indicates that this behaviour was not to rid 'Abd al-Malik of his problem. The latter could have been achieved by selling the books. 'Abd al-Malik would not have been ordered to destroy his books if their very presence was not problematic. This is not enough to assume an advisory aspect within the incident unless we say that the order to burn the books involves an educational and psychological dimension that achieves a personal feeling of being saved from these books, severing attachments to them and purifying oneself of them. Such a possibility is not improbable.

14 Muḥammad ibn 'Alī ibn al-Ḥusayn ibn Bābawayh al-Qummī al-Ṣadūq, *Kitāb Man lā yaḥḍuruh al-faqīh*, ed. 'Alī Akbar Ghaffārī, 2nd ed. (Qom: Mu'assasat al-Nashr al-Islāmī al-Tābi'a li-Jamā'at al-Mudarrisīn, 1983), 2:267.

15 Quṭb al-Dīn Sa'īd ibn Hibat Allāh al-Rāwandī, *al-Da'awāt* (*Salwat al-ḥazīn*) (Qom: Madrasat al-Imām al-Mahdī, 1986), 112.

16 Murtaḍā ibn Muḥammad Amīn al-Anṣārī, *al-Makāsib* (Qom: Majma' al-Fikr al-Islāmī, 2001), 1:234. See also Muṣṭafā al-Khumaynī, *Mustanad taḥrīr al-wasīla* (Qom: Mu'assasat Tanẓīm wa-Nashr Āthār al-Imām al-Khumaynī, 1997), 1:412; and Muṭahharī, *Majmū'a-yi āthār*, 30:571.

Second, Shaykh al-Anṣārī also mentioned that the narration involves a separation (*istifṣāl*) between obeying and not obeying the order. When 'Abd al-Malik told the Imām that he would indeed obey, the Imām pronounced that the ruling was to burn the books. This means that the ruling of burning the books is not permanent. If 'Abd al-Malik said that he would be unable to fulfil this demand, keeping them would have been permissible. The narration does not prove a universal ruling about the prohibition of keeping books of misguidance.[17]

This is a noteworthy observation. This means that the presence and keeping of the books of misguidance is unobjectionable if its corrupting influence does not enter into effect. If the presence, publication and viewing of such books had the corrupting influence of misguidance, the books would be prohibited. Nevertheless, this is not an absolute ruling. If such books should be burned in all cases, the Imām's question would have been pointless.

Third, the chain of transmission of this narration includes Muḥammad ibn 'Alī Mājīlawayh (the nephew), as well as Muḥammad ibn Khālid al-Barqī whose trustworthiness has not been established for us.[18] Therefore, the chain of transmission of this narration that only Shaykh al-Ṣadūq transmitted is not sound, according to al-Sayyid al-Khū'ī. The second narration is the sound narration from Abū 'Ubayda al-Ḥadhdhā' from Abū Ja'far where he said, 'Whoever teaches others a branch of guidance gains the reward of whoever applies it without the reward of those people being lessened, and whoever teaches a branch of misguidance bears the burdens of whoever applies it without the burdens of those people being lessened.'[19] The same report was narrated from the Imām, with a slight difference, through Muḥammad ibn Muslim in *al-Maḥāsin al-Barqī*.[20] Al-Muḥaqqiq al-Narāqī relied on this report when discussing the books of misguidance.[21]

17 al-Anṣārī, *al-Makāsib*, 1:234. See also Abū al-Qāsim al-Khū'ī, *Miṣbāḥ al-faqāha*, 4th ed. (Qom: Anṣāriyān, 1996), 1:405; and Taqī al-Ṭabāṭabā'ī, *Mabānī minhāj al-ṣāliḥīn*, 2nd ed. (Qom: Manshūrāt Qalam al-Sharq, 2008), 7:290.

18 See Ḥaydar Ḥubb Allāh, *Iḍā'āt fī al-fikr wa-l-dīn wa-l-ijtimā'* (Beirut: Mu'assasat al-Buḥūth al-Mu'āṣira, 2013), 2:152–59.

19 Muḥammad ibn Ya'qūb al-Kulaynī, *al-Kāfī*, ed. 'Alī Akbar Ghaffārī, 3rd ed. (Qom: Dār al-Kutub al-Islāmiyya, 1988), 1:35; Abū Muḥammad al-Ḥasan ibn 'Alī al-Ḥusayn Ibn Shu'ba al-Ḥarrānī, *Tuḥaf al-'uqūl* (Qom: Manshūrāt Dhawī al-Qurbā, 2003), 297.

20 Abū Ja'far Aḥmad ibn Muḥammad ibn Khālid al-Barqī, *al-Maḥāsin*, ed. al-Sayyid Mahdī al-Rajā'ī (Qom: al-Mu'āwiniyya al-Thaqāfiyya li-l-Majma' al-'Ālamī li-Ahl al-Bayt, 1992), 1:27.

21 al-Narāqī, *Mustanad al-Shī'a*, 14:157.

However, this tradition may be discussed from a number of angles. First, it points to the prohibition of teaching misguidance, but it does not indicate seizing the books of misguidance or forbidding their authors from having their freedom of thought. The narration equally does not indicate the prohibition of keeping the books of misguidance, and so on.

Second, what is understood from this tradition, as some commentators of *al-Kāfī* said, is that it concerns paving the way for teaching guidance and misguidance.[22] This means that the tradition concerns a person who misguides people by opening the door of misguidance for them and not a person who misguides people in a certain matter. Misguidance is of two kinds: partial and specific, which is not mentioned in the verse, and total and general, which is the misguidance mentioned in the verse. In this latter case, misguidance would be a gateway for a series of misguidances. This second kind is the one forbidden here, as it entails establishing and teaching a trend of misguidance, which necessitates a series of deviations.

This verse states the prohibition of teaching misguidance to misguide people away from the Truth. We must assume that this is not specific to teaching misguidance. In this case, the meaning would be that teaching the people a branch of misguidance while knowing that it is misguidance with the people applying it would be prohibited. Of course, if he did not know that it was misguidance he would be excused, as in the case of the differences among the *mujtahids* in Islamic sciences. The tradition also implies that teaching or conveying misguidance without opening the gateway of misguidance before others, such as in the case of teaching misguidance with the goal of knowledge or criticism, and without the presence of danger, is not problematic at all.

The third narration is that of al-Ḥarrānī, narrated directly (*mursala*) from al-Ṣādiq. It is the long narration with which Shaykh al-Anṣārī prefaced *al-Makāsib*. Listing the prohibited deeds within the mercantile domain, it says, 'Every forbidden thing that is used to draw nearer to anyone but God or that strengthens faithlessness and polytheism, including all acts of disobedience and acts that strengthen the branches of misguidance, falsehood or any other aspect that weakens the Truth, is illicit and prohibited. It is prohibited to buy it, sell it, hold it, own it, gift it, lend it and use it in any way, except when necessary.'[23]

22 Rafīʿ al-Dīn Muḥammad ibn Ḥaydar al-Nāʾīnī, *al-Ḥāshiya ʿalā Uṣūl al-Kāfī*, ed. Muḥammad Ḥusayn Darāyatī (Qom: Dār al-Ḥadīth, 2003), 109.

23 al-Ḥarrānī, *Tuḥaf al-ʿuqūl*, 333.

Some jurists used this text as proof in this regard,[24] and Muṭahharī considered it useful despite not containing anything new for bolstering the reasonable ruling concerning eradicating the substance of corruption.[25]

Some arguments may be presented here. First, the narration is narrated directly (*mursala*) from al-Ṣādiq. It does not have a chain of transmission. All the opinions counting it as sound have been refuted by those who followed the generation of the late scholars (*muta'akhkhirī al-muta'akhkhirīn*), so I will not spend much time on their arguments. What concerns us is that this narration cannot be relied on alone. Al-Muḥaqqiq al-Īrwānī said, 'This narration is problematic because of a disconnected chain (*irsāl*) and because it was ignored by the *ḥadīth* compilers. It is improbable that the latter were not acquainted with it considering the confusion in its content. In its branches and divisions, it is similar to the books of compilers, which means that relying on it is problematic unless it was bolstered by an external proof.'[26]

Second, the narration itself permits all those prohibited activities when necessary. Necessity in cultural and intellectual life is different from necessity in personal life. The issue also requires calculating instances of public welfare and corruption, which we will attend to later with God's help. For this reason, al-Muḥaqqiq al-Narāqī permitted these books when they are needed to raise the scholarly level, gain the skills of research and debate, and cultivate insight by viewing other opinions and schools of thought, and so on.[27] This is an instance of permissible welfare. If we can point out other instances of permissible welfares, they would fall under the same ruling.

Al-Muḥaqqiq al-Najafī made the exception of refuting these books lawful because refuting them is destroying them all, which is preferable to physically destroying one book among them.[28] This welfare-based understanding of al-Muḥaqqiq al-Najafī is absolutely correct. The most important thing in our age is to uncover the means that are actually more effective in limiting misguidance despite having the appearance of licensing the propagation of misguidance. There is no text limiting these means to refutation; these means are the result of human legal opinions that may change based on time, place, circumstance and condition.

24 See al-ʿĀmilī, *Miftāḥ al-karāma*, 12:206; al-Narāqī, *Mustanad al-Shīʿa*, 14:157; al-Najafī, *Jawāhir al-kalām*, 22:56; and al-Anṣārī, *al-Makāsib*, 29.

25 Muṭahharī, *Majmūʿa-yi āthār*, 30:572.

26 al-Mīrzā ʿAlī al-Najafī al-Īrwānī, *Ḥāshiyat Kitāb al-Makāsib*, ed. Bāqir al-Fakhkhār al-Iṣfahānī (Qom: Dār Dhawī al-Qurbā, 2000), 1:17.

27 al-Narāqī, *Mustanad al-Shīʿa*, 14:158.

28 al-Najafī, *Jawāhir al-kalām*, 22:57.

The fourth narration was transmitted by al-ʿAllāma al-Ḥillī, in which he says that the Prophet (peace be upon him) went out one day, and he saw ʿUmar carrying a scroll. He (peace be upon him) asked what the scroll was and ʿUmar said, 'It's from the Torah.' The Prophet (peace be upon him) got angry at him and threw the scroll to the ground, saying, 'If Moses and Jesus were alive, they would have been obligated to follow me.' Al-ʿAllāma al-Ḥillī included this narration in another book of his, but there he mentioned that ʿAlī was the one who went out.[29] The final part of this narration, the Prophet's (peace be upon him) saying in the end, also appears in both Ibn Kathīr's and al-Qurṭubī's respective *tafsīr* works without reference to the command of throwing the scroll away.[30] I also found this narration mentioned by Abū Ṭālib al-Makkī (d. 386) in *Qūt al-qulūb* using the same chain of transmission as Ibn Kathīr.[31]

However, further tracing the origin of this report indicates that it exists in Sunnī sources of jurisprudence as well. Al-Nawawī narrated it in his *al-Majmūʿ* and elsewhere, adding words with which the Prophet (peace be upon him) addressed ʿUmar such as, 'Are you in doubt, O Ibn al-Khaṭṭāb, are you having doubts?' or 'Are you all perplexed, then?' or 'Didn't I bring [a message] of purest white?'[32]

Sunnī traditionists indexed this report (*takhrīj*) as present in their own tradition compilations such as Aḥmad's *Musnad*, al-Dārimī's *Sunan*, Ibn Abī ʿĀṣim's *al-Sunna*, al-Harawī's *Dhamm al-kalām* and al-Ḍiyāʾ al-Maqdisī's *al-Muntaqā*.[33] The tradition has multiple channels, but all of them have prob-

29 Jamāl al-Dīn al-Ḥasan ibn Yūsuf ibn al-Muṭahhar al-ʿAllāma al-Ḥillī, *Nihāyat al-iḥkām fī maʿrifat al-aḥkām*, 2nd ed. (Qom: Muʾassasat Ismāʿīliyyān), 2:471.

30 See Abū al-Fidāʾ Ibn Kathīr, *Tafsīr al-Qurʾān*, ed. Yūsuf ʿAbd al-Raḥmān al-Marʿashlī (Beirut: Dār al-Maʿrifa, 1992), 1:387, 3:105; and Abū ʿAbd Allāh Muḥammad ibn Aḥmad al-Anṣārī al-Qurṭubī, *al-Jāmiʿ li-aḥkām al-Qurʾān*, ed. Aḥmad ʿAbd al-Ḥalīm al-Bardūnī (Beirut: Dār Iḥyāʾ al-Turāth al-ʿArabī, 1985), 13:355.

31 Muḥammad ibn ʿAlī ibn ʿAṭiyya al-Ḥārithī al-Mashhūr bi-Abī Ṭālib al-Makkī, *Qūt al-qulūb fī muʿāmalat al-maḥjūb wa-waṣf ṭarīq al-murīd ilā maqām al-tawḥīd*, ed. Bāsil ʿUyūn al-Sūd (Beirut: Dār al-Kutub al-ʿIlmiyya, 1997), 2:139.

32 Muḥyī al-Dīn Yaḥyā ibn Sharaf al-Nawawī, *al-Majmūʿ sharḥ al-Muhadhdhab* (Beirut: Dār al-Fikr, n.d.), 15:328; Muwaffaq al-Dīn ʿAbd Allāh ibn Aḥmad ibn Muḥammad Ibn Qudāma, *al-Mughnī* (Beirut: Dār al-Kitāb al-ʿArabī, n.d.), 6:240; al-Bahūtī, *Kashshāf al-qināʿ*, 1:525, 4:300.

33 See Aḥmad ibn Ḥanbal, *al-Musnad* (Beirut: Dār al-Ṣādir, n.d.), 3:387; Muḥammad al-Dārimī (Damascus: Maṭbaʿat al-Iʿtidāl, n.d.), *Sunan*, 1:115; Ibn Abī ʿĀṣim al-Shaybānī, *Kitāb al-Sunna*, 3rd ed. (Beirut: al-Maktab al-Islāmī, 1993), 5:2; Ibn ʿAbd al-Barr al-Qurṭubī, *Jāmiʿ bayān al-ʿilm wa-faḍluhu wa-mā yanbaghī fī riwāyatihi wa-ḥamlihi*, ed. Muḥammad ʿAbd al-Qādir Aḥmad ʿAṭā (Beirut:

lems in their chains. They were examined by both Ibn Ḥajar in his *Fatḥ al-Bārī* and al-Albānī in his *Irwā' al-ghalīl*.[34] The versions differ in the details of the story and the name of the person whom the Prophet (peace be upon him) castigated or blamed. The reason for using this tradition as proof is that the Prophet (peace be upon him) ordered the throwing of the scroll for its misguiding function. This means that keeping such materials is prohibited and throwing them away is obligatory.

We can question this narration from different angles. First, the Imāmiyya do not acknowledge it in their books, and it has no chain of transmission. It only appeared with al-'Allāma al-Ḥillī (d. 726/1325) in legal works. This proves that its channels and chains of transmission are distinctly Sunnī.

If we go back to its Sunnī chains of transmission, we will find that they include weak or criticised narrators, such as Mujālid, 'Abd al-Raḥmān ibn Isḥāq al-Wāsiṭī and al-Qāsim ibn Muḥammad al-Asadī. In a number of sources, the tradition was interrupted (*munqaṭi'*) or missing certain links (*mu'ḍal*) in a number of sources. The claim that its four channels strengthen one another is unsound because there is a difference in the body of the text itself. Some narrations claim that the story involved Ḥafṣa and that it had nothing to do with 'Umar. They are two separate incidents. Therefore, the tradition involving Ḥafṣa cannot be used to support the tradition involving 'Umar because it is improbable that the story is the same but that people got mixed up and confused the two names so often. This means that it is difficult to prove the veracity of this tradition based on its chain of transmission.

Second, all the contexts of this tradition in its different variations imply the Prophet's fear about his *umma* going astray after seeing these books while being so new to Islam. This means it is a special case restricted to misguidance taking place due to these books' presence in the community. It might even be a verdict of guardianship (*ḥukm walā'ī*).

Mu'assasat al-Kutub al-Thaqāfiyya, 1995), 2:42; Abū Ismā'īl 'Abd Allāh ibn Muḥammad ibn 'Alī al-Harawī, *Dhamm al-kalām wa-ahluhu*, ed. 'Abd al-Raḥmān ibn 'Abd al-'Azīz al-Shabal (Medina: Maktabat al-'Ulūm wa-l-Ḥikam, 1998), 4:67; and Ḍiyā' al-Dīn Muḥammad ibn 'Abd al-Wāḥid al-Maqdisī, *al-Muntaqā min akhbār al-Aṣma'ī*, ed. 'Izz al-Dīn al-Tanwakhī (Damascus: al-Majma' al-'Ilmī al-'Arabī, 1935), 2:33, among others.

34 Aḥmad ibn 'Alī Ibn Ḥajar al-'Asqalānī, *Fatḥ al-Bārī sharḥ Ṣaḥīḥ al-Bukhārī*, 2nd ed. (Beirut: Dār al-Ma'rifa, n.d.), 13:438; Muḥammad Nāṣir al-Dīn al-Albānī, *Irwā' al-ghalīl fī takhrīj aḥādīth Manār al-sabīl*, 2nd ed. (Beirut: al-Maktab al-Islāmī, 1985), 6:34–38.

Third, some of the narrations that transmit this story only state that the Prophet cautioned the community from these books and called on them to hold fast to their faith. These versions do not feature any order to destroy or burn these books. In these versions, the Prophet expressed no legal stance on these books. He only said that 'if you were to abandon me, you would go astray'. He told them that he brought them a pure clear message and cautioned them against doubt because he was given comprehensive speech (*jawāmiʿ al-kalim*). The Prophet is simply calling to himself; the narration does not indicate the prohibition of books of misguidance or the necessity of destroying and seizing them as an independent subheading of Islamic law.

Fourth, what can be gleaned from this story is the fear of misguidance and the abandonment of Islam by converting to Judaism or Christianity. We cannot use this incident to say that it is prohibited to keep all kinds of books of misguidance, even those that do not cause the commitment to another religion. We have already seen that the command to burn the books was due to the fear of polytheism and faithlessness as they relate to astrology. This was also the case concerning the aforementioned verses. That is the most that may be inferred. Generalising this conclusion to include all instances of innovation or misguidance would be very difficult to do. The conclusion of this discussion is that the field of traditions contains a few narrations – about four. All of them except one are weak. It is difficult to achieve certainty about the attribution of these traditions. One of them, the narration of the *Tuḥaf*, is abandoned in the books of traditions and it has no chain of transmission, in addition to what's already been said.

Even if we move past that, the most that may be gleaned from these narrations is that they call for misguidance or promote it in a way that causes fear of misguiding people from religion and the basics of Islam. Inferring any additional layers is difficult based on the above. Even the Qur'anic texts, supposing they allow for such a meaning, do not exceed this limit. This is why Muṭahharī said that aside from the idea of misguidance itself, the Book or Sunna contain no ruling here.[35]

— Counter-evidence in the Narrative Tradition

There is another point here. The followers of Ahl al-Bayt have lived for three centuries alongside other sects. They witnessed the translation movement

35 Muṭahharī, *Majmūʿa-yī āthār*, 30:567.

and the emergence of schools of thought, opinions, books and trends. The books of different sects were readily available, and yet there were no questions about the possibility of buying them, having them copied or owning them, nor about the necessity of destroying them, seizing them or stealing them with the purpose of destroying them, and so on. No text has mentioned the necessity of imprisoning or incarcerating the promoters of misguidance for their acts. What the biographies of the Imāms do feature, however, are argumentations, invitations and debates – as early as the time of Imām 'Alī and Imām al-Ḥasan – and warnings about not being influenced by the misguidances of others. Not once do we witness Imām Riḍā calling for proscribing or stifling the other schools of thought, or at least the weaker ones of them, that had a public presence in the Abbasid court. He never said that such phenomena had to be proscribed and forbidden from expressing their radical opinions that mostly concern theology, the first principles and jurisprudence. I have not come across a significant text in which the Imāms denounce the translation movement in philosophy and other fields, nor did they criticise the ruling powers for allowing it. Although, according to some modern scholars, the translation movement might have been a deliberate move on the behalf of the ruling powers to weaken the 'Alids and the school of Ahl al-Bayt.[36]

In addition, some of the known narrations concerning the books of some of the Shī'a who left the Imāmī school, such as Banū Faḍḍāl, imply that keeping their books is not prohibited. Rather, a faithful person should make use of their narrations without believing in their ideas or acting upon them. These narrations did not state that it was required to destroy these books and eradicate them from the houses of the Shī'a, or remove those narrations or ideas that are considered misguidance, even though this was possible. There is an absence of texts that support such an opinion and an absence of any counter-measures against other groups, such as the Khārijites during the reign of Imām 'Alī. There is also an absence of questions and answers about such matters, and we have never heard that the Prophet burned or destroyed the books of the Jews, Christians or other groups that he vanquished. In the absence of relevant Qur'anic verses and texts relating to the policy of Imām al-Mahdī when he comes to power, this proves that the rubric is not misguiding others and not promoting

36 See, for instance, al-Namāzī al-Shāhrūdī, *Tārīkh al-falsafa wa-l-taṣawwuf* (Qom: Mu'assasat al-Nabā al-Thaqāfiyya, 2012), 118–22.

misguidance. As for the rest of the details, such as forbidding, proscribing and destroying the books of misguidance and prohibiting the keeping of them, they cannot be inferred from the Qur'an and the Sunna.

All of these circumstances lead to confusion and prevent attaining certainty or proof about a primary Islamic legal ruling that concerns seizing, prohibiting or burning the scholarly and cultural materials of falsehood. The most that can be said is that there is a principle of not misguiding people, and in parallel, there is the principle of guiding people to the Truth. However, the texts that we referred to remain silent on the legal procedures that put those two principles into effect. To that end, one should refer to the judgements of human reason in an effort to specify the circumstantial interests and corruptions (*maṣāliḥ* and *mafāsid*) that might emerge. This idea will become clearer later in our discussion, God willing. Perhaps, this normalisation of suppression and subjection resulted from the heinous, dark past of the states that ruled over the Islamic history, and was categorically renowned for repression and stifling dissent voices among other injustices, like many a period during the reigns of the Umayyads and Abbasids, and their ilk; and God knows better.

4. The Argument of Juridical Consensus or the Authority of Tradition

A close reading of the corpus of literature put down by jurists reveals that they have attended to the question of consensus in terms of the prohibition of the books of misguidance with some nuanced considerations that one could trace in their discussions.[37]

Perhaps the most striking view that sets itself apart amongst the Shīʿī consensus is the question of keeping the books of misguidance, foregrounded by Shaykh Yūsuf al-Baḥrānī (d. 1772), and it seems that later scholars after him reconsidered the question of prohibition.

37 See, for example, Jamāl al-Dīn al-Ḥasan ibn Yūsuf ibn al-Muṭahhar al-ʿAllāma al-Ḥillī, *Muntahā al-maṭlab fī taḥqīq al-madhhab* (Mashhad: Majmaʿ al-Buḥūth al-Islāmiyya, 1991), 2:1013; Aḥmad al-Ardabīlī, *Majmaʿ al-fāʾida wa-l-burhān fī sharḥ Irshād al-adhhān*, ed. Mujtabā al-ʿIrāqī, ʿAlī Banāh al-Ishtihārī and Ḥusayn al-Yazdī al-Iṣfahānī (Qom: Muʾassasat al-Nashr al-Islāmī al-Tābiʿa li-Jamāʿat al-Mudarrisīn, n.d.), 8:76; and ʿAlī al-Ṭabāṭabāʾī, *Riyāḍ al-masāʾil fī bayān aḥkām al-sharʿ bi-l-dalāʾil* (Qom: Muʾassasat al-Nashr al-Islāmī al-Tābiʿa li-Jamāʿat al-Mudarrisīn, 1993), 1:503, among others.

Discussing the very precept of the prohibition of keeping the books of misguidance, al-Baḥrānī argues that, 'In my opinion, the ruling [of the prohibition of the books of misguidance] is refuted altogether on the grounds of the absence of textual proof. Prohibition and obligatoriness and their ilk are legal rulings that could be rebutted based on legal proof. The common justifications that are deployed by them [i.e. the jurists] do not suffice, in my opinion, to establish a legal judgement.'[38] Al-Baḥrānī later proceeds to criticise the principles of jurisprudence. Surprisingly, al-Sayyid Jawād al-ʿĀmilī considers those words of al-Baḥrānī as referents to misguidance, proposing that, 'Those words of the writer of *al-Ḥadāʾiq* represent clear misguidance that should be destroyed and addressed following the teachings of al-Shahīd II, for he [al-Baḥrānī] falsely and elaborately claimed that our companions and the masters of our school of thought (*madhhab*) had favourably followed the Shāfiʿīs in stipulating the principles.'[39]

The following points can be gleaned from the words of al-Muḥaddith al-Baḥrānī and al-ʿĀmilī: First, it seems that relying on the Qurʾanic verses and narrations to prove a legal position or ruling in terms of keeping the books of misguidance was not a common practice until the time of al-Muḥaddith al-Baḥrānī as we conclude from his words, for he deployed the term 'justifications' in reference to the jurists' judgements, which we will discuss later, God willing.

That is true, for the aforementioned argument of the Qur'an and tradition was brought to the fore after the thirteenth Hijrī century with writers of *Miftāḥ al-karāma*, *al-Jawāhir* and *al-Mustand*, when then Shaykh al-Anṣārī continued until today. Conversely, most early scholars either did not argue for [keeping the books of misguidance], or rather relied on consensus or other justifications that we will discuss later.

Second, clearly, the Akhbārī leaning of al-Baḥrānī urged him to adopt this position following the lack of direct texts on the subject. However – as we will discuss later – even in the Akhbārī school some of the arguments that we will present below could be considered direct proofs. Even forbidding the encouragement to assist in sin – if understood in light of the above-mentioned verse – could be considered a textual proof in this context on the fundaments of the Akhbārīs.

Third, the excerpt of al-Sayyid al-ʿĀmilī hints at the negative mentality that undergirded the approaches of some jurists throughout history towards the intellectual currents that widely differed from their own beliefs. Hence, it

38 Yūsuf al-Baḥrānī, *al-Ḥadāʾiq al-nāḍira* (Qom: Muʾassasat al-Nashr al-Islāmī al-Tābiʿa li-Jamāʿat al-Mudarrisīn, n.d.), 18:141.

39 al-ʿĀmilī, *Miftāḥ al-karāma*, 12:209.

is logical to consider a set of the books (or parts thereof) authored by jurists, exegetes, philosophers, traditionists, among others, as books or texts of misguidance that should be destroyed and prohibited. For instance, looking at the Imāmī scholars who accused the early scholars of taking the science of jurisprudence from the Sunnī school of thought as perpetuating a form of misguidance signals an even broader understanding of the very concept of misguidance.

Relying on consensus (*ijmā'*) is insignificant here, since its perception is clear for the legal mind – its textual basis (*mustanad*) is either the Qur'an or the Sunna as elucidated above or the other forms that we will encounter later; let alone if we primarily agreed on the existence of consensus in this question,[40] and if we disregarded the subsequent discussions foregrounded by later scholars since the times of al-Baḥrānī. Now if we assume for the sake of argument that consensus did exist, it emerged as a result of the fear for people being misguided without any greater public interest or provisional necessity.

5. The Rational or Conceptual Proof: A Review

We should, here, grapple with a set of rational and conceptual proofs inferred by Muslim jurists and examine their scopes. Some jurists, such as al-Sayyid Aḥmad al-Khawānsārī,[41] considered that the most important proof is that of rational ruling.

5.1 The Ruling of Reason concerning the Necessity of Eradicating the Substance of Corruption

The first proof: the ruling of reason concerning the necessity of eradicating the substance of corruption.[42] This proof consists of two premises: The first premise: the books of misguidance represent a substance of corruption, as

40 For more on the historical development of the question of the books of misguidance, see Muḥammad 'Alī Ṣulṭānī, 'Kutub ḍālla', in *Ketāb-e naqd wa-naqd-e ketāb* (Qom: Mu'assasey-e Khāneh Ketāb, 2007), 379–428.

41 See Aḥmad al-Khawānsārī, *Jāmi' al-madārik fī sharḥ al-Mukhtaṣar al-nāfi'*, 2nd ed. (Qom: Mu'assasat Ismā'īliyyān, 1984), 3:21.

42 See al-Anṣārī, *al-Makāsib*, 1:233; and al-Khawānsārī, *Jāmi' al-madārik*.

they would eventually result in misguiding the society. The second premise: the general maxim of reason implies the necessity of eradicating or warding off corruption and repudiating oppression and deviation. The following conclusion may be gleaned as a result: the books of misguidance should be eradicated and essentially proscribed within the society. In other words, keeping, distributing, teaching, learning, publishing, printing or advertising whatever is tied to misguidance, whether books, periodicals, journals or advertisements, and so on, should be proscribed on the grounds of eradicating the substance of corruption and categorically averting all forms of misguidance.

However, some counter arguments and further discussions are presented here. Most importantly, al-Sayyid al-Khūʾī opines that if the major premise in this rational proof stands true (i.e. the general necessity of eradicating the substance of misguidance), God would have, according to the stipulations of reason, existentially prevented evil, even through compulsion and predeterminism, although the very creation of this universe categorically contradicts this dictum, for it was built on free will and freedom. Surely, it is good to eradicate the substance of corruption in hopes of obeying the commands of God; however, there is no divine command that indicates the *necessity* of eradicating the substance of corruption except in specific cases, such as the demolition of idols, crosses and temples.[43]

Similarly, al-Muḥaqqiq al-Īrwānī argues that if eradicating the substance of corruption was a general ruling of reason it would have been necessary to kill every faithless or whoever has gone astray from the path of God. Such a ruling would rather necessitate the preservation of the assets and properties of others among other improbable cases.[44]

Shaykh al-Muntaẓarī also comments on this question, dividing the rulings of reason into two different categories: First: after observing potential public interests and corruption, the human reason judges according to the things as they are in themselves (*nafs al-amriyya*), such as reason's judgement that justice is good and that oppression is evil. This sort of reason's ruling implies correlation (*mulāzama*), and thus rules according to the judgments of reason for legal rulings do observe interests and corruption.

Second: the rulings of reason that emerge after the legal commands, such as reason's judgment of the necessity of obeying God. In this case, the law of

43 See al-Khūʾī, *Miṣbāḥ al-faqāha*, 1:402; and Taqī al-Ṭabāṭabāʾī, *Mabānī minhāj al-ṣāliḥīn*, 7:288.

44 al-Īrwānī, *Ḥāshiyat Kitāb al-Makāsib*, 1:25.

correlation is improbable, as it requires infinite (*tasalsul*) regress and others.[45] This means that the jurists who seek proof should be aware that the ruling of reason falls under the first category on the basis that the rule of divine assistance (*luṭf*) is not general; it does not fall under the second category. The rule of divine assistance requires that God commands others to eradicate the substance of corruption not that He Himself eradicates it. This is the very kindness that is furnished through free will and absence of enforcement (*iljāʾ*). The legal ruling thus is established and proven here without God being the subject and doer.[46]

In response to Shaykh al-Muntaẓarī, I argue that: First, al-Sayyid al-Khūʾī's argument is true with this nuance: if it is assumed that the very existence of those books entails oppression, how would God then have kept these books without removing them from the society? Hence, the very existence, qua existence, of these books does not entail oppression; however, their existence may result in oppression if mediated by the acts of the servants of God through the conflict of interests (*tanāzuʿ*). God the Almighty considers that the public interest of humans lies in creating them in a milieu that comprises both good and evil. This way, testing (*ibtilāʾ*) will be grounded on free will and thus, unlike what most of the jurists proposed in several cases, no general rulings would emerge in this regard. According to God there are conflicting interests in the aim and ends of creation and becoming.

This discussion is not limited to the books of misguidance. The same is also true for the oppression that people incite. So one might ask: why did not God existentially prevent oppression from being created and conversely allowed its existence in the external world? In response we say that interests and good are the keystones of the divine action; however, those considerations are not always lucid or evident before us in real life, driven by the multiplicity of disturbances (*tazāḥumāt*) and the inability of the human reason to always identify interests in all times and contexts, for what might appear at first glance to the human reason as evil would, upon further consideration, be actually good.

That is the reason why I agree with al-Muḥaqqiq al-Narāqī,[47] who proposed that the principle of divine assistance (*luṭf*) that was one of the pillars of the

45 Ḥusayn ʿAlī al-Muntaẓarī, *Dirāsāt fī al-makāsib al-muḥarrama* (Qom: Tafakkur, 1994), 3:92.

46 Ibid., 2:353–54.

47 Aḥmad ibn Muḥammad Mahdī al-Narāqī, *ʿAwāʾid al-ayyām*, ed. Markaz al-Abḥāth wa-l-Dirāsāt al-Islāmiyya (Qom: Markaz al-Nashr li-Maktab al-Iʿlām al-Islāmī, 1996), 197, 705–9.

rational understanding of divine action for the 'Adliyya is valid and true; however, identifying its external referents is improbable on the grounds of limitedness of the human understanding of their interests throughout history and of the ends of the creation itself. Perhaps, that is why some of the jurists, including some of the 'Adliyya, refuse the principle of divine assistance (*luṭf*) categorically, as we understand from the proposition of Imām Khomeini.[48] The 'Adliyya who deny the principle of divine assistance may well rely on the improbability of this principle in relation to the limitation of the human reason in terms of discerning good from evil at all times, for what we could perceive as evil under certain considerations may be good under others. Hence, we conclude that keeping the books of misguidance does not generally fall under the rubric of oppression.

Second, Shaykh al-Muntaẓarī's argument that the principle of divine assistance implies God's *command* to eradicate the substance of oppression rather than He Himself eradicating the existential oppression in the external world is also problematic. It follows from his argument that the subject of this command is us rather than God on the grounds of the fear of enforcement (*iljā'*), and one might ask if this is the *only* case in which it is allowed to apply the principle of divine assistance without enforcement.

The absence of the books of misguidance is *merely* one path towards preventing misguidance in the world. So why did not God, for instance, use His power to prevent the actualisation of misguidance in the world without any enforcement through sending messengers incessantly and creating miracles as a proof for people; or even why did He not provide them with some signs in their dreams, for instance, to guard them against misguidance, and the likes of these actions? One might also ask, why did not God create us infallible so that enforcement would be ruled out of the whole question? These arguments reveal the futility of the approaches of some jurists and the improbability of their arguments.

Third, certainly God has established the order of human life on the creative will, which means the invalidity of any proof that claims the categorical inclusion of God in the ruling of reason. The most that we can understand is that God does not accept misguidance and disbelief; however, He does not use His absolute power to prevent [misguidance and disbelief]. Certainly, He wants to remove misguidance and disbelief in such a fashion that humans themselves would strive to ward off misguidance and disbelief from their societies, without

48 Rūḥ Allāh al-Khumaynī, *Anwār al-hidāya* (Qom: Mu'assasat Tanẓīm wa-Nashr Āthār al-Imām al-Khumaynī), 1:257.

laying down a certain and determined method for them to so do. In this regard, al-Muḥaqqiq al-Īrwānī pointed out that methods should not be generalised.

Hence, in conclusion, we say that confronting disbelief and misguidance are incumbent on the grounds of the ruling of the human reason, as they both represent oppression. However, the method of confrontation may vary as there is no one and only external referent to that method; that is the reason why social activists, religious reformers, thinkers and intellectuals in all times did not arrive at a consensus in terms of the methods that should be advanced to confront misguided thought. For some, it is permissible to keep misguided thought; however, others impose some restrictions on such a thought. And yet some others categorically prohibit this kind of thought. Human reason does not prescribe one general method for eradicating and destroying the books of misguidance, for instance, unless there is a proof that implies otherwise. The most that human reason proposes is productive confrontation in conformity with the general, established and divine decrees, while taking into consideration the nuances of time, space, circumstances and conditions.

As a result the following three strands of thought emerge:

- The [validity of the] principle of the prevention and removal of misguidance and disbelief.

- This principle should conform with the divine law and the postulates of human reason.

- The principle of the law of the conflict of interest should be taken into consideration upon applying the principle of eradicating misguidance and disbelief.

Accordingly, upon the application of the principle of eradicating misguidance and disbelief, one should be aware that it is legally impermissible to seize the books of misguidance of the respected souls; as the general principle necessitates deploying legal methods that the Islamic law approves. Obviously, Islamic law prohibits using the assets and properties of others without their consent, and the books of misguidance represent no exception. Hence, in conformity with Islamic law, it is impermissible, for example, to confront misguidance *through* killing and incarcerating, those who are protected against being killed or incarcerated [by Islamic law]. So this legal restriction prevents us from recourse to these types of methods in efforts to confront misguidance.

However, one might argue here that this is a specification (*takhṣīṣ*) of the ruling of human reason, which is prohibited; further still, it is a legal restriction imposed on the rulings of human reason which essentially contradicts the principle of mutual implication (*mulāzama*); even more, it denies the principle of the lack of contradiction between reason and law in Islam. In response, I argue that it is only with the universal axioms that the human reason gives a general ruling that should not observe any specification or opposition, such as the principle of the evilness of oppression and the goodness of justice. However, the application of these general axioms on external referents and cases is not subject to generalisation. Otherwise, lying would have been generally prohibited on the grounds of its general prohibition by the ruling of human reason. However, Islamic law allows it in very specific and narrow cases provided that a specific interest was at stake. Similarly, killing would have been generally delegitimised even in legal *jihād*.

Thus, one should differentiate between the general axiom and its specific manifestations. If human reason is able to perceive the entirety of the subtle details of a specific case, it will accordingly apply the general axiom to that case. However, in most instances, human reason falls short of so doing, as how could it do so in light of the abundant texts whose general propositions elaborate on such external referents, such as the prohibition of destroying one's or someone else's wealth or the incompatibility of reason in applying the general rule on divine actions as al-Muḥaqqiq al-Narāqī makes mention.

The conclusion is that it is obligatory, pursuant to the rulings of reason, to confront misguidance and disbelief, as they entail oppression. However, human reason remains silent on the general principle concerning the very method of confrontation, for it is subject to the principles implied in the texts and to the principle of the conflict of interests (*tazāḥum*), provided that both private and human interests are considered. In that way, we will be able to better grapple with the argument put forward by al-Muḥaqqiq al-Īrwānī.

Fourth, the title of disbelief does not generally apply to the books of misguidance. Conversely, reason would determine whether those texts might result in misguidance upon scrutinising their ramifications and influences. Hence, if keeping these books does not represent any danger or threat, such as being kept in the library of a scholar, or even more if they represent a threat that should be guarded against, we could not argue that reason would prohibit keeping these books per se or equally destroying them. The [jurists'] channelling of the argument from the very origin of misguidance into the books of misguidance and any other expressions of misguidance was not quite accurate, on the grounds that if reason generally prohibited keeping these books without any specifications in regards to particular cases, then keeping them in an effort to be criticised or rebutted would be also forbidden. Hence, we conclude that the ruling of reason should be entwined to goals, aims, interests and corruption, rather than being general or universal. Moreover, this proof should hold true of any nuances that are subject to jurisprudential or theological debates amongst scholars who are certain of the invalidity of the conviction or the fatwa of other scholars, for in such a case the titles of corruption and misguidance could also be applied to the convictions and fatwas of others; however, I think that none of the scholars would adhere to that.

In conclusion, we did not arrive at any definitive ruling of reason that would make the very eradication of the substance of corruption necessary; meaning to destroy every misguidance. The endeavour of reason lies in the general ruling rather than specific cases which are subject to legal conflict of interest.

5.2 The Ruling of Reason concerning the Necessity of the Prevention of Potential Harm: A Critical Approach

The second proof: the ruling of reason concerning the necessity of the prevention of potential harm, for harm might emerge as a result of allowing the books and media of misguidance and of giving them freedom – harm here lies in consolidating misguidance and thus leading people astray, which, in turn, necessitates the prevention of harm. We culled this proof from the proofs of al-Sayyid Murtaḍā and Shaykh Ibn Idrīs on the rational necessity of enjoining good.[49]

However, we argue that: (1) If what is at stake is one's worldly harm, then the most that can be proven in this case is the necessity of destroying the books that one owns, as destroying the books of others might entail a harm in the hereafter resulting from destroying the possessions of others without their consent. In this case, it is not valid to deploy the ruling of reason upon the existence of the possibility of two harms, as long as the law of conflict of interest does not apply

49 See ʿAlī ibn al-Ḥusayn ibn Mūsā al-Murtaḍā al-Mūsawī al-Baghdādī, *al-Dhakhīra fī ʿilm al-kalām*, ed. al-Sayyid Aḥmad al-Ḥusaynī (Qom: Mu'assasat al-Nashr al-Islāmī al-Tābiʿa li-Jamāʿat al-Mudarrisīn, 1990), 553; and Muḥammad ibn Manṣūr ibn Aḥmad Ibn Idrīs al-Ḥillī, *al-Sarā'ir al-ḥāwī li-taḥrīr al-fatāwī* (Qom: Mu'assasat al-Nashr al-Islāmī al-Tābiʿa li-Jamāʿat al-Mudarrisīn, 1990), 2:22.

here. However, if what is at stake is the worldly harm of the society at large and of others through the influence of misguided media and thought, I argue that there is no rational ruling that stipulates the necessity of preventing the harm that might be inflicted on others under this consideration; otherwise, it would have been necessary for the rich to give the entirety of their money as a charity for the poor to prevent the harm that is inflicted upon them, among other possibilities. Some might further argue that misguidance, in this world regardless of the hereafter, is not harm per se, but rather it might be a lack of benefit (*manfaʿa*) or a missing of an interest.

The proposition that the potential worldly harm consists of [divine] punishment, for instance, necessitates the prohibition of every action whose prohibition is doubted, and the incumbent of every action whose incumbent is doubted, on the grounds that prohibited acts once performed entail harmful existential ramifications. I do not think that scholars and jurists have endorsed such an argument, including those who argued for *iḥṭiyāṭ* (precaution) amongst the Akhbārīs. This is tantamount to the belief in the prohibition of living in the non-Muslim countries on the grounds that they might be subject to [divine] punishment as a result of their disbelief, or the prohibition of living in earthquake-prone countries or countries with active volcanos, driven by the fear of earthquakes or volcanos that might erupt. Do rationalists or jurists pay mind to such possibilities?

(2) Conversely, if what is at stake is the harm in the hereafter, we would say that it is a result of the legal prohibition of keeping the books of misguidance; and as we mentioned above, , such a prohibition is not tenable. In this case, what should be invoked is the legal and rational exemption of duty (*aṣālaṭ al-barāʾa*) that reveals the lack of proof of harm in the hereafter. Accordingly, this proof is quite unclear from its rational perspective; indeed, if it were true, then it would be necessary to adopt some invalid positions, such as the position that we alluded to above with al-Muḥaqqiq al-Īrwānī.

5.3 The Ruling of Reason concerning the Necessity of the Prevention and Removal of Wrong (*Munkar*): A Critical Approach

The third proof: the reliance on the ruling of reason concerning the necessity of the prevention of wrong and destroying the books of misguidance – wrong meaning here turning away from the way of God.

Shaykh al-Ṣāniʿī suggests that this argument proposes a set of propositions and premises: (1) The books of misguidance represent wrong. (2) The prevention of wrong is incumbent. (3) Pursuant to the ruling of reason, prevention (*dafʿ*) and removal (*rafʿ*) are one. (4) And the result is that the removal of wrong is incumbent as well.[50] Some counter arguments may be presented here. First, concerning the proposition that prevention and removal are one, Shaykh al-Ṣāniʿī notes that prevention refers to resolution and decision-making; however, removal refers to the action taken afterwards.[51] It is true to structure the proof this way; however, its aim is to advance the deduction through saying that reason necessitates the removal and prevention of wrong, while the final outcome of the seekers of this proof is merely the inclusiveness of the ruling of reason of both removal and prevention.

Second, with further consideration, we will find that this proof is yet another specific re-expression of the first, which is the obligation to eradicate the substance of corruption. What undergirds this argument is the necessity of universally eradicating corruption. Clearly, corruption is wrong; and it must be eradicated, whether after being actuated or before through prevention. It is worth noting here that unlike textual interpretations, in rational judgements and rulings the dispute over the nuances between removal and prevention is peripheral; however, what undergirds the argument is *quintessential*, which is the absence of corruption and wrong in the external world. That said, the discussions that we proposed in discussing the first argument hold true here as well.

Third, Shaykh al-Ṣāniʿī mentions that the books of misguidance are not wrong by themselves; nevertheless, if used improperly, they will result in wrong and thus the ruling of reason could not be channelled into them.[52] However, it might be that the seekers of this proof aimed at this very latter point, which is the reason why they prevented misguidance through the removal of its books.

Fourth, Shaykh al-Ṣāniʿī also argues that some of what falls under the rubric of the books of misguidance is not wrong, on the grounds that if the writers of these books deployed rational methods and were persuaded and convinced of their arguments, and then author their books and distribute them in markets, these writers are excused and there is no proof of the permissibility of inflicting punishment on them or on the necessity of prevention in this case;

50 al-Ṣāniʿī, *Muqārabāt fī al-tajdīd al-fiqhī*, 79.
51 Ibid.
52 Ibid., 80.

and likewise of preventing them from composing these books, as long as the arguments put forward in them do not fall within the categories that the Law-giver would repudiate; in such a case the proof would be more specific than what it claims to prove.[53]

This discussion is entrenched in the intentions of wrongdoing as proposed by the jurists in the theme of enjoining good and forbidding wrong. Jurists suggest that in order to enjoin good and forbid wrong the person who is being enjoined or forbidden from doing a certain action should be necessarily familiar with the legal prohibition of that very action, and nevertheless violated the rule; otherwise forbidding or enjoining him to do certain actions would fall under the consideration of guiding those who have gone astray and teaching the ignorant rather than the consideration of enjoining good and forbidding wrong. We aptly discussed elsewhere that this foundation (*mabnā*) is untrue on the grounds of its generalisation;[54] knowing that if the aforementioned argument of Shaykh al-Ṣāniʿī was invalid the books of misguidance would have been in themselves wrong; and the prevention of wrong in this case is not associated with the writers of those books but rather with the books themselves; and if his first argument was valid the writers of the books of misguidance would be the agents [of misguidance].

Fifth, in the inquiries of enjoining good and forbidding wrong we argued that enjoining and forbidding are incumbent through legal and permissible methods pursuant to the postulates of reason and law. Every method that is in itself impermissible or forbidden hence must not be deployed in enjoining good and forbidding wrong. If this rational proof is substantiated, then any method that is not in itself impermissible or forbidden could be deployed in confronting the books of misguidance, such as critiquing these books. However, the methods that are in themselves prohibited, such as destroying the books, scientific works, and software of others, or even imprisoning or physical punishment, are very problematic. There is a small nuance here, though: according to the theory of the guardianship of the Islamic jurist with its exercised guardianship over the souls, money and honour of believers it might be possible to deploy such a method in specific contexts as we have discussed in the inquiries of enjoining good.[55]

53 Ibid.

54 Ḥaydar Ḥubb Allāh, *Fiqh al-amr bi-l-maʿrūf wa-l-nahy ʿan al-munkar* (Beirut: Muʾassasat al-Intishār al-ʿArabī, 2014), 399–411.

55 Ibid., 481–82.

5.4 Keeping the Books of Misguidance Reflects Their Acceptance: A Critical Approach

The fourth proof: the keeping of the books of misguidance, let alone their distribution, and so on, manifests jurists' acceptance of their arguments and content, and that is undoubtedly prohibited.[56] I argue here that: First, there is no concomitance whatsoever between keeping these books and accepting their arguments or believing in them; does the existence of any book in a house means agreeing with the propositions of that book even if the intention of keeping that book was not primarily critiquing it?

We should thoroughly discuss this point, as some of the legal mindsets are entrenched in such an approach for they are not truly familiar with healthy scientific inquiry. If the Islamic government worked out an intellectual plan for development in an effort to provide impetus for scientific inquiry and research, it will be necessary for it, sometimes at least, to allow for the distribution and presence of the thought of the other which consists of other readings and understanding of religion, as it might result in an active intellectual exchange; and after a period of time a prodigious leap in religious scientific research would take place, which in the end would serve the religious thought altogether. That is the reason why Muṭahharī pointed out that the religious thought only developed when it was in contact with the thought that contradicts it.[57]

However, *when* does the Islamic government abstain from so doing? When the religious people in the community at large are unable to actively engage in intellectual conversations and milieus; conversely, if they demonstrate intellectual and scholarly knowledge, the government would consider that allowing room for the other would place that other in its natural context, limit its influences and eventually be less attractive in the eyes of the youth, for instance. This mode of thinking and planning is not cherished by some of the pious, religious people who limit themselves within the context of mosque circles only, and who are not open to different intellectual schools and scientific milieus which would allow for an encounter with the other in an attempt to establish intellectual, deep conversations and engagement with ideas that flow from different intellectual schools. The Islamic government in such a case refuses to accede to the arguments of the misguided thought that looms

56 See al-Ardabīlī, *Majmaʿ al-fāʾida wa-l-burhān*, 8:76; and al-ʿĀmilī, *Miftāḥ al-karāma*, 12:207.

57 Muṭahharī, *Majmūʿa-yi āthār*, 30:575–76.

large in the books of misguidance; however, it believes that allowing room for such books would eventually help in weakening their arguments and lessening their readership, rather than silencing this kind of thought which might make the readership of these books increase, and in tandem might lead to a public rage against religion.

Another example that would also show that keeping, distributing or allowing the misguided thought does not reflect its acceptance is the curriculum of some of the Islamic seminaries and institutes which includes teaching different schools of thought and religions. If we look at the issue from one perspective only, we will see that teaching the thought of the other schools and religions has truly adversely affected some students, who were influenced, to a certain extent, by some philosophical or other schools of religious thought. It is true that broadly some students would be influenced by this thought even if it were appended to its critique; however, Islamic seminaries continued to so do in their efforts to train an entire generation of scholars that is capable of standing up to other intellectual currents.

To that end, some of the religious institutes set out to send their students to study abroad in the West, from within, from its very sources, for they wanted to promote an in-depth scholarly and active critique. Some of the comments that were raised against the Islamic thought is its weakness in critiquing the West in certain regards. Some of the students who went to study abroad in Western countries were surely influenced by Western thought; however, the general outcome was educating a generation that is more familiar with Western thought, and capable through a scientific discourse, rather than mobilising, decree-prone or rhetorical discourse, with all our respect to all types of discourse, of having an influence in different academic avenues and universities. The balance between public interest, on the one hand, and corruption, on the other, leads by implication to a limited loss in hopes of achieving greater aims; and that does not mean that Islamic seminaries accept the propositions of the materialistic Western thought, for instance. Accordingly, there is no concomitance between keeping, distributing or allowing the books of misguidance, on the one hand, and accepting the arguments of these books, on the other. The association between both results from a nebulous, simple approach to religion. If such an approach was used to gain currency in the times of al-Muḥaqqiq al-Ardabīlī, for instance, it is no longer convincing these days.

How could one critique the thought of the other without understanding its nuances at first? How could one critique the other without a well-educated generation? How could one guarantee to train an educated generation that is familiar with the thought of the other without internalising it? This is all possible in limited scopes of activity, such as small villages or mosques; however, this is not the case when what is at stake is strategic intellectual policies developed for countries, scientific institutions, Islamic seminaries and institutes, research centres or universities, especially that the other in our time is actively present and will continue to publish books whether we accept them or not. As a result, the consideration of public interest and corruption necessitates, sometimes, that we publish the thought of the other while critiquing it, before its being published without any critique. This approach of intellectual engagement differs widely from the first approach that we brought to the fore in this proof.

This balance between public interest and corruption manifests itself in yet another example gleaned from a letter that al-Shahīd al-Ṣadr penned to al-Sayyid al-Gharawī in which he comments on owning a television. In principle, al-Ṣadr averred that owning a television is legally problematic yet he allowed selling it. He writes:

> In terms of television, we have permitted its selling and buying for trade purposes; as its prohibition will not decrease its use. It would rather result in increasing the revenues of impious traders, on the grounds that we could not assume that the external world includes only pious traders. Let us assume that there are two pious and impious traders, and the average of what they sell is 10 [pounds]. If we prohibited selling televisions, one of them only would abstain from selling; which means that the average of what the other would sell would increase to 20 [pounds]. This way, we will be doing nothing except increasing the revenues of the second seller, which is quite different from the prohibition of owning and having a television, which might result in decreasing the average number of television owners. Surely, that is all based on not listing television under the category of distraction (*lahw*) instruments, and its prohibition falls under the consideration of eliminating corruption not on the primary level (*'unwān awwalī*). However, had it been listed under the category of distraction (*lahw*) instruments, its selling would have been prohibited on the primary level, regardless of whether it would eliminate corruption or not.[58]

58 See Aḥmad Abū Zayd 'Āmilī, *Muḥammad Bāqir al-Ṣadr: al-sīra wa-l-masīra fī ḥaqā'iq wa-wathā'iq* (Beirut: Mu'assasat al-'Ārif li-l-Maṭbū'āt, 2006), 2:386.

Similarly, books and media of misguidance are not prohibited on the primary level; however, the prohibition is for misguiding people, and the other considerations are avenues into the latter. So if we aim at eliminating the misguidance of people the only option at hand is not necessarily the general prohibition of the books and media of misguidance, for they will not cease to exist as long as others are producing them. That said, the legal prohibition of those books or media will only result in increasing the unfamiliarity of the pious with modern doubtful arguments (*shubuhāt*), which will consequently seclude them in their own circles and they will fail to confront the thought of the other with their knowledge. That is the reason why [some scholars] adopt methods of mobilisation, fatwa and incitement, as a sort of compensation for their weak knowledge. The prohibition of these books by implication means that they will be published and distributed by the other, and they will reach their readerships without being critiqued. Otherwise, if the religious and pious people make these books available, they will gain the trust of their readership through publishing the arguments and the counter arguments concurrently, and through critiquing the arguments of others while maintaining respect; by so doing, the influence on readership would ultimately be better; if not always oftentimes.

In the same vein, some modern jurists permitted collecting taxes on wine from the municipalities that are under the authority of Muslims, for if Muslims refrain from collecting these taxes while having taken control over municipalities or the Ministry of Tourism, for instance, the value of wine will decrease in markets, and then it will be abundantly available, and thus it will eventually lead to graver consequences; hence, from this vantage point, it should not be generally prohibited.

Along these lines, some of the religious authorities in the Arab world prohibited the Shīʿa from taking up governmental jobs and positions, which meant that others would take power and authority over governmental facilities – a fact that, in turn, brought forth bad consequences. However, Shīʿī jurisprudence nowadays is reconsidering this question on the grounds that the public interest of occupying those positions and jobs outweighs secluding or isolating our own selves.

All these examples assert that the public interest is the starting point, for there is no textual proof that singles out a particular method to deploy in responding to the books or media of misguidance; moreover, there is no general fatwa that espouses that whoever keeps or allows the books of misguidance actually consents to those books; had it been the case, it would eventually hinder the intellectual advancement of the Islamic communities. This accentuates, even more, the importance of the very context of time and place in *ijtihād*, in issuing and structuring the fatwa, and elucidates how things are not moulded in one rigid form; conversely, they are naturally fluid and they change in light of different circumstances. There is no singular text or rational ruling that would categorically and universally define the methods that must be deployed to react to the books of misguidance. If anything, we should investigate which methods are best to be deployed from the perspective of the general moral ends (*maqāṣid*), while ruminating over the myriad aspects of the subject in question.

Through exploration and accumulation of fatwa-related and equally hands-on experiences, we can decide on the best methods. Such methods are subject to change pursuant to different times, places, communities and circumstances. It is worth noting here that we are not advocating for the exclusivity of one method. Moreover, some modern scholars were even sceptical about the very origin of the prohibition of accepting these books, depicting its end goal as inner vileness (*qubḥ*);[59] however, that is a different discussion that needs no further elaboration in light of what has been mentioned thus far.

5.5 The Classification of the Books and Media of Misguidance under the Concept of Innovation (*Bidʿa*)

The fifth proof: what can be gleaned from the propositions of some jurists that the books of misguidance are books of innovation (*bidʿa*) and that standing up to the people of innovation, and thus the removal of these books, is one of the referents of enjoining good and forbidding wrong, which is legally incumbent.[60]

Some counter arguments may be presented here. First, probative and authentic traditions mention that the ways of confronting the adherents to innovation (*ahl al-bidʿa*) consist of insulting, backbiting, slandering, boycotting and demonstrating knowledge in their milieus; none of the traditions on the adherents to innovation imply that they should be imprisoned, silenced or prevented from publishing, or that their books, journals or media should be seized. Surely, supporting the adherents to innovation and advancing their innovations and misguidedness or even keeping silent on their innovations is strictly prohibited.

59 al-Ṣāniʿī, *Muqārabāt fī al-tajdīd al-fiqhī*, 82.

60 See Shams al-Dīn Muḥammad ibn Makkī al-ʿĀmilī, *al-Durūs al-sharʿiyya fī fiqh al-Imāmiyya* (Qom: Muʾassasat al-Nashr al-Islāmī al-Tābiʿa li-Jamāʿat al-Mudarrisīn, 1991), 326; al-Ardabīlī, *Majmaʿ al-fāʾida wa-l-burhān*, 8:75; and al-ʿĀmilī, *Miftāḥ al-karāma*, 4:62.

Second, some of the modern jurists proposed that the conceptual scope of the adherents to innovation is more specific than that of misguidance itself, for not every misguidance is branded as religious innovation. Rather, innovation is defined as any addition to or elimination from Islam, or even establishing a sect or religion that finds no roots in Islam.[61] And that is true; as a result, one might ask, could *ijtihād* be bracketed together with innovation?! Shall we brand the opinions that challenge consensus or major opinions in exegesis and interpretation, theology, jurisprudence or principles as innovation? Also, are the opinions that contradict religious or political authorities deemed as innovation? Elsewhere, we have traced the concept of innovation and we proved that it is narrow and limited in scope.[62]

Third, we have also demonstrated in the same book that the degree of deploying [one's] 'hand' [*viz.* power] in enjoining good and forbidding wrong, meaning resorting to violence, oppression, hitting, imprisoning, freely using the properties and assets of others without their consent, preventing them from exercising their legal freedom pursuant to the first level (*ʿunwān awwalī*),[63] is not yet established and proven. As a result, the most that we can do in confronting the adherents to innovation is to turn to legal and scientific confrontations, as long as these adherents are not subjects to penal sentences, such as apostasy, and so on; in the latter case, judgements will be inferred according to specific conditions and circumstances.

5.6 The Primacy of the Ruling concerning Confronting and Weakening the Adherents to Misguidance

The sixth proof: al-Muḥaqqiq al-Najafī argued that we should hold on to the evidence that proves that confrontation with the adherents to misguidance is incumbent and thus they should be weakened in every possible way; and by so doing their sect, in his words, should perish upon destroying whoever adheres to it.[64]

In this vein, the following counter arguments are presented. First, we might come to terms with this argument only if the conditions of *jihād* (confronta-

61 al-Ṣāniʿī, *Muqārabāt fī al-tajdīd al-fiqhī*, 82–83.
62 Ḥubballāh, *Fiqh al-amr bi-l-maʿrūf wa-l-nahy ʿan al-munkar*, 411–31.
63 Ibid., 470–516.
64 al-Najafī, *Jawāhir al-kalām*, 22:75.

tion) against disbelievers and adherents to dissension (*baghī*) are achieved. Otherwise, the argument does not hold true and if that is the case, then what reason do we have to accept this evidence? We have proven elsewhere that there is no initiated (*ibtidāʾī*) *jihād* in Islam.[65] And equally, we have proven that not every inconsistency with the leader of the Muslims or deviation from the path of truth is necessarily dissension; and that not every political or intellectual dissonance represents dissension that requires the application of *jihād* and rules of engagement against it. The scope of these rules of *jihād* includes only the cases of defending against armed revolts waged against the licit Islamic government.[66]

Second, one might ask if all books of misguidance are associated with disbelievers and the adherents to dissension whose confrontation is incumbent. Again, this proof is more specific than what it claims to prove. The most that can be inferred from this proof is that the books (and media) of misguidance that are associated with a conspiracy mapped out by the enemy within the context of war tactics could fall in line with this proof; otherwise, the books that the enemy makes use of or the books that are not related to war and *jihād* fall outside its scope. What undergirds this proof is problematic in that it channels war-related rulings into intellectual issues.

In conclusion, if these books assisted the transgressors and were part of war, we could respond to them according to the propositions of this proof. Otherwise, it would be problematic if we channel the proof from a military context into intellectual avenues. In Islamic law, there is no heading labelled 'the adherents to misguidance' that stands on its own and that has its own effective rules, such as the concepts of Islam and disbelief.

6. Between *Ijtihād* and Confronting Corruption: The Predicament of Seizing Theory

The heart of the problem in most rational and mental arguments lies in the principle of distinguishing between the permissible, or even incumbent, *ijtihād* in all Islamic sciences, and the concepts of misguidance, innovation, disbelief, corruption and falsehood, which still lack accurate definitions.

65 Ḥaydar Ḥubb Allāh, *Dirāsāt fī al-fiqh al-Islāmī al-muʿāṣir* (Beirut: Muʾassasat al-Fiqh al-Muʿāṣir, 2015), 1:59, 4:287–335.

66 Ibid., 3:393–451.

(1) If we label every book that we categorically do not agree with and certainly refuse its arguments with the label of misguidance, this requires us to include in the same category the books of many exegetes, jurists, traditionists, and so on, as some of the books of narrations, for instance, include misguidance. Do not the books of the principles of jurisprudence and doctrine include misguidance? The concept of misguidance is very broad and it is unlikely that anyone would commit himself to such an understanding of misguidance; the result of which would be what we have encountered earlier with al-Sayyid al-ʿĀmilī's opinion in his *Miftāḥ al-karāma* on al-Baḥrānī's book titled *al-Ḥadā'iq*, and by implication preventing, destroying and seizing all these books would be incumbent!

(2) However, if we consider that the books of misguidance are the very books that openly undermine the principles of religion, in the sense that they hope to invalidate and nullify the prophethood of the Prophet or the Imāmate of the Imām, or the divinity of God or His Oneness, or the like, this understanding of misguidance necessitates the following:

First, the language of those books should be critical rather than commentarial, as there is a difference between whoever nullifies and disavows the Imāmate and between whoever believes that the Imāmate theory entails the affairs of religion rather than worldly affairs. The first wants to clearly destroy the Imāmate; whereas the second hopes to offer a new understanding of the theory. And one should not compare between the first and the second because their end points vary.

Second, this understanding of misguidance also requires a clear definition of the principles of Islam and the principles of our school of thought. This is very instrumental, as one might ask whether the infallibility of the Imāms outside the context of transmitting and summoning others to religion is part of the principles of our school of thought and why. Is the integrity of the Companions of the Prophet part of the principles and why? Is consensus and indisputability part of the principles of our school of law and how? Our readers should heed the fact that we are considering our religion and school of thought from the actual prism rather than an historical lens. If Shaykh al-Ṣadūq, for instance, considered that believing in the forgetfulness (*sahw*) of the Prophet is permissible, would repudiating forgetfulness, as a result, no longer be considered a principle of our school of thought or would it nevertheless stay part of the principles, and hence it follows that the books of Shaykh al-Ṣadūq must be destroyed?!

Certainty in such concepts of the principles of the school of thought or the principles of religion, and the axioms thereof, is scant and limited. It is unclear to us how the scope of certainty got widened to include more principles and axioms. Is it because some issues gained currency amongst scholars and were thus deemed as principles or did it rather result from the availability of a Qur'anic evidence? We should seriously consider these questions, as their answers are not readily available or easy to find. Also, one might ask if a scholar considers an issue a principle of religion in variance to the opinion of yet another scholar, is he entitled the right to consider the latter's books as books of misguidance and act accordingly?

Why was the denial of the infallibility of the Prophet and his household considered misguidance, while casting aside dozens of the unauthentic narrations that are allegedly associated with them after applying biographical evaluations – such as the cases of al-Sayyid al-Khū'ī, al-Sayyid Āṣaf Muḥsinī, Shaykh Ḥasan Ṣāḥib al-Ma'ālim – was not so considered? Likewise, why was believing in the historicity of legal regulations (*tashrī'*) considered misguidance; however, the Akhbārīs' denial of the probative force (*ḥujjiya*) of the *ẓāhir* (apparent meaning) of the Qur'an, which partially suspended this book, is not considered misguidance? Why is the theory of the influence of human knowledge on religious knowledge considered misguidance, while believing in the suspension of the Islamic governance, Friday prayer, initiated *jihād*, *al-ḥudūd* (punishments) in the time of occultation are not so considered? Why is the denial of breaking the rib of Fāṭima al-Zahrā' considered misguidance, while the fatwas that prohibited self-flagellation and a set of other mourning rituals are not so considered? Why are the fatwas of self-flagellation painted as misguidance; however, the arguments of Shaykh al-Tabrīzī concerning the knowledge of the household of the Prophet are painted differently? Why was arguing for the lack of proof on the miscarriage of Fāṭima al-Zahrā' considered misguidance, and journals that used to perpetuate that narrative were seized, while believing that the household of the Prophet is the perfect manifestation of the divine Names and Attributes was not so considered? The foregoing is to merely name a few examples from dozens of others that clearly delineate the double standards established in applying those nebulous and elusive concepts. A thorough consideration of these examples clarifies that the grounds of all these hotly debated discussions is the fear for the very existence of religion itself in a certain historical moment, and that the public interest necessitated the confrontation of a number of arguments or intellectual currents.

The scope of *ijtihād* in religious thought is ample. If jurists disagreed among themselves on a question their respect is preserved and maintained; even more, the respect of theologians, philosophers, traditionists, scholars in *rijāl* studies, historians, exegetes, mystics, *uṣūlī* scholars is also equally preserved even if they purported a different understanding of religion. Whoever does not agree with the arguments and opinions put forward by the other is entitled to critique these arguments; however, there is no legal proof that demonstrates that he can actually restrict the freedom of the other accordingly as long as they are, at least, still abiding by Islam. We did not arrive at any convincing proof that demonstrates otherwise. Inasmuch as reading the books of so many different jurists with their diverging opinions does not bring about any fear for religion, and equally so the *taqlīd* of different *marājiʿ al-taqlīd*, reading the opinions and arguments of other scholars should not intimate any fear for religion, as long as everyone engaged does believe in the Oneness of God and message of the Prophet. Everyone employs their own proofs and evidence; if you assume that the proofs of others are weak, they might actually consider your proofs as frail as a spider's web. Certainly, one should stand up to double standards, while keeping to our initial proposition that every rule has its exception that might come to the fore as a result of specific conditions and urgent circumstances. Surely, everyone is entitled the right to refute and critique the viewpoints and arguments of others whether in jurisprudence or in other fields.

Hence, the reference that should guide us is the extent of fear for religion and the best methods to be deployed given a certain context and there is no textual proof or primary ruling concerning the media and misguidance per se. This is why scholars deploy preponderating external referents in their arguments, for their authoritative reference to which they resort is not a general textual evidence, but rather the legal law of defending and upholding the principles and values of Islam against disbelief, misguidance and innovation, and their influences. However, their course of action and method vary in view of their assessments which, in turn, result from the intellectual, social and political horizons of the religious or political authority or *marājiʿ al-taqlīd*, on the one hand, and the circumstances, possibilities, public interests and corruption, on the other.

This is what we attempt to prove: the heart of the question lies in defining and assessing the subject matter of the case at hand. For instance, I might consider that keeping the books of misguidance is better for the public interest rather than destroying them. Conversely, I might believe that preventing these books is better for the public interest given some specific circumstances. With everything being said, there are only two principles: (1) the right [of scholars] to exercise *ijtihād* in the general sense that we argued for, and (2) the right [of scholars] to stand up to disbelief and misguidance. The principle that should be applied is surely not the prohibition of these books; however, on the secondary level (*'unwān thānawī*) we permit these books; proving this principle is quite problematic.[67] Muṭahharī, for instance, pointed out that the jurists did not delve into this question as every jurist believes that what he asserts is true and is a form of *ijtihād* in religion.[68]

It is worth mentioning here that we are not apologetic concerning the restriction of media or intellectual freedoms. The West itself imposes restrictions that would limit these freedoms, such as the principle of the restriction of hate speech, through which the West legally imposed restrictions on Islamic and Arabic media outlets because they simply defended the rights of Palestinians and spoke truth to power about the Palestinians' expulsion from their lands. And also on the pretext of antisemitism, the West legally prosecuted a number of intellectuals, such as Roger Garaudy.

Indeed, what we care for here is the very principle: does the principle lie in prohibiting or conversely allowing the books and media of misguidance? I argue that Islamic Sharī'a adopts the principle of confrontation; however, there is no direct textual, legal evidence that necessitates their prohibition or that defines the methods that should be deployed in confrontation. Surely, misguidance itself and supporting misguidance are both prohibited; while keeping and concurrently rebutting these books is not.

7. The Results of Research into Texts and Tradition (Chosen Theory on General Principles)

This is the sum of Islamic jurisprudence (*fiqh*) texts regarding the books of misguidance. Upon researching them, we can deduce the following:

- It is forbidden to misguide oneself and others, and it is forbidden to take any path leading to misguidance of oneself and others. It is, however, utterly forbidden when it is done deliberately or due to negligence.

---

67 The 'secondary' title is a term in Islamic jurisprudence that means that a thing has a ruling in itself, but cases may arise that require it to be described in another capacity, and as a result of that another ruling will follow. An example of this is drinking water, for it is permissible with the title that it is water, which is the primary title. But if this water becomes impure, then it becomes forbidden because it has a secondary title, which is the title of impure water.

68 Muṭahharī, *Majmū'a-yi āthār*, 30:574–75.

- It is forbidden to support misguidance and acts of misguiding in all shapes and forms (financial, intellectual and moral) with the intention of reinforcing corruption, disbelief (*kufr*) as well as intellectual and moral deviation. In other words, it is forbidden to reinforce falsehood (*bāṭil*) in any fashion.

- It has not been proven lawful to use an impermissible method towards confronting misguidance, excluding verbal forms of expression stipulated in the authentic narration (*ṣaḥīḥa*) of Dāwūd ibn Sarhān, such as cursing, slandering and backbiting, etc., regardless of the details and nuances of this narration, since we do not adopt it, nor do we adhere to its substance, based on consensus, save for one of the later jurists. If the external referent of this narration is substantiated and, equally, all conditions are met, it would be possible to implement this narration in the questions that involve legal penalties, *al-ḥudūd* (punishments) of the sort stipulated by Sharīʿa law, or that are *jihād* related.

- It is obligatory to utilise every productive means of protection against misguidance, for oneself and others, without being forbidden in itself for others.

- There should be precise differentiation between the principle of legitimate freedom of *ijtihād*, on the one hand, and the principle of innovation and misguidance, on the other, and all forms of confusing them with each other should be rejected.

- One should resort to the principles of conflict, priorities and weighing of public interests and corruption during the process of countering misguidance, and select the best ways, methods and means, while taking into consideration the time, place, circumstance and situations, and reject having a primary legitimate principle that would allow eradicating misguidance, no matter how it is done. Hence, if a certain method results in strengthening misguidance in a certain time, it will be necessary to take on another approach, and perhaps the situation would be the opposite at a different time.

8. The Position of Sharīʿa Law towards Misguidance and How to Counter and Grapple with It (The Chosen Theory)

In light of these results, we can discuss misguided thought and media under four categories: (1) production of misguidance; (2) distribution and dissemination of misguidance; (3) consumption and utilisation of misguidance; (4) countering misguidance.

8.1 Production of Misguidance

Production here means when one brings about misguided thought and all elements that support this production process, such as establishing organisations, centres or circles that produce anti-Islamic ideas, so any financial or emotional support of the creation of such projects is deemed legally forbidden in Islam. That is because it would be supporting disbelief and deviance, unless one is unaware of that. However, if one thought he was doing the right thing without being neglectful of the preliminaries, then he would be excused, based on the details mentioned. Similarly, intellectual work in such organisations like writing books of misguidance and so forth falls under this consideration.

One might say that the very act of writing is not forbidden, but the act of publishing is, since the actual prohibition lies in the act of misguiding people and steering them away from the path of God. Authorship is not forbidden, nor is establishing research centres and other entities, unless it is associated with publication, distribution and promotion of misguided books, since the act of misguiding would not occur.

The first aforementioned Qur'anic verse indicates that any attempt to lead people astray from faith without a legitimate justification or particular excuse is utterly prohibited. If one does so, believing that this is Islam or not intending to misguide, then it is not prohibited. If one writes misleading content or produces misguiding programmes, one can keep them on the condition that they are not published with the intention of causing misguidance, as clearly stated. If one also creates misguiding content for the purpose of refuting it, as in presenting an argument, 'if you say this, I say …', then it is not prohibited, since it does not fall under the intention to misguide others. In short, this clarifies the direction to take when dealing with different examples and cases of the question of misguidance.

8.2 Distribution and Dissemination of Misguidance

Distribution here means causing misguidance to reach others – fully aware of it being an act of misguidance – in any way possible with the intention of causing misguidance, or knowing that misguidance will take place, or being informed that it will take place. In this vein, some jurists have ruled that making copies of books of misguidance is prohibited.[69] And it is evident – according to the indication of the aforementioned verses and others – that it is prohibited and impermissible. This is not limited to copying books, as it also includes today printing, distributing and promoting books, as well as broadcasting media programmes and disseminating misguiding ideas in newspapers, media outlets, online and by any other means. Moreover, teaching, promoting and defending misguidance, and any other means that allow ideas of misguidance to reach people, leading them astray as a result, are all prohibited, based on the aforementioned.

Here, clarifications are also necessary: First, it is a condition for the prohibition to be proven and established here that the author of the publication does not believe, out of ignorance without negligence, that this is the truth, and that he thus calls for the truth and the straight path (*al-ṣirāṭ al-mustaqīm*). However, if he reached through *ijtihād* a false conclusion, he is excused, in the event he did not neglect the preliminaries, for one should be insightful. This also applies if one followed the other with justification and an excuse for following the said person, such as the case with followers of religious authorities (*al-marāji'*) and scholars.

Second, if books and media projects included both the truth and falsehood, such as interviewing two people on television, one advocating misguided thought and another refuting it, or interviewing a person, knowing that among the dozens of statements of truth he makes there is a false statement being said, would this be prohibited or not? Put differently, if the media, in all its forms, whether political, artistic or intellectual, was aware that it was airing misleading ideas of some individuals, would broadcasting that be permissible or not?

The answer: what matters here is the intention. If the publisher and distributor intended to misguide people, it is prohibited. However, if he did not intend to so do, but what he did necessarily caused misguidance in a way without any public interest in return, it is also prohibited. Nonetheless, the mere possibility of causing misguidance, strictly being a possibility while having qualitative

69 al-'Āmilī, *Miftāḥ al-karāma*, 4:62.

interests resulting from broadcasting and publishing, is not prohibited and there is no evidence of it being so, because prohibition, as aforementioned, is based on the intention, which is misguiding people. If it is not guaranteed to happen, then there is no proof for it to be prohibited.

Third, if adopting the approach of presenting opposing points of view via media outlets was done for certain public interests, but in turn could possibly lead to misguiding some people, it is a matter that has not been proven to be prohibited for that possibility. However, if one was made aware, in general, of causing the misguidance of some people, though, for instance, being influenced by a person who is being hosted at a talk show and who has misleading views, while being unaffected by the propositions of his critics, then in this case, it could be deemed forbidden as well on the grounds of having general knowledge of that.

On the other hand, one can refer to the principle of conflict of interests (*tazāḥum*), that is, when conflict takes place between a media policy that is completely close-minded towards different opinions and an open-minded media policy, whose open-mindedness may lead to some negative effects while, concurrently, creating an atmosphere of general awareness, intellectual development and revival of awareness in this regard. Here, one looks into what is best for the interests of religion in every time and place, for if general books of knowledge were adopted as a whole, it would have been ruled forbidden to publish many books of Muslim scholars and even scholars of the same school of thought, such as the books of philosophers, Sufis, mystics and exegetes, and even some books of jurists and narrators, which comprise evidence presented by others from various schools – supposing that their statements are considered misguided – so it depends. If we were in a time when myths of Sufism are being promoted, causing deviation from the Sharīʿa as a result, it would have been possible to prohibit spreading such ideas since they would influence the youth, for instance. However, this may not be the case in another time, even if it was known that one person was influenced, for there is no book, broadly speaking, that is not known to mislead, if only partially or only one person. How is it not so when some books of jurists and their statements were used as material for defaming religion itself!

8.3 Consumption and Utilisation of Misguidance

What we mean by consumption of misguidance are acts like reading books, magazines, publications, newspapers and misleading statements, as well as listening to lectures, speeches, lessons or misleading words, in addition to watching television and surfing the Internet which include misguidance and corruption, such as learning about misguidance and reading from its sources, particularly without reading rebuttals.

ʿAlī al-Ṭabāṭabāʾī states that whoever does not guarantee remaining steadfast in his faith is forbidden from reading misguidance, as he is not sure of remaining unaffected by it; that said, it is not permissible for him to review it, and the evidence for that is the obligation to prevent potential harm.[70]

Also, some contemporary jurists mention that after choosing faith consciously and out of belief, it is necessary to avoid what spoils it in an attempt to prevent potential harm, but before choosing it, one can search for various opinions to arrive at the truth, pursuant to the verses and *ḥadīth*s that call for reflection, thinking, contemplation and searching for answers.[71]

Nonetheless, both cases could be more nuanced, because sometimes we want to express our opinion to this person [who has access to misguided thought] if we believe that this thought is harmful, driven by our initial belief in its misguidance; and other times we want to look into the person's condition, and in both cases our point of reference is the very prevention of potential harm.

(1) So if we believe that this thought is a thought of misguidance, we will tell this person: 'It is not permissible for you to read these books due to the potential harm that it might bring about, as reason calls for the necessity of the prevention of potential harm.'

The question, however, is this: what is it that obligates this person to listen to us or even take into consideration what we say? You will see the response below.

(1) As for the person, if he actually has any doubts and second thoughts about the truth and the different schools of thought and currents, then his reason, which is his rational reference, implies the necessity of researching and examining, even if he is already adhering to a particular religion or school. In this situation, his hesitation means that he might be misguided at that moment, so remaining without research poses potential harm by negligence towards research, not vice versa.

70 ʿAlī al-Ṭabāṭabāʾī, *Riyāḍ al-masāʾil*, 1:503.

71 al-Ṣāniʿī, *Muqārabāt fī al-tajdīd al-fiqhī*, 86.

However, if he does not have any doubts, then it does not necessitate research by relying on the ruling of reason, especially after assuming he is aware of the correctness of his ideology. There is, however, a point here concerning the permissibility of research, since being influenced by the thoughts of others is not always like being influenced by deviant behaviour. As for the person who meets immoral and perverted individuals, he will be influenced by them although knowing that he is wrong theoretically, and even though he has not himself responded to this conscious recognition. Behavioural deviance usually does not result from awareness – even with compounded ignorance – as much as it results from either desires or interests. It is the contrary with regards to the intellectual issue, for when this person looks into different intellectual currents which he considers as misguided and becomes influenced by them, it indicates the lack of his prior conviction and newfound belief that he was misguided before and has now become guided. Thereby, as there is potential harm from refraining, there is the possibility – even if slight – of becoming influenced by these books, so he detects the harm in adhering to what he believed in. Otherwise, if there is no possibility of detecting that basically, as it would not be possible if he read these books to discover misguidance in what he adheres to, hence abandoning it due to these books, there would be no potential harm in this case, which would require him based on reason to prevent potential harm. Here, one faces two scenarios: either he does not become influenced by these books so there would not be any potential harm that would need to be prevented, or he does become influenced by these books; meaning, he is now misguided. Therefore, how could we forbid him to research efforts to prevent harm?!

Yes, it is probable that a person could be influenced, not from the perspective of conviction, but rather another perspective. Here, he shall be obligated to conduct thorough scientific research and evaluation of these books without being emotionally involved. If he becomes misguided, he shall be punished – as a result of his own choice – for misguidance. Or else, how would reason prevent him from setting out on such research?

If this was deemed true, it would not be permissible for the disbelievers, like the Jews, Christians and Magians, or the people of other sects, or people of different views under the same school of thought, to read the books of truth, because as soon as they intend to read, their minds would forbid them in efforts to prevent potential harm. Supposedly, they perceive the real truth as misguidance. Should this be followed? Does not our scholastic approach of handling this topic reveal that there are paradoxes within it?

What may be concluded here is that a person is allowed to read about or come across misguidance with the condition of setting his personal behaviour right; as in teaching oneself to deal objectively with occurring thoughts. If he based his readings on objectiveness and prepared himself beforehand, his mind would not forbid him to dive in, especially if he was, in fact, doubting things.

Accordingly, it becomes known that the human being's reason in itself is the reference here, not the Islamic scholar who has chosen a specific belief for himself. From the perspective of an Islamic scholar, he has the right to issue a fatwa prohibiting this, but this fatwa cannot counter the reality of what human reason rules from the perspective of individuals themselves. If one is a doubter of the truth, how can his mind prohibit him from coming across what others – the religious authority – see as misguidance? I invite the readers to look carefully here; it is just an assessment (*tashkhīṣ*) made by the Islamic jurist and not a fatwa per se. This assessment is not binding according to the picture we have painted. Even if this fatwa or statement is one of the rights of the jurist, since he sees that he is protecting the faithful from doom and deviance based on his assessment, it is still deemed a didactic fatwa or statement that is not binding to the *mukallaf*, when it comes to making an analysis. For example, if the jurist said that the books of so-and-so are books of ideological misguidance, or that the books of such-and-such ideological current are books of misguidance, what is the binding factor to follow his words when there is no *taqlīd* (lit. imitation or conformity) when it comes to ideologies and thoughts? Being a person of expertise is not enough for the jurist here, as other experts, including scholars of other religions, schools of thought, groups and movements, might take an opposing stance. Therefore, the words of the jurist, in this context, would not be binding on the *mukallaf* – i.e. someone upon whom there is a legal responsibility — only in the case of the greater duty, that is, protecting oneself from being led astray from the truth, and from deviation and temptation. This duty should be well established within the practical intellect without the need of a fatwa from the jurist. We find similar instances in some *fiqh*-related cases, like the case of referring to *taqlīd* in regards to the very root of the question, as well as the case of the *taqlīd* of the most learned of jurists. There are cases where there is no meaning for the probativity of *taqlīd*; a subject I have tackeled in my book *Iḍā'āt*.

Finally, I point out the attempt of some contemporary researchers who use Qur'anic prohibition, with regards to sitting with those who mock the verses of God only when they get into a different subject, as a reference and claim that this ruling includes reading the books and publications that mock and ridicule the religion. This is strange, as mere reading, like we mentioned before, does not constitute acknowledgement. Similarly, not reading does not always translate to making a stance, unlike what is stated in this verse, which refers to a stance taken against the disbelievers who practise mockery of the religion and confronting it. It is a faulty analogical reasoning and does not fulfil the conditions. The verse forbade mingling with them, but did not forbid the disbelievers from speaking, which contradicts the attempt to refer to this verse in order to forbid the books of misguidance in Muslim markets. In addition, it is evident that not every book of misguidance is a book of mockery.

8.4 Countering Misguidance

According to all of the aforementioned, we know that countering misguidance is an Islamic duty, where only all, initially legitimate, means are permissible. We have not based our words on anything but the authority of authentically issued narrations. We are not certain about the report of Dāwūd ibn Sarhān, since it was only narrated by al-Kulaynī and was not mentioned after him by anyone until the tenth century Hijrī, and since it only has one *isnād* (chain of narration), in addition to some context-related remarks.

But today, the question is: how do we counter misguidance in the Islamic society internally? We are facing two directions in this regard. The first direction calls for severing and disputing. It is the direction that believes in the necessity of severing all connections with the phenomenon of misguidance and going under social, political and economic quarantine as much as possible. It also calls for launching an attack on this phenomenon by various available means, such as issuing fatwas, confiscating its intellectual works, preventing people from referring to it, prohibiting scientific communication with the people who are considered misguided and distorting their image so that people look down on them, even through the use of lies and slander. The matter may even reach the extent of imprisonment, expulsion, exile, killing, closure of their centres and confiscation of their work, in addition to taking away their salaries, expelling them from their jobs and imposing financial restrictions on them; all of this, of course, is coupled with scientific and research-related critique.

The second direction is that of connection, engagement and dialogue. This direction sees that the first approach of severing and disputing is not feasible today, except in very rare and limited cases, and that the best way lies in adopting a strategic cultural policy. Some of its steps can be summarised in the following.

(1) Carrying out an immediate and comprehensive revitalisation in religious centres, institutes and seminaries, with the aim of preparing a new and capable scientific cadre versed in contemporary studies and modern intellectual climates that generate most of these ideas. This requires several years to achieve, and its pursuit should be taken seriously and supported by the supreme religious authorities as well as political authorities, where possible. This huge cadre should have roles in various media fields, such as authorship, journalism, audio-visual social media, and so forth, so that we could have a well-equipped army for this noble intellectual confrontation.

(2) Educational work to establish what we called in the *Fiqh al-amr bi-l-maʿrūf wa-l-nahy ʿan al-munkar* book the principle of moderation in expressing religious concern. It is the principle that teaches scholars, preachers and workers psychological and mental calmness and strategic planning, in addition to abandoning anger, tension and inflammatory speeches, replacing them with calm, objective and composed methods, because, nowadays, this approach is of a great influence with regards to the next generation. This requires moral and educational efforts, since it is not easy to create a completely new culture.

(3) Promoting the use of scientific rather than ideological or individual-interest reasoning, which is the logic that the Holy Qurʾan has taught us: to tell the truth, even if against ourselves, and to tell the truth, even if for the benefit of those with whom we are quarrelling, and so on. This principle, when practised and included in our political discourse, will help create great credibility for us instead of using the logic of covering up our flaws, obscuring the merits of the other party, painting others in a distorted light, justifying and simplifying our mistakes, not acknowledging the truth or our weaknesses, as well as neither seeking to justify others' mistakes, nor giving them the benefit of the doubt, while exaggerating their faults and not recognising any of their positive elements.

This double standard is what is ruining the image of religion, the religious institution, and religious figures and activists. We are in need of a method similar to that of al-Sayyid al-Ṣadr, a calm critical scientific approach, even when addressing atheist groups. We should not allow agitation to take us over and rather devise plans calmly in a sound scientific manner. It is a war where empty words and rhetoric do not matter, since preparation and planning is what is important.

(4) Striving to use demonstrative logic, without relying on dialectical logic except when necessary; since demonstrative logic would reinforce our scientific structure, and present us as genuine intellectuals in the nation, rather than the disputatious approach that paints us as mere hot-tempered individuals. The

combination of both critique and a constructive strategy – which al-Sayyid al-Ṣadr adopted in his *Iqtiṣādunā* and *al-Usus al-manṭiqiyya* – is of the utmost importance today.

In this context, I point to the failure of selective text-cutting and 'sentence-level' critical approach of thought. It is a method that has undermined us, limited our intellectual dimension and transformed us into something similar to the inquisition courts of the Middle Ages, as we only concern ourselves with exposing people, and luring them to see whether they say this or that. Once they are exposed, we tear into their image, causing them to lose their status in life by any means possible, even if dishonourable.

(5) Developing a cultural policy that tolerates differing opinions, and does not shut out foreign or new ideas, but rather contemplates and critiques if one is not persuaded. Acknowledging others does not mean correcting their thought, as much as it means that they are actively searching, and that they have the right to do so, and that what is required of one today is defending one's thought by acquiring more sophisticated means of influence.

However, this does not mean that we accept anything but scientific research – no matter how weak – from others. We do not accept ridicule, mockery or offense towards our sanctities, since these are our convictions and we have the right to have them. This, however, does not mean that others' scientific critique of our ideas always amounts to irony. Nonetheless, whoever does not want his thought and belief to be mocked should not mock the belief of others, for whoever knocks on a door shall hear an answer.

(6) Not ruling out the conspiracy logic, since Muslims have been on the receiving end of conspiracies for over two centuries, but this does not mean playing the conspiracy card – without any scientific, legitimate or judicial evidence – to accuse others. And if we prove someone has conspired against the nation and homeland, we have the right to prosecute them without hesitation.

Conclusion

I think this is the best way, today, to confront all the phenomena of intellectual perversions, and religious misguidance in the nation. As for the approach of accusing others of disbelief, ignorance, corruption, treason, as well as using defamation, violence, obscenity, insults, conspiracy and slander, it has very adverse effects on the upcoming generations. Refusing to practise these methods or suppress the books of misguidance does not mean we are practising silence or we are failing to enjoin what is right and forbid what is wrong. We rather believe in confronting those whose opinions we disagree with, but the question at hand is how to do so and what are the effective methods at this moment or the next, especially since there is a lack of religious texts that determine which methods we should use, so we should not muddle things up.

I say: this is what I see fit today, and for every matter there is an exception. We should not compensate for our weaknesses and negligence by attacking and cursing others, so let us ask ourselves a question: have not people abandoned religion because of us? They have not renounced it out of conviction, but out of psychological pressure, and not only did some renounce religion, but also took it upon themselves to take revenge and retaliate against it.

MOHSEN KADIVAR

Free Speech and Critique of Religion in Contemporary Islam

Free speech (and the limits of expression) is one of the important issues of contemporary human rights and undoubtedly started with the Universal Declaration of Human Rights (UDHR) (1948). It does not mean that it is perfect or beyond critique.[1] It ignored 'human duties and responsibilities' before him/herself and God,[2] on the one hand, and it was written in a specific secular atmosphere in the aftermath of World War II,[3] on the other.

There are three concerns here. First, is the impossibility of a comprehensive universal declaration including both human rights and human duties and responsibilities especially in the regions of conflict between believers and atheists.[4] Second, a comprehensive universal declaration between believers including Abrahamic and non-Abrahamic traditions is not realistic.[5] It is not clear that such a declaration is practically accessible between different denominations of each tradition such as Catholics and Protestants in Christianity, and Sunnīs and Shīʿites in Islam. Third, freedom of expression and religious freedom are among those rights that reconciliation between these camps are so difficult.

Beyond these practical concerns, the articles of the UDHR have become the norms of international law and scholarly discussions of human rights since the mid-twentieth century. We can say that many of these articles including

1 See, for example, Roger, Ruston, *Human Rights and the Image of God* (London: SCM Press, 2004); and Carrie Gustafson and Peter Juviler, eds, *Religion and Human Rights: Competing Claims?* (Armonk: M. E. Sharpe, 1999).

2 Seyyed Hossein Nasr, 'Standing before God: Human Responsibilities and Human Rights', in *Humanity before God: Contemporary Faces of Jewish, Christian and Islamic Ethics*, ed. William Schweiker, Michael A. Johnson and Kevin Jung (Minneapolis: Fortress Press, 2006), 299–320.

3 Johannes Morsink, *The Universal Declaration of Human Rights: Origins, Drafting, and Intent* (Philadelphia: University of Pennsylvania Press, 1999).

4 Mohsen Kadivar, *Human Rights and Reformist Islam*, trans. Nikky Akhavan (Edinburgh: Edinburgh University Press, 2021), chapter 7.

5 For example, see Mirsolav Volf, ed., *Do We Worship the Same God? Jews, Christians, and Muslims in Dialogue* (Grand Rapids: William B. Eerdmans Publishing, 2012).

freedom of expression and religious freedom are considered as 'the disciplines of the reasonable people' (*sīrat al-'uqalā'*). It means that the reasonable people in view of their being reasonable (*al-'uqalā' bi-mā hum 'uqalā'*) support freedom of expression and religion. Although Muslim reformists welcome this approach, most Muslim conservatives deny it absolutely or partially.[6]

Free speech and its limits include several issues. I focus here on merely one: a critique of religion, which means the common ground between freedom of expression and religious freedom. This common ground includes several issues of its own. To focus and deepen my discussion, I have chosen only six of them: first, the decriminalization of apostasy and blasphemy versus capital punishment for an apostate and blasphemer or at least civil penalty for the latter; second, critique of Islam in Muslim-majority countries versus critique in those with Muslim minorities; third, critique of Islam by non-Muslims versus critique by Muslims; fourth, scholarly critique of Islam versus non-scholarly criticism; fifth, critique of Islam in public for the masses versus critique in closed circles; sixth, respectful critique of Islam versus defamation of Islam and blasphemy.

The context of these six issues are Articles 18 and 19 of the UDHR.[7] While the UDHR is not a treaty, and as such does not directly create legal obligations for countries, the 1967 International Covenant on Civil and Political Rights (ICCPR) is a legally binding treaty, for the states which ratified it. There are two related articles in the ICCPR in support of religious freedom[8] and freedom of

6 Kadivar, *Human Rights and Reformist Islam*, chapter 8.

7 Article 18: 'Everyone has the right to freedom of thought, conscience and religion; this right includes freedom to change his religion or belief and freedom, either alone or in community with others and in public or private to manifest his religion or belief in teaching, practice, worship and observance.' Article 19: 'Everyone has the right to freedom of opinion and expression; this right includes freedom to hold opinions without interference and to seek, receive and impart information and ideas through any media and regardless of frontiers.'

8 The first one is Article 18: '1. Everyone shall have the right to freedom of thought, conscience and religion. This right shall include freedom to have or to adopt a religion or belief of his choice, and freedom, either individually or in community with others and in public or private, to manifest his religion or belief in worship, observance, practice and teaching. 2. No one shall be subject to coercion which would impair his freedom to have or to adopt a religion or belief of his choice. 3. Freedom to manifest one's religion or beliefs may be subject only to such limitations as are prescribed by law and are necessary to protect public safety, order, health, or morals or the fundamental rights and freedoms of others. 4. The States Parties to the present Covenant undertake to have respect for the liberty of parents and, when applicable, legal guardians to ensure the religious and

expression. Although the wording of Article 18.1 in the ICCPR is similar to the UDHR, the former does not specifically mention the freedom to change religion.

Article 19 (ICCPR) reads:

> 1. Everyone shall have the right to hold opinions without interference. 2. Everyone shall have the right to freedom of expression; this right shall include freedom to seek, receive and impart information and ideas of all kinds, regardless of frontiers, either orally, in writing or in print, in the form of art, or through any other media of his choice. 3. The exercise of the rights provided for in paragraph 2 of this article carries with it special duties and responsibilities. It may therefore be subject to certain restrictions, but these shall only be such as are provided by law and are necessary: (a) For respect of the rights or reputations of others; (b) For the protection of national security or of public order (ordre public), or of public health or morals.

This is the standard of freedom of speech and freedom of religion in our time. As can be seen, it acknowledges large and broad regions for these two types of freedom as two basic rights for human beings. Before any judgement is made, it is necessary to consider the related articles of the 1990 Cairo Declaration on Human Rights in Islam (CDHRI). It is the declaration of the member states of the Organization of Islamic Cooperation (OIC) (Conference of Foreign Ministers) which provides an overview on the conservative Islamic perspective on human rights. The CDHRI declares its purpose to be 'general guidance for Member States [of the OIC] in the field of human rights'.

Article 10 (CDHRI) reads:

> Islam is the religion of true unspoiled nature. It is prohibited to exercise any form of pressure on man or to exploit his poverty or ignorance in order to force him to change his religion to another religion or to atheism.

And Article 22 (CDHRI) states:

> (a) Everyone shall have the right to express his opinion freely in such manner as would not be contrary to the principles of the Sharīʿa. (b) Everyone shall have the right to advocate what is right, and propagate

moral education of their children in conformity with their own convictions.'

> what is good, and warn against what is wrong and evil according to the norms of Islamic Sharīʿa. (c) Information is a vital necessity to society. It may not be exploited or misused in such a way as may violate sanctities and the dignity of prophets, undermine moral and ethical values or disintegrate, corrupt or harm society or weaken its faith.

It is obvious that religious freedom and freedom of expression are unqualified forms of freedom in the UDHR and ICCPR, but both are restricted to the Sharīʿa in the CDHRI. There is a big difference between UN documents and the conservative Islam that is presented in the CDHRI.

1. Decriminalisation of Apostasy and Blasphemy

(A) According to Article 18 of the UDHR explicitly, and Article 18.1 of the ICCPR, changing religion or belief is not only not a crime but also an essential part of freedom of religion. CDHRI Article 10 prohibited any 'compulsion' or 'exploitation' in conversion *from* Islam, but it does not condemn the same techniques in conversion *to* Islam.[9] While apostasy is a crime in traditional Sharīʿa (the explicit framework of the CDHRI) with severe punishments, these punishments are not removed, nor is apostasy decriminalised.

The best sources of criminalisation of apostasy in Sunnī Islam is *al-Fiqh al-Islāmī wa-adillatuh* (*Islamic Jurisprudence and Its Evidences*, 1996);[10] and in Shīʿite Islam, the long and detailed article on *irtidād* (apostasy) in *Mawsūʿat al-fiqh al-Islāmī tibqan li-madhhab Ahl al-Bayt* (*Encyclopaedia of Islamic Jurisprudence according to the Doctrine of the Household [of the Prophet]*, 2007).[11] This is the encyclopaedia of the Iranian Supreme Leader's office and represents conservative Shīʿī jurisprudence. There are many similarities between these

9 For more information, see Ann Elizabeth Mayer, *Islam and Human Rights: Tradition and Politics* (Colorado: Westview Press, 2012), chapter 9.

10 Wahba al-Zuḥaylī (1932–2015), *al-Fiqh al-Islāmī wa-adillatuh* (Damascus: Dār al-Fikr, 1996), 6:183–90, 7:621.

11 *Mawsūʿat al-fiqh al-Islāmī tibqan li-madhhab Ahl al-Bayt*, ed. al-Sayyid Maḥmūd al-Hāshimī al-Shāhrūdī (Qom: Mu'assasat Dā'irat Maʿārif al-Fiqh al-Islāmī, 2002–12), 8:353–457. Al-Shāhrūdī (1948–2018), its chief editor, was Chief Justice of the Islamic Republic of Iran (1999–2009) and Chairman of the Expediency Discernment Council (*Majmaʿ-i Tashkis-i Maslahat-i Niẓam*) from 2017 until his death. In addition, he was one of the main writers of the Iranian penal code (*Qānun-i Mujāzāt-i Islāmī*, 2013).

two schools. I have narrated both of them in detail elsewhere,[12] but here I omit the former and focus on the main parts of the latter.

The penalty of a *fiṭrī*[13] male apostate is immediate execution without *istitāba* (being given a chance to repent). As for a *millī*[14] male apostate: if he is asked to repent, he does so, and returns to Islam, then there is no punishment. If not, his execution is consensual. A female *fiṭrī* or *millī* apostate is asked to repent. If she refuses, she is imprisoned, pressured, whipped during the prayer times, and subjected to severe punishments until she repents or dies. The second punishment is dividing the apostate's property among his heirs before his death. The third punishment is annulling the marriage.

Apostasy is criminalised in about twenty Muslim-majority countries including Iran.[15] The most important particular of Article 220 of Iran's penal code is punishment of apostasy that was expressed indirectly and implicitly.

Blasphemy is decriminalised in the UDHR and ICCPR. Article 22, clause (c), of the CDHRI states: 'It [information] may not be exploited or misused in such a way as may violate sanctities and the dignity of prophets', referring to the prohibition of blasphemy, and it is obvious that the framework of this declaration is the Sharīʿa. In conservative Islam, and for the Sunnīs, this is the Sharīʿa ruling in the case of blasphemy: 'The four Sunni legal schools have reached consensus that a Muslim man who insults a prophet or one of the angels (*malāʾika*) is to be executed. The Mālikī school, based upon a widespread opinion, says that repenting is not an option.'[16]

For the Shīʿites: 'The jurists have reached a consensus that blasphemy [*sabb Allāh, sabb al-rasūl* or *sabb* of one of the Imāms] is apostasy and the person is considered *mahdūr al-dam* (a guilty person whose blood may be shed with

12 Mohsen Kadivar, *Blasphemy and Apostasy in Islam: Debates in Shi'a Jurisprudence*, trans. Hamid Mavani (Edinburgh: Edinburgh University Press, 2021), 2–4, 27–34.

13 One who was born into Islam.

14 One whose parents were disbelievers at the time of sexual intercourse, and the child converted to Islam and later on left it.

15 Article 220 of Iran's penal code (2013): 'It should be done according to the Article 167 of the Constitution of the Islamic Republic of Iran in the cases of *ḥudūd* punishments which are not mentioned in this bill.' Article 167 of the Iranian Constitution (1989): 'The judge is bound to endeavour to judge each case on the basis of the codified law. In case of the absence of any such law, he has to deliver his judgement on the basis of authoritative Islamic sources and authentic *fatāwā*. He, on the pretext of the silence of or deficiency of law in the matter, or its brevity or contradictory nature, cannot refrain from admitting and examining cases and delivering his judgement.'

16 al-Zuḥaylī, *al-Fiqh al-Islāmī wa-adillatuh*, 6:184.

impunity). Blaspheming Fāṭima [the Prophet's daughter] and other prophets is attached to apostasy. Blasphemy and apostasy are not the same, even though sometimes they do occur together; executing a blasphemer does not require the ruler's permission.'[17] Blasphemy (*sabb al-nabī*) is explicitly expressed in Iran's penal code (*Qānun-i mojāzāt-i Islāmi*, 2013).[18]

(B) I have rejected penalising apostasy and blasphemy in the following way: from an Islamic perspective, people have the freedom to choose a religion and a belief system and cannot be compelled to accept the 'true religion' and the 'right belief system'. Islam recognised the diversity of religions and beliefs after its revelation as the divine call to the true religion, in the sense that some responded and others persisted in error. The latter are divided into many groups and sects.

Those who knowingly decide to ignore this invitation out of stubbornness and obstinacy will be punished only in the afterlife. Islam's invitation to others is based on reasoned logic, peace and compassion, as opposed to violence and despotism. Faith pertains to the heart and, as such, it is impossible to force a person to change his or her religion. However, if his or her denial was due to spite and hostility, such a person will face a severe retribution in the afterlife. Given that Islam has inscribed the freedom of religion and faith, any *ḥadīth* that sanctions killing or shedding an apostate's blood with impunity is incompatible with the noble Qur'an and must be rejected. There is no reliable proof from the Qur'an, Sunna, consensus (*ijmāʿ*) or reason that can establish the validity of executing anyone accused of apostasy or blaspheming the Prophet. On the contrary, such actions violate both the Qur'an and human reason. Moreover, the negative effects of allowing such a practice would be numerous and, as such, would certainly weaken Islam.

Only a sound judicial system can issue a judgement and supervise its implementation. The issuance of a ruling by a *mujtahid* who is qualified to issue a legal opinion (*fatwā*) in the community without undergoing due process in the state's judicial system does not suffice.

The Qur'an absolutely pronounces no death penalty on an apostate and a blasphemer of the Prophet. Traditionalist jurists, by employing derivative *ijtihād*,

17 *Mawsūʿat al-fiqh*, 8:364–67.

18 Article 262: 'Anyone who curses the Prophet or the each of the messengers of God or falsely accused them of unchastity (*qadhf*) is a blasphemer (*sābb al-nabī*) and is sentenced to the death penalty. Note: Accusing each of the Shīʿite infallible Imāms of unchastity (*qadhf*) or Fāṭima al-Zahrāʾ [daughter of the Prophet] or cursing them is blasphemy.'

have arrived at this judgement and claimed consensus by relying on 'isolated' *ḥadīth*s (*khabar al-wāḥid*). The ruling on killing apostates and blasphemers is incorrect and cannot be implemented on account of the following seven proofs:

First, the necessity of stopping the execution of an apostate or a blasphemer by invoking the secondary injunction (*ḥukm thanawī*) of '*wahn* Islam' (i.e. implementing the punishment would impair or debilitate Islam; avoiding the harm or seeking public welfare or governmental injunction). Second, the necessity of suspending or stopping the *ḥudūd* punishment absolutely or at least the *ḥudūd* that would lead to killing a person during the Imām's occultation (since the mid-tenth century). Third, since the judgement on killing is based on *thiqa* 'isolated reports' (*khabar al-wāḥid*), it is mandatory to exercise caution on matters that lead to shedding someone's blood (human life). Fourth, when dealing with vital and critical issues, all *thiqa* 'isolated *ḥadīth*s' (*khabar al-wāḥid*) are rendered non-probative and non-authoritative. Fifth, removing the death penalty for the apostate because of alteration of the subject matter of a ruling or situational context (*mawḍū'*). Sixth, *ḥadīth*s that are contrary to explicit and univocal (*muḥkamāt*) Qur'anic verses are rendered non-probative and non-authoritative. Seventh, reason dictates that it is abominable to terrorise a person merely for abandoning Islam or insulting its holy personages or primary injunction (*ḥukm awwalī*) of '*wahn* of Islam'.

In conclusion, given that no temporal punishment has been mandated for apostasy, executing anyone for insulting the Prophet, the Qur'an or any of Islam's other sacred objects is indefensible. The right to life has no relationship to one's beliefs and convictions. As the results and consequences of one's faith will only appear in the afterlife, no reward or punishment should be assigned in this world, irrespective of the validity of one's faith. The prescribed punishments to be carried out in this world pertain to the perpetration of crimes. As no worldly punishment has been assigned for committing sins, apostasy by itself cannot be punished in any way, let alone by capital punishment. Likewise, there is no worldly punishment for remaining an unbeliever and refusing to embrace Islam. A sound judicial system cannot convict and punish such people, because religion is a matter of the heart and personal choice. In addition, the Lawmaker did not proclaim any punishment in this world or in the hereafter for erring in one's research and study. Of course, in the afterlife an apostate who rebelled and exhibited hostility and enmity to truth will receive a severe retribution.

I classified blasphemy under 'hate speech', hence the blasphemer's execution is rejected, and punishment is possible only by the judicial system. This light civil punishment can be suspended depending on the level of the society's development.[19]

To summarise this section: religious freedom and freedom of expression are not defined in terms of the criminalisation of apostasy and blasphemy. That is to say, there is a deep contradiction between these two types of freedom and the penalisation of apostasy and blasphemy. It is impossible to believe in them both. We can choose only one of them. The claim of religious freedom and freedom of speech of those who did not decriminalise apostasy and blasphemy is baseless and unacceptable.

2. Critique of Islam, Muslim-Majority Countries and Muslim Minorities

The subject of this section is comparing the ruling of critique of Islam as a constant with two variables, Muslim-majority countries and Muslim minorities. Is there any difference between these two situations? Practically, there is no room for critique of Islam in countries or societies where Muslims constitute the majority, while the critique of Islam is smoother and easier in countries or societies where Muslims are a minority. When the Muslims are a majority, they prevent critique of their tradition in legal and even illegal ways. When they are a minority, they do not have authority to do so, and it leads them to tolerate the critique of Islam.

Does this mean that there is a problem in Islam in the case of critique of itself? The answer depends on the types of Islam, or one can say, interpretations of Islam. Conservative Muslims[20] do not tolerate any critique of Islam and interpret it as animosity or a plot for weakening or removing Islam. Public media and pedagogy are restricted and censored in this case by the dictatorship of the majority. Islamic states or theocracies intensify this restriction and

19 This is the topic of my book *Blasphemy and Apostasy in Islam.*

20 Traditionalists, sometimes called conservatives, are those jurists who adhere to classical *fiqh* rulings and methodology; they constitute a strong majority in religious centres of learning.

censorship. Most of the cases of critique of Islam are classified under apostasy and blasphemy in such countries and the critics are sentenced to death or assassinated. There are many examples of this in Asia and Africa.[21]

In contrast, reformist Muslims[22] not only do not fear critique of Islam, but also believe that such critiques strengthen the Muslims in competition with other cultures and traditions, on the one hand, and manifest the advantages of Islam and eliminate the probable weaknesses of their religious knowledge, on the other. They argue that even if the critiques of Islam are harmful, it is impossible to prevent them in the time of the Internet and satellites. From their perspective, a 'closed society' is not an Islamic one.

Reformist Muslims compared Muslim minorities who do not only loss their faith, but also find the most progressive tactics for defending their faith, with Muslim-majority countries which tried to reduce or remove the critique of Islam and conclude that the Muslims who live in free societies without any restriction of such critique are better and more up-to-date believers in the case of defence of their faith in modern times than the Muslims who live in closed societies.

I have a memoir very close to this section. I was put in jail by an 'Islamic state' for delivering a critical speech on the Night of Destiny (*laylat al-qadr*), 23 Ramadan 1419 (12 January 1999), in Hussain-Abad Congregational Mosque in Isfahan regarding the 'prohibition of terror in Sharīʿa', and for a critical inter-

---

21 Abdullah Saeed, *Human Rights and Islam: An Introduction to Key Debates between Islamic Law and International Human Rights Law* (Massachusetts: Edward Elgar Publishing, Inc., 2018), 198–200.

22 Reformist Muslims are a spectrum of Muslims who have these characteristics: first, they are aware of the tremendous impact of modernity on humanity and human life, and strive to reconcile religious knowledge with modernity. Secondly, they believe in the necessity of separating the institution of religion from the state (objective secularism). Thirdly, they do not consider traditional *ijtihād* to be sufficient in the derivatives of jurisprudence (*al-furūʿ al-fiqhī*), but advocate a holistic and comprehensive reform based on the core foundation and principles of Islamic thought and jurisprudence. In contrast to 'semi-reformists', who concentrate on piecemeal reforms, reformists argue that it is not enough to simply reinterpret rulings within the traditional framework, that is, traditional *ijtihād*; what is required is rethinking the underpinnings of classical juristic methodology. They contend that meaningful reform in *fiqh* rulings is the fruit of two deep reforms: that of the juristic methodology (*uṣūl al-fiqh*) and that of its foundations (*mabānī*), which involves other areas of Islamic intellectual thought; in other words, structural *ijtihād*. It is only then that modern issues, such as the emergence of nation-states and the expansion of discourses of citizenship, human rights, gender equality and democracy, can be addressed from within an Islamic framework.

view ('An overview of the twenty-year record of the Islamic Republic', *Khurdad Daily*, February 14–16 1999) and spent eighteen months of my conviction period.[23] It was precisely the violation of freedom of expression. In May 2000, I received a new book from my family entitled *Violence, Human Rights and Civil Society*, which was written by an atheist author.[24] The following question, posed by the author, impressed me a lot: 'If you ever had to live abroad for any reason, where would you rather be? Where do you think your rights may be protected, your opinions may be respected and you're not told to give up your ideas lest you be crucified: in Baghdad, Kabul, Riyadh, Khartoum, Damascus, or Washington, London, Paris and Berlin?!' It was a serious question. After being released from jail, I tried to live in that closed society under the ruling of fundamentalist Muslims,[25] but I was restricted more and more. I was fired from my tenured academic job, all of my publications including my websites were banned and now I am writing from exile (United States of America). This is a lived experience of freedom of expression in contemporary Islam. I criticised the weaponisation of Islam or abusing Islam as an instrument for political purposes by the governments of the Islamic state, and one can imagine what happens to someone who criticises Islam.

I can conclude that critique of Islam is permissible with no difference between Muslims in the majority or minority according to reformist Islam. Conservative Muslims, however, use a double-standard criterion: they do not support critique of Islam in Muslim-majority countries, while they use religious freedom and freedom of expression when they are the minority in other countries. This double-standard approach is certainly questionable.

---

23 *Bahā-yi Azādi: defāʿiyyāt-i Mohsen Kadivar dar dadgah-i viji-y- ruḥāniyyāt* [The price of freedom: Mohsen Kadivar's defence in the cleric court], comp. Zahra Roodi [Kadivar] (Tehran: Nashr-i Nay, 2000).

24 Mohammad Reza Nikfar, *Khosounat, Hoquq-Bashar va Jāmiʿi-yi Madani* (Tehran: Tarh-i Now, 1999).

25 Fundamentalists (or radical Muslims or extremists – I do not have any reservations on the name) are a spectrum of Muslims with the following characteristics: first, they are dogmatic in their religious views and consider themselves empowered to impose their beliefs and ideas on others. Secondly, the establishment of an Islamic state is considered a prerequisite for the main task of implementation of the Sharīʿa. Thirdly, in order to achieve this main purpose, *violence* is allowed to the extent that is expedient. Fourth, the Sharīʿa is considered the main source of Islamic state laws. Fifth, among the Shīʿites, the Islamic state is considered equivalent to the political Guardianship of the Jurist-Ruler (*wilāyat al-faqīh*). They constitute a much smaller group than traditionalists.

3. Critique of Islam by Non-Muslims and Muslims

In this section, I try to compare the constant of critique of Islam with two other variables, that is, the religion of the critics. Is there any difference between Muslim and non-Muslim critics? We know that Muslims have more restrictions in the case of apostasy according to the conservative understanding of Islam which criminalises apostasy. A non-Muslim would not be accused of apostasy and be executed, for example. From the same perspective (criminalisation of blasphemy) a blasphemer would be punished severely regardless of being Muslim or non-Muslim.

Critique by a non-Muslim is usually justified as the religious hostility that is predictable, such that the critic would necessarily be a non-Muslim, because he or she did not find Islam perfect and complete. Critique of Islam by a Muslim is divided into at least three types. The first is the critique that easily could be attributed to the misunderstanding or deviation of Muslims' actions from the standards of Islam that are mentioned in the Qur'an and the tradition of the Prophet and his household. This type of critique has been tolerated without any difficulty. The second is the critique of Islam, but not critique of the Qur'an and the tradition of the Prophet and his household. It is the critique of superstitions or local customs or understanding of past jurists or abrogated or time-bound rulings that are considered as Islamic. This type of critique or purification of Islamic teachings is introduced in the authentic *ḥadīth* of Imām Ja'far al-Ṣādiq:

> The scholars are the heirs of the prophets because the prophets did not leave any Dirham or Dinar (units of money) as their legacy. What they left was certain pieces of their statements. Those who acquired anything of these pieces of their statements they have certainly gained a large share. You must be very careful, when acquiring such knowledge, to see from what kinds of people you receive them. Among us (the Ahl al-Bayt, household of the Prophet) after every one there comes a just person who removes (and exposes) the forgeries of the exaggerators from it (knowledge), the infiltrated materials of the fallacious ones and the interpretations of the ignorant ones.[26]

This is the precise job of the true *'ulamā'*. These reforms or corrections or cul-

26 Muhammad ibn Ya'qub al-Kulayni, *al-Kafi*, trans. Muhammad Sarwar (New York: The Islamic Seminary, Inc., 1999), 1:61.

tural surgery are on controversial issues. Many conservative or ultra conservative *'ulamā'* and their followers insist on their old-fashioned understandings and do not listen to reformist *'ulamā'*. Public acceptance of these reforms depends on religious and cultural authority of reformist *'ulamā'*. These Islamic reforms are not acceptable by many conservative *'ulamā'*, while they are the only way of reviving Islamic teachings. We should tolerate these contradictory viewpoints. Imposing each of these two viewpoints, fanatic and reformist, that each of them are supported by two types of *'ulamā'* is not acceptable. Freedom of expression requires tolerance of both. Critique of each of them is an academic right.

The third type of critique of Islam is the critique of God, His Prophet, the Qur'an and the Shī'ite Imāms by a Muslim. The critiques by non-Muslims are understandable, tolerated and justified as the hostility or hatred or misunderstanding of a disbeliever, but these critiques by Muslims are problematic. These critiques are the signs of inconsistency with Islamic faith according to the mainstream of Islamic thought.[27]

The key question in this type is, how can a person believe in these statements and simultaneously consider him/herself a Muslim? We can criticise these statements and argue that they are wrong and could not be introduced as Islamic teachings, on the one hand, and give evidence for their inconsistency with Islamic teachings, on the other, but we are not allowed to call such a critic non-Muslim as long as he or she considers him/herself a Muslim. The only judge for the claim of Islam is God in the hereafter. We are in charge of

27 The following viewpoints could be examples of this type: the Qur'an is not the word of God but it was written by Muhammad; the revelation is the Prophet's dreams, and the Qur'an needs *ta'wīl* (spiritual interpretation) not *tafsīr* (exegesis); the revelation followed the human personality of Muhammad; Muhammad was an authoritarian figure who forced people of his time to convert to Islam; Islam meant submission to his political power even without faith and believing in God and His Prophet; the real meaning of God's servant (*'abd Allāh*) is His slaves; the Qur'an is the book of fear (*kitāb al-khawf*); the Qur'an and Islam were imperfect and incomplete because of the lack of 'love' – it was the Sufis such as Rumi who added love to Islamic teachings, and as such the *Mathnawī* and *Diwan-i Shams* of Rumi are the references/criteria not the Qur'an; God is an arbitrary ruler who should be worshipped to be immune of His punishment; the real meaning of God's punishment in the Qur'an is torture; the Qur'an, Muhammad as a prophet and even God are not free of error and mistake; the Qur'an is Muhammad's interpretation of the world; it is doubtful that the Qur'an was written by one person in the name of the Prophet – it could have been written by a team of Arabs and non-Arabs before or after the Prophet's life; there is no required worship in Islam, but prayer or worship are totally optional and voluntarily.

accepting the appearance of people in the matter of faith and religion. And this is an important principle of the decriminalisation of apostasy and blasphemy. Critique of Islam is free, but responding to such critiques and arguing against them also is free. The authority of the arguments of each side determines the winner, not removing or killing the critics. In other words, the logic of Islam is the logic of demonstration not the logic of force and coercion. There is a big difference between the two.

We should tolerate dissidence, innovation, new ideas or critique of Islam. It means that these viewpoints, even when we are convinced that they are wrong, are not crimes and their producers are not to be punished. This is the meaning of freedom of expression. But it does not mean that no one has the right to criticise these innovative ideas. We should be ready to participate in a fair competition. It is not acceptable to cover our weakness or laziness with the concern of restriction of the freedom of expression.

4. Scholarly Critique of Islam versus Non-scholarly Criticism

The subject of this section is two other variations, that is, scholarly and non-scholarly critique in relation to our constant, critique of Islam. Non-scholarly criticism of Islam was not considered in the pre-modern period. Although most of such critiques may be deemed baseless, irrational or hedonistic, we cannot ignore the impact and importance of non-scholarly criticism of Islam in mass media, global social networks and the Internet in the modern era. Many of these critiques are organised to shape Islamophobia, and they help form the attitudes of Western audiences to Islam.

The world is described as a small village in modern times. If this is true, we should acknowledge that the influence of these critiques of Islam on the Muslim masses is undeniable. Banning them is not possible, issuing fatwas of prohibition (*taḥrīm*) of reading or listening or watching them is not effective and sentencing the producers to severe punishment is not the solution. What can Muslims do in such a case? First, we should acknowledge the non-scholarly critique of Islam in the modern period as an unpleasant reality. Second, we should respond to these critiques in a scholarly way, using language and style that is understandable by the masses. These arguments will start competing with those critiques and the non-scholarly defamation of Islam. This is exactly the implementation of a Qur'anic teaching: 'Call unto the way of thy Lord with wisdom and goodly exhortation. And dispute with them in the most virtuous manner. Surely thy Lord is He who knows best those who stray from His way, and He knows best the rightly guided' (16:125).[28]

Scholarly critique of Islam has a rich history in the lived experience of Muslims. There was not any red tape for scholarly critiques in the traditional seminary. The most important issues in Islamic theology and philosophy are the unity of God, the hereafter and prophesy. For example, all of them were criticised respectively by Sa'd ibn Manṣūr Ibn Kammūna[29] (1215–84) in his *Shubha* (*Dubious Issue*), Omar Khayyam (1048–1131) in his *Rubā'iyyāt* (poetry in the form of quatrains)[30] and Abū Bakr Muḥammad ibn Zakariyā al-Rāzī (854–925) in his attributed theory of religion.[31]

Although the martyrs of Sufism al-Husayn ibn Manṣūr al-Ḥallāj[32] (858–922), 'Ayn-al-Qużāt Hamadānī[33] (1098–1131) and Shihāb al-Dīn Yaḥyā ibn Ḥabash Suhrawardī[34] (1154–91) were executed by the fatwas of close-minded conservative jurists of their times, they were exceptions, and Sufis grew and produced their masterpieces in the margins of *fiqh* (jurisprudence) and *kalam* (scholastic theology) works. There were pressures and restrictions on some of the philosophers, mystics and dissidents by the close-minded conservative jurists in the time of the Safavids (15701–1736) and Qajarids (1789–1925) but Islamic philosophy and mysticism continued their academic lives successfully.[35] I confine myself to two examples from these two periods. Ṣadr al-Dīn Muḥammad Shīrāzī, also called Mullā Ṣadrā[36] (1572–1640), one of the foremost Muslim philosophers in

28 Seyyed Hossein Nasr, editor-in-chief, *The Study Quran: A New Translation and Commentary* (New York: HarperOne, 2017).

29 Ibn Kammūna, *al-Kāshif (al-jadīd fī al-ḥikma)*, ed. Ḥāmid Nājī Iṣfahānī (Berlin: Freie Universität Berlin, Institut für Islamwissenschaft; Tehran: Iranian Research Institute of Philosophy, 2008), chapter 7, section 2. He himself tried to respond to the 'dubious issue'.

30 Edward FitzGerald, ed., *The Rubā'iyyāt of Omar Khayyam* (New York, 1942).

31 Sarah Stroumsa, *Freethinkers of Medieval Islam: Ibn al-Rāwandī, Abū Bakr al-Rāzī and Their Impact on Islamic Thought* (Leiden: Brill, 2016).

32 Carl W. Ernst, ed., *Hallaj: Poems of a Sufi Martyr* (Chicago: Northwestern University Press, 2018).

33 Arthur John Arberry, *A Sufi Martyr: The 'Apologia' of 'Ain al-Qudat al-Hamadhani* (London and New York: Routledge, 2008).

34 Mehdi Aminrazavi, *Suhrawardi and the School of Illumination* (New York: Routledge, 2013).

35 Seyyed Hossein Nasr and Oliver Leaman, eds, *History of Islamic Philosophy* (New York: Routledge, 2015).

36 Fazlur Rahman, *The Philosophy of Mulla Sadra Shirazi* (Albany: State University of

Islamic history and the founder of *al-ḥikma al-muta'āliya* (the transcendent philosophy), in some of his works described some of the pressures and restrictions of his time.[37] He was accused of apostasy because of his theory of *waḥdat al-wujūd* (unity of existence). Shaykh Mohammad Hadi Tehrani (1835–1903), one of the leaders of Constitutionalist movement, was accused of blasphemy and because of that he was called Shaykh Hadi Mukaffar ('the Unbeliever').[38]

Despite some of its tragic exceptions, scholarly critique of Islam has been the best examples of freedom of expression among Muslims, and has continued to the present.

5. Critique of Islam in Public for the Masses versus Critique in Closed Circles

The subject of this section is comparing the constant of critique of Islam with two other variations, 'in public for the masses' and 'in closed circles'. The conventional image of this comparison could be described in the following way: freedom of expression including critique of Islam is acceptable in closed circles especially academic ones. The correct place of responding to critiques of Islam is closed academic circles. *'Ulamā'*, or the scholars of Islam, clarify the perfection of Islam, and prove the invalidity of any suspicions or dubious issues about Islam. They also welcome debate with critics of Islam. Closed non-academic circles are somehow tolerated, not because of their theoretical permission in conservative Islam, but because of the difficulty or even impossibility of monitoring such circles. Imagining their low influence on the masses, these circles are ignored by *'ulamā'* or Islamic states.

The story of critique of Islam in public for the masses is something else. Conservative Islam requires hard restrictions in public. The concern is not shaking the faith of the masses due to weak public information. This concern

---

New York Press, 1976).

37 Ṣadr al-Dīn Muḥammad Shīrāzī, *al-Ḥikma al-muta'āliya fī al-asfār al-'aqliyya al-arba'a* [The transcendent philosophy of the four journeys of the intellect] (Beirut: Dār Iḥyā' al-Turāth al-'Arabī, 1990), 1:6–7; *Risāla-yi Sih Asl*, ed. Mohammad Khajavi (Tehran: Mawla, 1997); *Majmū'i-ye Ash'ār Ṣadr al-Dīn Shīrāzī*, ed. Mohammad Khajavi (Tehran: Mawla, 1997); *Masnavi-yi Mullā Ṣadrā*, ed. M. Fayzi (Qom: Kitābkhāna-yi Mar'ashi Najafi, 1999). The latter two are editions of selections of Mullā Ṣadrā's poetry.

38 Ne'matullah Safari Forishani, 'Resali-yi Haqq wa Hukm wa Sharh-i Hal-i Shaykh Muhammad Hadi Tehran', *Nami-yi Mufid* 1, no. 4 (Spring 1996).

is a thoughtful one, especially when we know that many of these suspicions or dubious issues about Islam are organised, and Islamophobia is a political agenda in the post-colonial period. The background of this approach is Plato's *Republic*, which justifies censoring for the protection of people's expediency and real goodness.[39]

There is a big question here. If the censor and restriction of the public sphere were possible in the pre-modern period, are they possible in the modern era? This type of closed society can be found in North Korea and China. Modern technology, especially the Internet and satellites, negate the possibility of restriction of the public sphere. Regional or local media (radio, television and magazines) in Muslim-majority countries restricted the critiques of Islam, but they could not deny that many citizens secretly listen, watch and read censored media. Comparing the believers of two different societies, the believers of open societies are more enlightened and immune of deviation than believers of closed societies. These are two types of anthropology. Conservative *'ulamā'* should be more optimistic regarding human beings. Islamic faith could be protected in open societies regarding the freedom of expression.

Freedom of expression in Muslim-majority countries does not mean preaching atheism or anti-Islam, or distributing propaganda against Islam, but it means that these ideas could be broadcast in private media, or could be taught or discussed in private academic centres. Discussing these issues in public media, academies and research centres would be done in the framework of regional law.

Morteza Motahhari (1919–79), the distinguished Islamic theologian, a few months before his assassination expressed very important points in his speech on the freedom of belief that was published in the *Future of the Islamic Revolution*. I narrate a brief segment of his detailed discussion, because of its high importance (the longest quotation in this paper). He mentioned the samples of freedom of discussion in the history of Islam:

> Non-Muslims and disbelievers came to the Mosque of the Prophet in Medina and freely denied the principles of Islam, rejected God or expressed that they did not believe in God; the other event [is that] they sat in the Holy Mosque (*Masjid al-Ḥarām*) in Mecca and said they disbelieved in God, in the Prophet, in the pilgrimage (*ḥajj*) and even mocked the pilgrimage. Islam could remind [us] because of these

39 Plato, *The Republic*, Book 3.

> freedoms. If those who denied God and Islamic teachings in Medina in early Islam were beaten or killed, Islam would not exist today. Islam has survived, because it encountered different thoughts which were in contradiction with Islam bravely and frankly.
>
> Al-Mufaḍḍal ibn ʿUmar al-Juʿfī [d. ca. 762], one of the companions of Imām Jaʿfar al-Ṣādiq and theologians of the eighth century, came to pray at the Mosque of the Prophet (*Masjid al-Nabī*) in Medina. A few materialists (*Dahrī*) started a discussion on the non-existence of God and rejected the prophecy of the Messenger of God. After his prayer, al-Mufaḍḍal, who was very angry, challenged them strongly. The materialists told him: 'First of all, tell us from which group you are. Are you a companion of Imām Jaʿfar al-Ṣādiq?' He confirmed [this]. The materialists told him: 'Okay! We discussed in his presence much more than this several times, and he did not get angry. He listened carefully to our discussions, and then criticised our claims one by one.' This is the method of our Imām, Jaʿfar ibn Muḥammad al-Ṣādiq. This is the reason of the survival of Islam.

He continued:

> The discussions and arguments of the materialists were written and protected by our *ʿulamāʾ*. The materialists' books, if there were any, have not survived and did not reach our time. Abū Jaʿfar Muḥammad b. ʿAlī, well known as Shaykh al-Ṣadūq or Ibn Bābawayh (after 917–91), in one of his books entitled *ʿUyūn akhbār al-Riḍā* (*The Sources of Traditions on [Imām] al-Riḍā*), compiled the *ḥadīth*s of the Eighth Shīʿite Imām, ʿAlī ibn Mūsā al-Riḍā. A large part of this book comprises the Imām's debates with Sunnī Muslims, Christians, Jews, the Sabaeans, Zoroastrians (*Majūs*) and materialists (*Dahrī*) in the time of al-Maʾmūn al-ʿAbbāsī (768–833). Some of these non-Muslim scholars expressed blasphemous ideas against the Prophet and Islam.
>
> Abū Manṣūr Aḥmad ibn ʿAlī al-Ṭabrisī, the twelfth-century scholar, compiled the arguments and debates of the Prophet and Imāms against their opponents in his book *al-Iḥtijāj ʿalā ahl al-lijāj* (*Argumentation against the People of Stubbornness*), best known as *al-Iḥtijāj*. Muḥammad Bāqir ibn Muḥammad Taqī al-Majlisī (1628–1699), in his narrative encyclopaedia *Biḥār al-anwār al-jāmiʿa li-durar akhbār al-aʾimmat al-āthār* (*Seas of Lights: The Collection of Pearls of the Reports of the Pure*

> *Imāms*), compiled the arguments and debates of the Prophet and Imāms in section four (volumes 9 and 10), *Kitāb al-Iḥtijājāt wa-l-munāẓirāt* ('on argumentations and debates'), containing eighty-three chapters. This is the way of survival of Islam.

Motahhari concluded:

> I advise the youths and proponents of Islam: do not imagine that the way of protection of Islam is negation of freedom of expression. Islamic beliefs and Islamic philosophy are not preserved by not letting others express their ideas. No! let them talk, do not let them betray [Islam]. Keep in your mind that Islam could not be guarded by preventing others to express their thoughts and beliefs. The only way that we can guard Islam is [by] *logic*, regarding freedom [of expression] and encountering opposite thoughts explicitly, frankly and clearly.[40]

He means by 'logic' demonstration (*burhān, istidlāl*), not force and suppression. Motahhari strongly advocated the freedom of expression. His colleague Hossein-Ali Montazeri Najaf-Abadi (1922–2009), my mentor of *fiqh* and ethics, continued this way for three decades.[41] My brief comment on Motahhari's speech is his last point: 'Do not let them betray [Islam].' Does it mean that *'ulamā'* or Muslim governments should examine each speaker before expressing his or her ideas, and be sure that there is no betrayal? If so, practically it opens the arbitrary restriction of freedom of expression in the name of prevention of betrayal. This is not acceptable.

Motahhari created the difference between the freedom of thought (*fikr*) and the freedom of belief (*'aqīda*) by accepting the reasonability of the former, and by denying the latter because of the rational possibility of incorrectness of some beliefs;[42] and it is not an acceptable position. This is because thinking does not require taking permission from any authority, and in general it is not preventable. Freedom of thought is neither the subject of challenge, nor a favour

40 Morteza Motahhari, *Ayandeye Enqelab-e Eslami* [Future of the Islamic Revolution] (Tehran: Sadra, 2006), 46–49.

41 Hossein-Ali Montazeri Najaf-Abadi, *Ḥukūmat-i dīnī va ḥuqūq-i insān* [Religious state and human rights] (Qom: Sarā'i, 2008).

42 Morteza Motahhari, *Piramoun-e Jomhuri-e Eslami* [On the Islamic Republic] (Tehran: Sadra, 1989), 87–136; Morteza Motahhari, *Piramoun-e Enqelab-e Eslami* [On the Islamic Revolution] (Tehran: Sadra, 1989), 6–22.

to be accepted from Motahhari. Where there is room for critique and dispute is the freedom to express one's views and the freedom to act in accordance with them. Thus, making a distinction between thinking and belief does not solve the problem. Which beliefs do introduce themselves as false or incorrect? Those who are faced with such a division will take their place on the side of those who deny the freedom of belief and religion.[43]

To conclude this section: freedom of expression in public and private is the best way of spreading Islam and strengthening Islamic thought. Freedom of expression provides a competitive sphere, and the winners will be those who are stronger in argumentation, theoretical knowledge, practical dialogue and in convincing the people. Censorship, banning media, restriction or violation of freedom of speech are not the solution.

6. Freedom of Expression and Blasphemy

The subject of this section is the most controversial issues related to the freedom of expression in Islam, and it is its key question: Does freedom of expression include blasphemy? Many believers including Muslims distinguish respectful critique of Islam, on the one hand, from defamation of Islam and insulting or cursing or mocking the Prophet, his household and his Companions, on the other. It means that the freedom of expression in Islam in both areas of individuals and religions does not include the freedom to ridicule, insult and make a mockery of anyone, especially prophets, while critique of religion is allowed.

The UDHR and ICCPR, which recognise freedom of expression, define its domain as 'respect of the rights or reputations of others, and the protection of national security or of public order, or of public health or morals'. Muslim countries have repeatedly tried to ban insults to Muslim beliefs by relying on this clause and have never succeeded. This is because the clause deals with violations of the rights of 'individuals', and no rights are recognised for 'religions' (or followers of religions). That is, insulting an 'individual' can be a crime, but insulting the 'religious beliefs' of individuals in these documents is not considered a crime in principle!

43 Kadivar, *Human Rights and Reformist Islam*, 225.

The Human Rights Council thus observes that 'in the framework of international human rights law, the combination of "defamation" with "religion" remains unclear'. The other problem is that many Muslim-majority countries do not have codified definitions of the crime.[44]

Unlike what I wrote a few years ago,[45] the argumentation based on 'hate speech' for excluding blasphemy from freedom of expression, in the framework of United Nations documents, is problematic. There is a deep conflict between Islamic thought and United Nations documents. What can we do or what should we do? Practically, although the Muslims' main purpose has been rejection or banning blasphemy, mockery or insulting the Prophet or Islam, in the West where the Muslims are a minority, they cannot do anything. In Muslim-majority countries, although they have restricted the freedom of expression, the blasphemy laws 'are often used by governments to suppress unorthodox religious views or the governments' oppositions under the guise of protecting religion'.[46]

As Abdullah Saeed continues: 'Even if blasphemy laws do not formally exist in a state, there have been cases where individuals have taken the law into their own hands and murdered accused blasphemers for their apparent violation. For instance, in 2017, Pakistani student Mashal Khan was accused of blasphemy and killed by fellow students after a debate in which he raised sensitive theological questions. NGOs in the country estimate 65 people have been killed extrajudicially in Pakistan since 1990 after being accused of blasphemy.'[47]

The other example is the gripping story of Rāfiq Taqī (1950–2011), an Azerbaijani journalist and writer, who was condemned to death by Iranian Shī'ite authority Mohammad Fazel Lankarini (1931–2007) for a blasphemous news article in 2006.[48]

Theoretically, defamation of Islam and insulting or cursing or mocking the Prophet or his household intentionally is a sin and ethically worthy of blame. But penalising these actions or utterances under the label of blasphemy is problematic. The Qur'an does not criminalise blasphemy. The *ḥadīth*s of

44 Paul Marshall, 'Exporting Blasphemy Restrictions: The Organization of the Islamic Conference and the United Nations', *The Review of Faith & International Affairs* 9, no. 2 (2011): 61. Marshall's article concentrates on OIC member countries.

45 Mohsen Kadivar, 'Islam: Between the Freedom of Expression and the Prohibition of Hate Speech', in *Human Rights and Reformist Islam*, 321–24.

46 Saeed, *Human Rights and Islam*, 183.

47 Ibid.

48 My book *Blasphemy and Apostasy in Islam* takes this event as a case study.

considering the blasphemer as *mahdūr al-dam* (a guilty person whose blood may be shed with impunity) are invalid for several reasons.[49] Undoubtedly, severe punishment for blasphemy is '*wahn* of Islam' (i.e. implementing the punishment would impair or debilitate Islam). Light civil punishment could be implemented in developing countries to pave the way for absolute decriminalisation of blasphemy.

I want to add one more essential point here. Islamic jurisprudence should be revisited in the light of freedom of expression and religious freedom. The Qur'an and the tradition of the Prophet and the Imāms support these two rights strongly. This revisiting is a return to Islamic standards.

Free speech and the limits of expression are the new problems (*al-masā'il al-mustaḥdatha*) in contemporary Islam. Its subject matter (*mawḍū'*) is new too. There are several new dimensions that cannot be found in early Islam, or in medieval times. Although we can learn from the Qur'anic teachings, as well as the method of the Prophet, Imām 'Alī and other Imāms, it is obvious that the traditional derivatives of jurisprudence or *ijtihād* (*al-furū' al-fiqhī*) are not sufficient and we need structural *ijtihād*, that is, *ijtihād* in principles and foundations (*al-uṣūl wa-l-mabādī*).[50] The problem of freedom of expression is less juridical (*fiqhī*) and more related to the *mabādī al-fiqh*, or pre-juridical principles, such as anthropology, criminology, international criminal law and history, which may be termed the requirement of one's time and place.

49 Kadivar, *Blasphemy and Apostasy in Islam*, 146–65.

50 Mohsen Kadivar, 'Reforming Islamic Thought through Structural Ijtihad', *Iran Nameh: A Persian–English Quarterly of Iranian Studies* 30, no. 3 (2015): xx–xxvii.

EBRAHIM MOOSA

Ghazālian Insights on Scholarly Critique and Freedom

1. Introduction

Thinking about scholarly critique and freedom of speech requires a historical sensibility as to how such categories would fit with tradition and history. All systems of thought, especially those developed in the pre-modern period, have a very different sense of liberty, rights, and responsibility. The Muslim tradition and Islamic thought are no exception. While accountability to God in Islamic ethics is often an individual burden and responsibility, especially in devotional matters (*ʿibādāt*), by contrast transactional (*muʿāmalāt*) matters are different. In matters of homicide and injury, we notice that the individual might have committed the offense, yet it is the kin of the deceased who are entitled to satisfaction, while the kin of the offender carry the burden of responsibility to offer reparations and blood money to the bereaved party. A communitarian ethos is baked into the Islamic ethical order. Centring individual freedom to the exclusion of all other freedoms in Islamic discourse might undo or undermine the communitarian ethos of Islamic moral and ethical thought.

Accountability, claims and entitlements are part of anthropological and sociological equations where the individual and the collective have complicated relations of shared responsibility, claims and entitlements. This also depends on the specific time in history where such moral and ethical systems were formed. It is also widely accepted that these Islamic ethical and legal formulas that I had just recounted were based on social systems that were derived from the imprints of seventh-century Arabia and parts of the Near East where Islamic theology and law in their formative periods were constructed based on lived practices. And, according to Fazlur Rahman, these practices were organic and part of dynamic societies where these social, legal and moral coordinates showed remarkable flexibility in everyday life, based on the larger political and cultural contexts.[1] Later, however, these teachings took on a more dogmatic posture.

1 Fazlur Rahman, *Islamic Methodology in History* (Islamabad: Islamic Research Institute,

The idea of freedom rings very differently in slave societies when the same concept is deployed in societies that had eliminated slavery. Early Islamic societies valorised both free individuals and slavery, with sympathetic pathways to manumission and freedom. Women were entitled to dispense with their property freely, even though some law schools even restricted this right to married women.[2] Yet women were indeed awarded limited autonomy over their sexuality to enter marriages or for that matter, to exit unions. While the law schools have some slight disagreements, the default and preferred option always gave the guardian the final say in contracting legally sound marriages. Appeals to political authority via courts could find grounds for the dissolution of the marriage. And a woman with means could financially negotiate her way out of an unsatisfactory marriage by inducing her spouse with a sum of money for release.

My larger point in these examples is to illustrate one key idea, the question of *ḥaqq*. In all these discussions the terms used would be *ḥaqq* and its plural *ḥuqūq*. While the term *ḥaqq* is translated as 'right' today, it did not have the same resonance in the past. In early and medieval Islam, the idea of an individual possessing a non-derogable right, namely, a right that cannot be infringed, would be a rarity. Yes, individuals possessed a certain dignity in the moral sense. Yet, dignity did not feature as an independent or an unembodied variable or a value possessing the power to veto a *sharʿī* rule or abrogate a practice. Dignity was embodied in practices, and practices, in turn, are embedded in cultural rhythms and logics. Dignity when embedded in the practice of respect or vested in male guardianship made total sense in that context. But on its own the appeal to dignity in the pre-modern world could not abrogate slavery, nor could appeals to dignity level believers to be equal to non-believers or create equality between women and men. But an appeal to dignity, as a famous prophetic tradition made known, could be part of the rhetorical repertoire of cautioning a slave-owner not to chastise a slave by hitting the poor man in the face, because the face is literally the epitome of dignity.

The conceptual history of dignity or the right to make certain claims and demand reciprocal obligations needs to be studied historically. Similarly, the right to respond to a doctrine or to disagree with a doctrine held by a firm

---

1984), 86.

2 Abū ʿAbd Allāh Muḥammad ibn Abī Bakr ibn Ayyūb Ibn Qayyim al-Jawziyya, *Ighāthat al-lahfān fī maṣāyid al-Shayṭān*, 2 vols (Doha: Wizārat al-Awqāf wa-l-Shuʾūn al-Islāmiyya, 2016), 2:748–49.

majority in pre-modern Muslim society was regulated by norms of compliance and obedience, or norms of knowledge-based disagreement, *khilāf*, not norms of freedom. The difference is subtle and requires reflection. One side, normally the majority point of view, claimed the right to respond to or sanction the minority point of view. The latter, depending on the severity of the disagreement, could cautiously respond. Polemics between Sunnīs and Shīʿas often rose to boiling point with mutual imprecations and anathematisation. Or witness the wounding rivalries between Ḥanafīs versus Shāfiʿīs, Ashʿarites versus Muʿtazilites in the early centuries. It would require the orchestration of mob violence to harm the offending party, or it would need some plot among contesting bureaucrats to get their opponents executed under some political or theological pretext. Only Abū Bakr al-Rāzī (d. *c.* 925 or 935) managed to get away with his radical ideas on prophecy without consequence.[3]

The past is a different world in terms of its conceptual vocabularies. That past had limits on what we today perceive as freedoms or the right to dissent, just as the modern world also places restrictions on freedoms. We cannot make irresponsible claims that endanger the lives of others by falsely shouting 'Fire!' in a packed cinema or in a sports stadium causing a stampede in a crowd where people are trampled to death.

And I want to caution against our use of categories and concepts that had very different resonances in the past, by merely transplanting them into the present without proper conceptual translation and adjustment. One is required to account for the discontinuities and explain the continuities and how they would or would not work today. And yet, even modern Muslims cannot journey in Islam without the memory of the past. Nor is it advisable to let the hold and grip of the past, namely tradition, be released on those living in the present. The German philosopher Hans-Georg Gadamer called that authority of the past 'effective-history'. For Gadamer, effective-history is the operative force of the tradition over those who belong to it. Even an acceptance or a rejection of tradition indicates the power and hold of tradition over us. As Abūl Kalām Āzād (d. 1958), the Indian Muslim religious scholar and politician, put it: 'No power can incarcerate a person as much as the chains of traditional convictions can fetter one.'[4] And at the same time, we also need to keep in mind that all these

3 Sarah Stroumsa, *Freethinkers of Medieval Islam: Ibn al-Rāwandī, Abū Bakr al-Rāzī, and Their Impact on Islamic Thought* (Leiden: Brill, 2016).

4 Abū al-Kalām Āzād, *Ghubār-i Khāṭir* (New Delhi: Sahitya Akademi, 1983), Letter no. 11, 99–100.

historical concepts and values are now operative in societies that are deeply secularised. To keep these conditions in perspective the caution of Michel de Certeau serves as valuable guidance: 'A society which is no longer religious imposes *its* rationality, *its* own categories, *its* problems, *its* type of organization upon religious formulations.'[5]

2. Ghazālī as Interlocutor for Scholarly Critique

Like many past and contemporary thinkers, I do find Abū Ḥāmid al-Ghazālī (d. 1111) to be a most insightful interlocutor. Of course, he also poses to be an enigmatic figure, but nevertheless a formidable character intellectually. Ghazālī allows me to think through the historical Muslim tradition and he gives me some openings to build out and construct concepts of tolerance that might have cache among Muslims today. Hopefully, I will build these concepts with the relevant attention to historical adaptation. While Ghazālī's intervention to lower the tensions between different Muslim sects to my mind cannot be viewed as 'freedom' understood in the modern sense, but it does offer toleration. Rather, the purpose of *The Decisive Separation between Islam and Subversion* (*Fayṣal al-tafriqa bayn al-Islām wa-l-zandaqa*) was twofold: one was to draw the proverbial boundaries of the theological red lines, so to speak.[6] The other was to create a range of interpretative possibilities of revealed discourses. Central was his effort to dissuade scholars from adhering to authority (*taqlīd*) in an uncritical and uninformed matter. And in his view, a version of the truth is available in every contending sect.

When I think of scholarly critique within an Islamic context, I always find it regrettable that Ghazālī himself used some very strong language to excoriate those he deemed to be his intellectual and political adversaries. I am referring to the Ismāʿīlīs whom he dubbed as the *taʿlīmīs*, because they relied so exclusively on the teachings of their absolute and infallible leader. He also did not spare the Imāmī Shīʿa his caustic criticisms, just as he found dumb-witted Ashʿarī and

5 Michel de Certeau, *The Writing of History*, trans. Tom Conley (New York: Columbia University Press, 1988), 141.

6 Muḥammad ibn Muḥammad Abū Ḥāmid al-Ghazālī, *Fayṣal al-tafriqa bayn al-Islām wa-l-zandaqa* (Damascus, 1993); Sherman A. Jackson, *On the Boundaries of Theological Tolerance in Islam: Abū Ḥāmid al-Ghāzalī's Fayṣal al-Tafriqa*, Studies in Islamic Philosophy, vol. 1 (Karachi: Oxford University Press, 2002).

Ḥanbalī scholars and theologians to be insufferable people to be around. And he had unkind things to say about law schools that rivalled the Shāfiʿīs, and he especially put down Abū Ḥanīfa in a youthful dissertation on legal theory.[7] But he reserved his strongest ire for the Muslim philosophers. He penned a well-known and elaborate critique of the Muslim philosophers, especially targeting Ibn Sīnā (d.1037), about which much ink has been spilt. *The Incoherence of the Philosophers* (*Tahāfut al-falāsifa*) has unfortunately for some people turned into a benchmark of how Ghazālī struck a blow to reason and philosophy.[8] In the eyes of some modern Muslim public intellectuals and historians who seek a short-cut explanation or analysis for the woes of Muslim societies in the modern period Ghazālī is turned into a scapegoat and unfortunately serves as grist for their polemical mill. This is less of an analysis but rather a poorly thought-out thought-experiment lacking historical credibility. Philosophy and reason in various shapes and sizes flourished in the post-Ghazālian era. The decline of Muslim political fortunes requires a much more serious diagnosis and to my mind the half-baked accounts that masquerade as analyses only cause more damage.

Ghazālī deemed the interpretative dissent of the Muslim philosophers to be so grave that it became tantamount to denying categorical doctrinal certainty. In his definition unbelief, *kufr*, constitutes a violation of tolerable dissent. Unbelief in his scholarly assessment is to 'falsify' (*takdhīb*) even a single teaching of what the Prophet Muḥammad delivered.[9] This is the nub of Ghazālī's charge against the philosophers on three issues – (1) the pre-eternity of the world and that all substances are eternal, (2) God's knowledge does not encompass the temporal particulars among existing things and (3) the denial of bodily resurrection.[10] It is clear that the philosophers' conception of the nature of the divine and how the divine acts in the world differed substantially from the way the theologians understood things.

Since Islamic theology was also a constructed discipline and blended with interpretations from the scripture and the teachings of the Prophet, the question arises: from where does this discipline gain its authority to outlaw beliefs

7 See Ebrahim Moosa, 'Abū Ḥāmid al-Ghazālī (d. 505/1111)', in *Islamic Legal Thought: A Compendium of Muslim Jurists*, ed. David Powers, Susan Spectorsky and Oussama Arabi, Studies in Islamic Law and Society (Leiden: Brill, 2013), 261–93.

8 Ghazzālī, *The Incoherence of the Philosophers = Tahāfut al-Falāsifah: A Parallel English-Arabic Text*, ed. Michael E. Marmura, 1st ed. (Provo: Brigham Young University Press, 1997).

9 al-Ghazālī, *Fayṣal al-tafriqa*, 25; Jackson, *On the Boundaries*, 92.

10 Ghazzālī, *The Incoherence of the Philosophers*, 230.

contrary to its own invented systematic programme of thinking? Ghazālī and others will claim that they are merely constructing a system of thinking, like dialectical theology (*ʿilm al-kalām*) and its disciplinary convention to protect the foundational dogma of a creed. As he put it, he is referring to those teachings that have 'been corroborated by innumerable reports, and belief in which is enjoined by religious law'.[11] The other argument Ghazālī makes is that the philosophers claim some teachings are anthropomorphic utterances or similes that are open to interpretation. He believes that utterances regarding paradise, hell and resurrection in the afterlife are not open to figurative interpretation in terms of the teachings of the religious law.[12] Interpretative possibilities must be in conformity with the conventions of the Arabic language to allow for such interpretative liberty, contrary to what the philosophers claim, he argued.

The development that we do observe is that after Ghazālī, theology, more correctly those who wield the authority of theology, gradually awarded it the authority of a master narrative and the authority to anathematise unacceptable ideas and their carriers. How? Theology now examined the complex implications of one's understanding of the universe by way of the resources of metaphysics or the natural sciences. In other words, if one denied God or the Prophet or the revelatory nature of the Qur'an in explicit terms, then one's membership of the Muslim community is obviously challenged. With the development of theology, micro-debates and implications of ideas were now subject to theological surveillance. Ghazālī creatively innovated – driven by his own passion to defend traditional Muslim doctrine and creed – a knowledge (epistemic) apparatus to surveil the granular implications of one's philosophical, natural science and cosmological convictions and how they squared or did not square with one's beliefs.

Ghazālī's epistemic apparatus to outlaw certain doctrines that were beyond the fold was gradually endorsed by different elements of the Muslim religious elites over time. And, for some, especially later Ashʿarīs, his apparatus became the touchstone to evaluate philosophical doctrines. Most ignore the fact that Ghazālī himself was deeply invested in philosophy. In addition to his voluminous and wide range of writings, his authority became quasi-sanctified in these matters and his authority is frequently invoked as a conversation-stopper on difficult questions. To further and deepen respectful but necessary scholarly critique this unofficial ban on questioning the boundaries of theological dissent ought to be revised. While Ghazālī identified with the Ashʿarī/Sunnī

11 Ibid., 177.

12 Ibid., 218.

perspective, the effect of this unofficial policing of the micro-implications of philosophical and scientific commitments is not limited to Sunnī circles. Gatekeepers across the various branches of Islamic thought often exercise limitations to the detriment of the development of religious thought itself.

Just to push the point a bit further. Why would it not be possible for there to be two or multiple accounts of how the universe works? One could be a metaphysical account related to an explanation of the natural sciences as the philosophers of the past held. Another account could be a narrative largely premised on scriptural and prophetic authority. This version would have no truck with metaphysics and philosophy. However, this scriptural account is surely unconvincing if it is unable to credibly answer existential and real questions about being-in-the-world. Yet, for argument's sake, it remains a theoretical possibility for those who believe it to express it. The best example is a previous Saudi mufti who stated that the earth is flat on the grounds of scripture. Such a person is dead wrong in the minds of those who disagree. And one should allow this disagreement to play out in knowledge circles where the less convincing narratives are discursively defeated. Many lay Muslims today possess some literacy of Islam, but they find it difficult to navigate between their convictions of the nature of the universe and those strict and literal versions of scriptural accounts that challenge their credulity. Yes, it would be most confusing to lay Muslims of this ilk when scripturalism absurdly concludes that the earth is flat. But to millions of other believers who do not delve into the literacy of the tradition, but for whom religion is about rituals and elementary beliefs requiring little or no religious literacy, such unthinking scripturalism would either be received with acceptance, rejection or in most cases an indifference as to its veracity.

Most sensible theologians attempt to combine both the metaphysical debates with scriptural theology as Ghazālī did. But Ghazālī found some of the literalist scripture-based propositions to fundamentally clash with some of the metaphysical propositions he held. This made him excoriate the unworthy and uncritical Muslim theologians for promoting false beliefs and views of the world. And the same impulse also drove his critique of the philosophers who gave priority to metaphysics and in doing so ignored scriptural teachings and consensus-based theological propositions. But Ghazālī failed to recognise that there could have been more than one metalanguage to understand the role of humans in the world. Ghazālī, among others, tried to make philosophy subordinate to the metalanguage of theology.

This game of knowledge gridlock in contemporary Muslim contexts where the framework for religious thought has become moribund does succeed to inhibit, or intimidate, conscientious Muslims from boldly engaging in scientific exploration and engage with social and philosophical challenges. How? Young Muslims and adult professionals are constantly petrified that their scientific inquiries or philosophical curiosities might leave them stranded in a theological heresy-land. While large numbers of Muslim scientists do undertake research and explore science with the presumptions of the big-bang theory and evolutionary biology at work, they are equally petrified about pronouncing their views on Darwinian evolution. The reason is that they fear the wrath of the Muslim theological thought-police who would unleash their fury on them if they violated official theological doctrines if they approved of evolution. In some instances, social ostracism would be a mild alternative when compared to harsh imprisonment or death if found guilty in heresy-related show-trials in some Muslim-majority contexts.

In the *Decisive Separation* Ghazālī created an opening for multiple shades of interpretation or interpretative keys to be tolerated in Islamic thought. These interpretative keys are established concepts. They are related to our ordinary and sophisticated conceptual systems, not just in language, but in the way we think and act, which are metaphorical in nature. Concepts structure how we perceive things, how we move around in the world, how we navigate both seen and unseen reality. This ranges from the most mundane acts and thoughts to the most profound thoughts and practices as well as their linguistic expression.[13]

So, in Ghazālī's proposal, one must first try and read any text in the interpretative key of 'essential existence'. This simply means to view things the way they occur to us in everyday life in obvious and unreflective terms. For instance, these are clouds in the sky, this is the earth or she is a woman. The way we see things in their essence. If it is not possible to understand something in this essential manner, then one proceeds to understand things in 'sensory' terms, namely, what your senses tell you if things are hot or cold or how you experience pain or happiness. Other times, and this is his third key, we understand things in terms of 'imaginary' existence: in other words, in 'mental' and abstract terms. Like we imagine the existence of an imaginary object like the reindeer or the mythical bird known as the phoenix. Also, the way you remember in your mind the way the pyramids look after you visited Giza in Cairo.

13 George Lakoff and Mark Johnson, *Metaphors We Live By* (Chicago and London: The University of Chicago Press, 1980), 13.

Once you left Giza, the pyramid becomes an imaginary object now located in your memory. Then there is the fourth key, 'rational' existence, meaning the implications that flow from rational discourses. One can say, for example, this pen is in my 'hand', when hand rationally signifies my power and my ability to physically grasp a writing object. Finally, the fifth key is 'analogical' existence, which occurs when a word or experience simulates something else. Anger, for example, is when one's blood pressure rises and causes a heightened emotional state. God's anger, for example, does not involve such bodily transformations, but results in an analogous sensibility of God's displeasure or imminent wrath, figuratively speaking. If an interpretation could sensibly and systematically fall into one of these five registers of interpretation, then to Ghazālī's mind one's understanding and interpretation falls within an acceptable level of toleration and thus one remained within the fold of a religious tradition and its boundaries.

With these hermeneutical keys in hand Ghazālī was hoping to introduce a level of sophistication, nuance. The key issue is toleration in order to reduce the contentious theological differences and interpretations among contending groups of Muslims. What he had mind was especially divisions within intra-Sunnī debates, but this could also possibly apply to some Shī'a groups. Therefore, Ghazālī's work gained a warm reception in Imāmī Shī'a circles, thanks to the labour of Fayḍ al-Kāshānī (d. 1680).[14] Ghazālī aimed to keep disagreement within a reasonable sphere of tolerable coherence and disagreement. However, despite a panoply of interpretative keys at his disposal, Ghazālī could not find a register to accommodate the interpretations of the philosophers in any of the keys of the five levels of interpretative possibilities he devised.

Ghazālī argued that those teachings that were derived from the Qur'an and prophetic reports must first be understood in the interpretative key of essential existence; in other words, it must be understood in realist terms. Only if such a statement amounts to incoherence and nonsense in that interpretative key, one should then turn to understanding it in sensory terms, followed by the sequences of the imaginary, rational and analogical interpretative keys, respectively. In the end Ghazālī himself admits that not a single group of scholars can avoid interpretation.

14 Kāshānī produced an adaptation of the *Iḥyā'* as Muḥammad ibn al-Murtaḍā al-Muḥsin (Fayḍ) al-Kāshānī, *Maḥajjat al-bayḍā' fī tahdhīb al-Iḥyā'*, 8 vols, 2nd ed. (Qom: Daftar-i Intishārāt-i Islāmī, *c.* 1964).

Now, one would have thought that these expansive interpretative registers would have reduced disagreement among rival Muslim schools or made them more tolerant of each other, but alas. The fact that Ghazālī's expansive interpretative framework did not foment tolerance is indicative of the absence of a sophisticated theological literacy among Muslims today. We have not yet fully deployed Ghazālī's helpful intervention. Or as the poet-philosopher Muhammad Iqbal put it: 'The ritual of the call to prayer (*adhān*) remains, but the spirit of Bilāl is missing; philosophy is found, but the conviction of Ghazālī is absent.'[15] Muslim theologians and their interlocutors have yet to properly deploy these Ghazālian hermeneutical keys to effectively create relations of toleration. So, toleration, not freedom, was the key issue in the medieval Islamic world. Perhaps toleration was a very elementary form of qualified freedom, the ability to deal with tolerable disagreement produced by the exercise of knowledge disciplines and growing human experiences in understanding faith teachings produced in a bygone world.

But even when one follows Ghazālī's hermeneutic and tries to rely on the realist understanding of things, one cannot always fully subscribe to an essential interpretation. Some figurative elements inevitably do insinuate themselves even in ordinary religious and everyday discourse. So, a prophetic report states that on the Day of Judgement one's actions will literally be weighed.[16] Linguists and logicians understand that actions are qualities. And, such entities, like qualities, cannot be weighed. In a bid to understand this teaching in a very elemental sense, Ashʿarī himself had to resort to an interpretative fiction. It is imagined that the actions of humans will be recorded on scrolls, and then ultimately the *scrolls* will be weighed on the Day of Judgement, not one's individual actions. Now this interpretation, while intelligible, clearly required the interpreter to step away from a literal interpretation in pursuit of a line of argument that stresses coherence and intelligibility. Of course, with this interpretative shift Ghazālī moved away from the literal words of what the Prophet had said, to grasp what the Messenger of God intended. At the end of the day, we need to understand that a sacred text or a teaching of significance is ultimately a conversation with the reader. While the reader cannot read his

15 Muhammad Iqbal, *Shikwa & Jawab Shikwa: The Complaint and the Answer: The Human Grievance and the Divine Response*, trans. Abdussalam Puthige, Muhammad Iqbal Memorial Series (Petaling Jaya, Selangor: The Other Press, 2015), 67.

16 al-Ghazālī, *Fayṣal al-tafrida*, 45–46.

or her own meaning into the text, disapproved as eisegesis or *tafsīr bi-l-ra'y*, the horizon of the text and the horizon of the reader will nevertheless have to find some meeting place.

Ghazālī also advocated that in matters of fundamental doctrine one could not abandon the apparent meaning of a text unless one was compelled by a categorical indicator to do so. It is a good question to ask: what constitutes such a categorical indicator? If one loyally follows the apparent meaning of a text and then it produces a rationally impossible meaning, then one is obliged to resort to an interpretation that will eliminate such incoherence. So, for instance, a prophetic report states that on the Day of Judgement death itself will appear in the form of an embodied ram and then the animal will be slaughtered.[17] On the face of it, this report invokes figurative language and hence makes us understand that in the afterlife death is no longer a possibility. But few scholars could agree on what constitutes a rationally impossible meaning. Many Ḥanbalīs literally accepted the report as mentioned. In short, Ghazālī himself realised that interpretation in any scheme of thought is a necessity, sometimes even in the most everyday and common-sense terms. Literal phrases are profoundly metaphorical in our everyday use because they are deeply embedded in our experiences. Reading and interpreting are what we denote as our experiences and '*every* experience takes place within a vast background of cultural presuppositions', write George Lakoff and Mark Johnson.[18] Philosophers and scholars who try to grasp the big picture of things often have to dig deep into the metaphors or provide interpretations that do not square with apparent meanings.[19]

So, when the Muslim philosophers refused to accept bodily resurrection, they were indeed wedded to their interpretative framework and principles. The key principle at work was this: if something is non-existent then it is rationally impossible to replicate it. On this basis the Muslim philosophers argued that once a human body is disintegrated then it becomes non-existent. Thus, it is impossible to resurrect that same non-existent body, rationally speaking. In doing so, they were consistent with their rational argument.

Ghazālī argued that the Muslim philosophers ought to have switched to authoritative discourse based on the teachings of scripture and the teaching of the Prophet Muḥammad in these matters. (When I use the term scriptural

17 Ibid., 33–34.

18 Lakoff and Johnson, *Metaphors We Live By*, 57.

19 For my extensive views, see Ebrahim Moosa, *Ghazali and the Poetics of Imagination* (Chapel Hill: University of North Carolina Press, 2005).

authority, I mean both the teachings of the Qur'an and the authoritative Sunna.) In other words, their philosophical rationality should give way to scriptural authority, he insisted. Ideally, he argued the best argument combines reason (*'aql*) and tradition (*naql*). Scriptural authority, in his view, trumped philosophical reason if there was an irreconcilable contestation between the two. In fact, scriptural authority generated its own tradition or authority-constitutive reason. In other words, reason bends to the tunes of the theological imperatives. So, the best way to explain this is to say, that our reason is often shot through with the experiences and logics of revelatory discourse. Ghazālī and the theologians believed that constructing such an edifice was a necessary and compelling requirement. The philosophers either never thought along those lines or they perhaps did not see the need to construct such an edifice. They thought philosophical reason was more compelling in understanding God and the cosmos.

The question arises: did the philosophers wilfully ignore the imperatives of the scripture and prophetic authority? They made it quite clear that religion and philosophy tried to accomplish the same goals, but each used different means. Both were catering to the truth but for different audiences. The philosophers believed they catered for the elites, while they thought religion catered for the needs of laypersons. Each audience required a different language of persuasion.

Ghazālī found this claim to be most nauseating and offensive. The implication that God spoke in a different idiom to common folk, while God gave humanity the gift of philosophy that only spoke to the elites, was a proposition that caused him great anguish and revulsion. The philosophers, he claimed, portrayed God as speaking in different tongues to different audiences. On their part, the philosophers were convinced that their language was the truth. What religion taught laypersons were teachings adapted to their level of common understanding, an approach we today would deem as being paternalistic or elitist. In other words, the philosophical discourse in essence, Ghazālī alleged, erased the discourse of religion. Philosophers opportunistically and superficially retained the discourse of religion to convince the less educated that their beliefs were identical when in truth it was not so. This provoked Ghazālī's ire to no end. If only the philosophers said, in my view, that the teachings of the Prophet could be understood in multiple ways, Ghazālī would have been satisfied. After all, Ghazālī too repeatedly spoke about appropriately addressing people according to their levels of understanding. But he did not claim that God spoke in different registers to different audiences. He also subscribed to the differences between the requirement of the elites (*khawāṣṣ*) as different from the needs of the laity (*'awāmm*). However, he often stated that something could mean both *x* and *y*, depending on which angle one stared at the problem, and provided one did not look at both angles simultaneously. The philosophers effectively viewed things from their singular and exclusive angle, which, in their view, was the correct or superior knowledge perspective. Knowledge, of course, we learn is highly dependent on epistemic virtues, namely, certain distinct ideals and specific ways of investigating and picturing nature and reality.[20] The Muslim philosophers were committed to a single set of epistemic virtues that excluded all others. Another way of looking at this is to agree that theologians and philosophers use different sets of metaphors. Reality is not entirely external to us, perhaps something neither the philosophers nor the theologians in the past fully recognised. The way each group conceptualises the world also involves human aspects of reality, such as their unique conceptualisations, motivations and actions that constitute their reality. By not accounting for the difference in metaphors can often result in deep misunderstanding of contesting sets of ideas.

Commenting on Ghazālī's attitude towards the philosophers, the legendary Indian Muslim scholar Muḥammad Shiblī Nu'mānī (d. 1914) was courageous enough to raise questions about Ghazālī's strictures to sustain a healthy conversation within Muslim theology.[21] Nu'mānī argued that Ghazālī often found sympathetic interpretative solutions to rescue several Sufis from being accused of doctrinal waywardness for their semi-heretical utterances. Why, he asked rhetorically, did Ghazālī not show the same generosity or hermeneutic charity to the Muslim philosophers as he did the Sufis? While this is a rhetorical question any conclusive reply is difficult unless we can pose the question to Ghazālī himself! One speculative reply would be that Ghazālī was invested in the experiences of the Sufis and shared their metaphors more empathetically. He possibly found philosophy useful as an epistemic framework but was less invested in its experiential reality. Politically also the stakes were too high for Ghazālī to give an inch to the Muslim philosophers, given that the philosophy-loving Ismā'īlīs posed a political threat from Egypt, challenging his Seljuk-Abbasid patrons. And the Ismā'īlī political propaganda was highly persuasive for some audiences and it relied heavily on philosophical discourses.

20 Lorraine Daston and Peter Galison, *Objectivity* (New York and Cambridge, MA: Zone Books, 2007), 28.

21 'Allāma Shiblī Nu'mānī, *'Ilm al-kalām aur kalām* (Karachi: Nafīs Academy, 1969).

In short, the invincible aura of philosophy had to be punctured, so to speak. In the meanwhile, some of Ghazālī's closest students claimed that he himself remained in thrall of philosophy.

3. Lessons

From the above journey with Ghazālī we might learn a few lessons of tolerance and deploy these in a broader framework of the discussion on freedom of speech. In doing so, I am aware of the observation by the Marquis de Vauvenargues that, 'It is easier to say original things than to reconcile things that have already been said.'[22] So my task of putting a medieval thinker into conversation with the present is daunting. All theological and philosophical thought claim to be in pursuit of the truth. We have no reason to doubt any of their claims at face value. What we do have to concede is that the truth always comes packaged with the passions and the interests of both the truth-seekers and the wider communities that subscribe to such truths. Hence the truth never stares one nakedly in the face, but it is always clothed in the most impressive and persuasive ideological apparel. In other words, there is always a politics, meaning a discourse of power attached to debates about the truth. This means, to be real, truth must first be a power discourse; it ought to have the power to convince others. Without power, the truth cannot possess our minds and our souls, hence power is intrinsic to the truth. We therefore must be alert to the politics of the truth. Such a politics is not a negative thing in and of itself. By recognising the politics of truth, we also recognise the constructive nature of the truth.

In pre-modern societies truth came packaged in the political-theological orders that governed societies. The emperor or monarch often exercised power in the name of an authority: as a delegatee (caliph) of the office of the Prophet, the caliphate in Sunnism. In the Shīʿī tradition the Imāmate at various times found some compact with political authority until the great occultation. In the absence of the Imāmate, the jurist governs in the aura of the absent Imām. Adherence to the truth and obedience to authority created the space for a domain free from political restraint, provided the absence of restraint did not threaten the stability of the political order. Obedience to authority was prior to absence of restraint or freedom. Freedom to dissent from the political order often came at a cost,

22 Antonio Gramsci, *Prison Notebooks*, ed. and trans. Joseph A. Buttigieg, 3 vols (New York: Columbia University Press, 2011), §192, 3:345.

since stability was a cherished norm and freedom always harboured chaos and disorder. And, in many Muslim-majority contexts, the priority of obedience in the interest of stability is still the preferred order of political institutions and Muslim religious leaders, the *'ulamā'*, with rare exceptions, of course.

Muslim political theology, even in the age of the nation-state, has not succeeded in calibrating a new political theology in the age of democracies. In most Muslim-majority nation-states, the preferred political model often favours authoritarian and coercive politics. That is because the political theology in place has yet to revise itself in a democratic key with a different kind of philosophical apparatus at its centre. At the centre of the political, the idea of sovereignty should be reconfigured from some symbolic sign of authority and could be reimagined as the imbrication of knowledge, freedom and obedience. How? Critical to any public debate is the density and sophistication of knowledge in a society. Knowledge allows one to aspire for the truth. A commitment to truth creates its own obligations and norms of obedience. When obedience is a choice based on knowledge the very nature of freedom is altered: it is freedom with responsibility. In Muslim theological circles in multiple modern contexts, in Muslim-majority or -minority contexts, freedom of speech and freedom of expression is always deeply threatening to political interests.

One reason why it is so threatening is that the dominant liberal notions of freedom are not always tethered to responsibility. With responsible freedom at the centre of political and theological debates, the dominant obedience-centred Muslim political-theology can be displaced with something different. Responsible discourse is not envisaged as a conversation-stopper, but should rather be an enabler of sensitive debates without a risk to the one initiating the debate and ought to be combined with a surplus of civility. Both the Ayatollah and the secular philosopher have a responsibility to the truth without demonising the other. Sensitive and difficult conversations should be conducted in the interests of the common good. To have freedom at the political and theological centre means the need to completely overhaul the dominant Muslim political-theology from an obedience-centred worldview to a responsible-freedom-centred polity and theology.

What I am proposing is a theoretical solution which might sound radical. Change happens incrementally. To move in the direction that I am gesturing would mean a tryst with a particular kind of liberty. In other words, Muslim theology and ethics should centre liberty and community as central elements of its moral philosophy. Liberty does not only have to be the liberal variant. There could be communitarian modes of liberty that values freedom, responsibility and the centrality of the community. By the latter I mean the importance of family, consensus-based decision-making and the right to creativity and innovation in the light of changing realities. Yes, this will create a host of contentious debates with the traditional modes of thinking but that is precisely the challenge: to create space for discussion and debate among Muslims on hard questions without the threat of fatwas of heresy and excommunication looming over the discussants and those who dissent. This would require intensifying the discursive traditions of Muslims by increasing the cultural, philosophical and political quotient of debates.

Here a few doctrinal elements could be debated. Among such issues would be what to do when scriptural teachings are literally adopted and then give rise to outcomes that would not be readily accepted by the sensibility of contemporary Muslims. The inheritance rules for daughters in the Sunnī tradition often elicits objections from females in a world seeking greater equality among the sexes. Could Muslim governance find a way in which a law passed by the majority would also allow a minority of legislators, scholars and members of the lay public to continue the debate about the suitability and validity of the law without any consequence to their safety, integrity and well-being? Can the inheritance laws or capital punishment laws of Pakistan and Iran, for instance, be publicly debated without an advocate of the unpopular perspective being harmed?

I do, however, advocate freedom within a communitarian ethos of individual and communal liberty. In socialist contexts Antonio Gramsci argued for certain political and intellectual freedoms in pursuit of improving the common good, especially the right to the freedom of association. What such freedoms require is some calibration of what purposes freedom would serve without turning it into a fetish. Political theorist Michael Oakeshott's support as well as caution deserves to be noted. 'The major part of mankind has nothing to say; the lives of most men do not revolve round a felt necessity to speak,' Oakeshott wrote. 'It may be supposed that this extraordinary emphasis upon freedom of speech is the work of small vocal section of our society and, in part, represents a legitimate self-interest. Nor is it an interest incapable of abuse ...'[23]

To revisit and revise theological concepts and to critique political practices, especially to explore the limits of theological and political tolerance, is a necessary task. Theology often posits itself as the search for the 'truth' about God. However, we need to distinguish between the political space and

23 Michael Oakeshott, *Rationalism in Politics and Other Essays*, new and expanded ed. (Indianapolis: Liberty Fund, 1991), 391.

the theological space. The freedoms associated with the political realm do not pave the way to the search for the truth. Rather, politics has to do with maintaining the public peace and tranquillity, not the search for the one 'truth'. Political conversation is free but becomes corrupted with lies which should be avoided at all costs. To combat lies one needs to cultivate 'peaceable decencies of conduct' among the public.[24]

Ghazālī in his day opened the door to viewing theological truths and convictions based on a more expansive scale of acceptable interpretative possibilities. Let's recall that he invented this convincing schema in his time in a bid to widen the theological circle of toleration. He was motivated to expand the circle of toleration to reduce the amount of heresy-mongering among contending Muslim groups. His moral sympathies were with the Sufis, and his schema shielded their utterances and practices from being delegitimised by bone-headed theologians and jurists. He also wanted to create space for the use of philosophical and logical arguments in theological debate, another qualified sympathy he had with the Greek-inspired philosophical tradition in Islamdom.

Finally, theological differences are embedded in our experiences and our theological metaphors ought to reflect those experiences and differences. While Ghazālī did not include selected Muslim philosophers in this circle of toleration, it does not prevent us to broaden that circle of toleration. This expansion will be based on our experiences and circumstances to include philosophers and philosophical thinking that are appropriate to our epistemological paradigm. This also requires a weakening of epistemic absolutes and an empathetic understanding of the experiences of one's rivals. To energetically pursue pluralism and toleration we need to ensure that the knowledge system contemporary Muslims pursue is capacious enough to include the experiences of the varieties of Muslim practices and beliefs as well as the shared experiences with people who retain different commitments to ours. Ghazālī provided one such model in his time. In doing so, he paved a way for us to find new formulations appropriate to our times.

24 Michael Oakeshott, *Religion, Politics, and the Moral Life*, ed. Timothy Fuller (New Haven: Yale University Press, 1993), 116.

LIYAKAT TAKIM

Freedom of Expression or Freedom to Ban: Delineating Boundaries in Islam

Islamic revelation came with a clear proclamation that human beings are to submit to and accept God's authority only. To be sure, Islam did not envision a priestly class that could mediate with the Divine or produce an ecclesiastic order capable of authoritatively defining and delineating parameters of a sacred canon or a set of beliefs. All believers are theologically at the same level, and each person is personally responsible for understanding and responding to God's revelation. Furthermore, scholars (*'ulamā'*) have no superior standing or claim to special status. Their authority is premised on their specialisation in navigating through the sacred sources, their interpretive skills and the ability to provide religious guidance to members of the community. Due to this factor, any Muslim can perform or lead a religious service. A person can perform his/her own marriage, and any person who is morally upright and knows the rules can lead a congregational prayer. There is no need for an imam to conduct a funeral or any other religious ritual.

Significantly, both Islamic law and the Muslim creed are inherently discursive and open to a multiplicity of interpretations, with no church or priesthood to define or monitor a singular or authoritative binding 'Islamic position' on any issue. In the absence of a centralised institution or procedure to rule on orthodoxy and heterodoxy Islam is, and has been since its inception, pluralistic in its structure. Due to this pluralistic ethos, Muslim scholars have always argued and disagreed on various issues. In theory at least, Muslims can hold a wide array of views on a particular topic and it is difficult, if not impossible, to privilege one view over another. Hence, freedom of speech, conscience and expression are important components of an Islamic society.

In this paper, I argue that despite Islam's 'pluralistic ethos', Muslim scholars have, on a number of issues, constructed normative parameters through which well-accepted beliefs can be distinguished from those embraced by their rivals. Through various forms of hermeneutics, boundaries that limit freedom of thought, conscience and expression have been constructed even though there were no such restrictions in the past. In the process, charges of misguidance, blasphemy and heresy were levelled to restrict or eliminate dissenting views. Punishments were applied to purported heretics even though the early sources did not prescribe any punitive measures. An important ramification of establishing an orthodox or canonical positions was the accentuation of the authority of the scholars as the guardians of Islamic law.[1]

1. Orthodoxy and Islam

The term orthodox, as is generally used, refers to conforming to and abiding by what is considered as the established and approved doctrine in a religion.[2] It also refers to 'conformity to an official formulation or truth, especially in religious beliefs or practices'.[3] Conceptually, orthodoxy is contingent on the establishment of authoritative structures and institutions that can delineate 'correct' doctrines. Since concepts such as the papacy, church and official creed do not exist in an Islamic context there is no authority or council that can definitively articulate or impose an 'official' rendition of Islam. Moreover, Islam has not created a legal mechanism that can articulate or enforce the 'right doctrine' or 'correct practices' or excommunicate a purported heretic. Neither is there an institution like a church that can accept or dismiss a member within its fold. The only exception to this would be if a person openly denies basic Islamic propositions regarding God, the Qur'an, the prophethood and the finality of Muḥammad's message, or declare him/herself to be an apostate. Hence, it is difficult to use the term orthodoxy in Islam.

In his report on a meeting with Ayatollah Sistani (b. 1930) regarding some of his controversial views, Abdulaziz Sachedina states:

> The Ayatollah opened his remarks by stating that he was not in a position to comment on the contents of the binder. Such matters were not within the jurisdiction of his authority as the *marja'* ... The Ayatollah then engaged in a long forty-minute monologue in which he exclusively addressed me, telling me that he did not doubt my faith and was not even

1 Liyakat Takim, *The Heirs of the Prophet: Charisma and Religious Authority in Shi'ite Islam* (Albany: State University of New York Press, 2006), xiii.

2 *Merriam-Webster*, s.v. 'orthodox', www.merriam-webster.com/dictionary/orthodox.

3 Encyclopedia.com, s.v. 'orthopraxy', www.encyclopedia.com/philosophy-and-religion/islam/islam/orthopraxy.

> in a position to 'try' me in the matter in which he had no jurisdiction.[4]

Since it was not in his jurisdiction, Ayatollah Sistani did not issue a religious edict (*fatwā*) against, ban or excommunicate Sachedina. He merely advised his followers not to invite him or listen to his lectures.[5]

Given the pluralistic process inherent in the Islamic legal system, rather than using the term orthodoxy to describe Islamic beliefs and practices, a more appropriate phrase is orthopraxy. The term refers to 'correctness of a practice or a body of practices accepted or recognized as correct'.[6] This definition provides an alternative and arguably better model for understanding the functioning of the religious mechanism in Islam. The term is especially appropriate for Islam since its primary religious obligation relates to the observance of a code of ritual and social behaviour as stipulated in religious texts and commentaries. In the Islamic instance, religiosity is not primarily a matter of holding correct opinions and beliefs as much as of conforming to a set of behaviours.[7]

2. Drawing Boundaries

Religious communities draw boundaries so as to demarcate and define correct beliefs and practices. Borders are erected to differentiate and separate concepts that may otherwise intersect. According to John Wansborough, scholars create a 'sectarian syndrome' or 'norm' through which proper and heretical beliefs and practices can be distinguished. Factors that lead to the formation of a syndrome include the acknowledgement of the 'saved' authoritative figures and beliefs, consolidation (defence of beliefs) and the concomitant creation of an 'orthodox' institution. In the process of associating themselves with 'orthodoxy', scholars identify their rivals or dissenters as 'heterodox', and as promoting erroneous beliefs. The distinct development of these strands of thought, although initially

4 Ali Teymoori, 'What Happened at the Meeting of Ayatollah Sistani and Sachedina', Ijtihad Network, 22 April 2018, http://ijtihadnet.com/happend-meeting-ayatollah-sistani-sachedina/.

5 This was confirmed to me by the Ayatollah's son, Muhammad Rida, in a conversation I had with him in 2013. Many members of the Shīʿī community had wrongly claimed that Sistani had prohibited his followers from listening to Sachedina.

6 According to *Webster's Third International Dictionary of the English language.*

7 Encyclopedia.com, s.v. 'orthopraxy'. Interestingly, of the five pillars of Islam, four of them relate to praxis.

not clear-cut, becomes more ensconced in subsequent literature where the beliefs of the respective schools are more clearly itemised.[8] Mapping boundaries is crucial because they identify a normative reading of texts and specify how to deal with those transgressing borders.

In constructing and defining boundaries, scholars often engage in various forms of hermeneutical enterprises that become cumulative and eventually evolve into a canonical representation of the norm while, simultaneously, creating a rigid reading of religious texts. The 'normative' and 'standardised' reading of texts is a construction that would be very difficult for subsequent generation of scholars to ignore. The appraisals of the scholars lay claim to an interpretation which can impose a normative or canonical reading of texts thereby limiting a text to a certain meaning. This determination is then posited to be the best interpretation of the text.[9]

Significantly, the hermeneutical terminologies employed homogenise readings of the texts based on scholars' preconceived ideas of what God or the Prophet meant by certain statements. The scholars' appraisals not only promote and define future renditions of texts but also restrict and limit textual pluralism culminating in a closing of the interpretive process. Gradually a scholarly consensus (*ijmāʿ*) emerges on the possible meanings of a text whereby anybody who disagrees with or deviates from the *ijmāʿ* is frequently labelled a deviant or even a blasphemer. In this way, freedom of expression is restricted within specified parameters.

Although initially there are a wide range of views a scholarly consensus is gradually reached on the boundaries of acceptable views. Furthermore, since there is no church in Islam to determine the canon, the principle of *takfīr* (declaring a person to be an infidel) is used by various groups to marginalise or exclude dissenting groups. Very frequently groups exclude and even kill those who do not subscribe to their views. It is here that the danger of religious despotism lies.

By appealing to the principle of *ijmāʿ* scholars employ textual hermeneutics and the views propounded by erstwhile scholars as shields to protect their pronouncements and to eliminate dissenting voices. Significantly, as I have discussed elsewhere, the pressure to adhere to and perpetuate the judgements of previous scholars means that a jurist may not share his research findings publicly. In this context, it is possible to discern two types of edicts: *al-fatwā*

8 John Wansborough, *The Sectarian Milieu: Content and Composition of Islamic Salvation History* (Oxford: Oxford University Press, 1978), 99–100.

9 Khaled Abou El-Fadl, *Speaking in God's Name: Islamic Law, Authority and Women* (Oxford: Oneworld, 2001), 5, 92; Takim, *The Heirs of the Prophet*, 155–56.

al-ʿilmī and *al-fatwā al-ʿamalī*. The former reflects the conclusion that a jurist has arrived at based on his research. However, to comply with the consensus reached by previous scholars or to avoid censure from his peers, he submits a legal opinion that is based on precaution or one that is more common (*mashhūr*). In reality, the same jurist has two different religious edicts on the same issue.[10]

Prominent jurists have, at times, not declared their *al-fatwā al-ʿilmī* publicly. For example, in his research, Ayatollah al-Khoei (d. 1992) had concluded that the correct time for the evening (*maghrib*) prayers is when the sun sets. This is the common view and is his *al-fatwā al-ʿilmī*. However, in order not to contravene an even more popular view (*ashhar*), he states in his juridical treatise that, based on obligatory precaution, the correct the time for *maghrib* prayers is after the redness in the sky has disappeared.[11]

Textual hermeneutics are also influenced by scholars' preconceived ideas or horizons of understanding. Due to this, scholarly interpretive enterprises can become subjective evaluations that reflect the times of the scholars rather than those of the author of the text. Gradually, the distinction between the past and its idealised form becomes blurred. This can apply to any dimension of Islam whether it be historical, exegetical, juridical, theological or even philosophical.

Boundaries are drawn in order to delineate what is acceptable and what is not. Borders are not only drawn but they are also 'policed' to exclude 'liberal' groups that reject the preponderant views. Penalties are then invoked to defend the dominant views and their symbols. Hence, charges of blasphemy or infidelity (*takfīr*) become very powerful tools to not only maintain control but also to intimidate and inject fear in potential dissenters. When constructing parameters of separation and differentiation, the boundaries of identity and exclusion conceive of soteriology along strictly defined borders.[12] It is here that freedom of expression and dissent are replaced by freedom to restrict speech.

The foregoing discussions suggests soteriology is conceived in terms of acknowledgement of the correct beliefs and practices and dissociation from dissenting groups. The role of the *ʿulamāʾ* in this venture is pivotal. They are seen as leading the laity to salvation. Without recognition of the correct beliefs and practices and detachment from all false doctrines, the community would

10 Liyakat Takim, *Shiʿism Revisited: Ijtihad and Reformation in Contemporary Times* (New York: Oxford University Press, 2022), 209.

11 Murtaḍā al-Burūjardī, *Mustanad al-ʿUrwa al-wuthqā* [compiled notes of lectures delivered by al-Khoei in Najaf], 5th ed. (Najaf: Muʾassasat al-Khūʾī al-Islāmiyya, 2013), 11:184, 186.

12 Takim, *The Heirs of the Prophet*, 130.

be led astray. In the process, the authority of the *'ulamā'*, as the interpreters and custodians of revelation, is inevitably augmented. The inherent motive for the scholarly interpretive exercises is to formulate textual hermeneutics as divinely endorsed. Amid competing factions that seek legitimacy by claiming divine approval, scholars are seen as having made a major contribution in neutralising the arguments of their opponents. Due to this, their authority as the 'guardians of the truth is ineluctably augmented'.[13]

3. Dealing with 'Heretical Opinions'

Throughout the centuries, Shī'ī jurists have struggled to deal with issues raised by scholars whom they deemed heretical. Since there is no formal process of excommunication, jurists sought different ways to silence and marginalise them. As I have discussed elsewhere, the Shī'ī Imāms prohibited their followers from following certain disciples who were seen as espousing or propagating dissenting views.[14] In fact, some eminent disciples like Zurāra ibn A'yan (d. 767), Muḥammad ibn Muslim al-Thaqafī (d. 767), Hishām ibn al-Ḥakam (d. 807) and Yūnus ibn 'Abd al-Raḥmān (d. 823) are reported to have held beliefs that contradicted the Imāms' teachings. Hishām is even reported to have accepted God's anthropomorphism.[15] Despite these seemingly heretical views, no punitive measures were stipulated by the Imāms against their associates. Instead Hishām and the other associates were merely rebuked for holding such views.

Differences arose not only between the Imāms and their disciples but also between the disciples themselves. The disciples argued and differed on various issues which resulted in major disputes and controversy within Shī'ī ranks. Some disciples labelled each other as *kuffār* (disbelievers). In fact, debates

13 Liyakatali Takim, 'The Rijāl of the Shī'ī Imāms as Depicted in Imāmī Biographical Literature' (PhD diss., School of Oriental and African Studies, University of London, 1990), 212.

14 Takim, *The Heirs of the Prophet*, chapter 3.

15 Muḥammad ibn Ya'qūb Kulaynī, *al-Kāfī fī 'ilm al-dīn* (Tehran: Daftar Farhang Ahl al-Bayt, n.d.), 1:136. See also 'Alī ibn Ismā'īl al-Ash'arī, *Maqālāt al-Islāmiyyīn* (Istanbul, 1929–30), 1:109, 283.

took place between the Imāms' disciples on various theological points. After the debate, 'Abd al-Raḥmān ibn Ḥajjāj (n.d.) labelled Hishām an infidel and heretic.[16] Books were written on the differences between the disciples.[17]

The Imāms and their disciples engaged in extensive discussions and debates with other schools of thoughts and even with non-Muslims. Although they refuted their arguments, the Imāms did not proscribe or ban their opponents. In his *'Uyūn akhbār al-Riḍā*, Muḥammad ibn 'Alī ibn al-Ḥusayn al-Ṣadūq (d. 991, also known as Ibn Bābawayh) narrates various genres of traditions from the eighth Imām, 'Alī al-Riḍā (d. 818). He also mentions al-Riḍā's debates with various groups ranging from Sunnīs, Christians and Jews, to the Sabaeans, Zoroastrians (*Majūs*) and materialists (*Dahrīs*). Some interlocutors expressed ideas that can be considered blasphemous yet the Imām did not call for any form of punishment.

Since the Imāms had purportedly criticised and rebuked some of their closest disciples, later scholars had to resort to various hermeneutical techniques so as to explain the derogatory remarks. They did this by pointing out to weak links in the chains of transmission (*asānīd*) or by claiming that they were uttered due to dissimulation (*taqiyya*). The presence of such traditions, reported especially in Muḥammad ibn 'Umar Kashshī's (d. 978) work, demonstrates that, initially, the boundaries of acceptable doctrines were not clearly demarcated hence they were frequently contested by the Imāms' closest disciples.

In other cases, a prominent figure like Aḥmad Muḥammad ibn Khālid al-Barqī (d. 888) was exiled from Qom by Aḥmad ibn Muḥammad ibn 'Īsā (n.d.). This was because al-Barqī reportedly transmitted traditions from 'weak' narrators.[18] It is not an exaggeration to state that boundaries of correct beliefs have been mapped and also contested by Shī'ī scholars throughout their history. In the process, what constituted acceptable beliefs and practices was also contested. The aforementioned al-Ṣadūq held many views that clearly opposed Shī'ī beliefs at that time. He believed, for example, that the Prophet was distracted in his prayers, that is, he committed *sahw* (inadvertence). He claimed the Prophet recited the *salām* in the second instead of the fourth

16 Muḥammad ibn 'Umar Kashshī, *Ikhtiyār ma'rifa al-rijāl*, ed. al-Muṣṭafawī (Mashhad: Dānishgāh-i Mashhad, 1969), 279.

17 Aḥmad ibn 'Alī Najāshī, *Kitāb al-Rijāl* (Qom: Maktabat al-Dāwarī, 1976), 152; Takim, *The Heirs of the Prophet*, chapter 3.

18 Ḥasan ibn Yūsuf ibn 'Alī al-Muṭahhar ('Allāma) al-Ḥillī, *Khulāṣat al-aqwāl fī 'ilm al-rijāl* (Najaf: Maṭba'at al-Ḥaydariyya, 1961), 14–15. Ṭūsī also agrees that al-Barqī reported from weak narrators (*du'afā'*). Muḥammad ibn Ja'far Ṭūsī, *Kitāb al-Fihrist* (Qom, 1983), 20.

unit of prayer. Al-Ṣadūq insisted on the authenticity of the tradition he cited and stated categorically that this was his belief. Al-Ṣadūq's student, Shaykh al-Mufīd (d. 1022), clearly disagreed with his teacher. He called him a *muqaṣṣir* (falling short in giving the Prophet his due respect).[19] In his *I'tiqādāt* (*A Shi'ite Creed*), al-Ṣadūq made other seemingly heretical statements. For example, he states that the *'arsh* (throne) of God is carried by eight angels each of whom had eight eyes. Each eye was as big as the world. The angels are in different shapes – of a human, a bull, a lion and a fowl.[20] The *'arsh* refers to God's kingdom. Al-Ṣadūq also claimed that God is seated on a throne and was carried by angels. Al-Mufīd wrote a correction (*taṣḥīḥ*) to al-Ṣadūq's treatise, rebutting what he claimed were many errors in al-Ṣadūq's work. Despite this, al-Ṣadūq was not excommunicated nor were his books banned or added to a list of erroneous works. Similarly, Muḥammad ibn Aḥmad al-Kātib al-Iskafī's (d. 991, also known as Ibn al-Junayd) juridical works were condemned by Shī'ī scholars for employing *qiyās* and *ijtihād*. Shaykh al-Mufīd criticises him for that and Sharīf al-Murtaḍā (d. 1044) attacks Ibn al-Junayd for his reliance on rare traditions, speculations and personal opinion.[21]

The list of Shī'ī scholars professing seemingly heretical views is almost endless. In more recent times, al-Ḥusayn ibn Muḥammad Taqī al-Nūrī al-Ṭabrisī (d. 1905, also known as Muḥaddith al-Nūrī) cites several traditions in his *Faṣl al-khiṭāb* to prove his thesis on the interpolation of the Uthmanic Codex.[22] Shī'ī scholars refuted his views but his books were neither banned nor was he silenced. Although beyond the scope of the present study it should be noted that many traditions cited in Shī'ī works mention that *taḥrīf* (alteration) had occurred in the Qur'an. This has been admitted by scholars 'Alī ibn Ibrāhīm al-Qummī, al-'Ayyāshī[23] and others. For example, Ja'far al-Ṣādiq is reported to have stated, 'If the Qur'an is recited as it was revealed, you will find us named

19 See Muḥammad ibn Muḥammad al-Mufīd, *Awā'il al-maqālāt fī al-madhāhib wa-l-mukhtārāt* (Qom: Maktabat al-Dāwarī, n.d.), 240–41.

20 See Muḥammad ibn 'Alī ibn al-Ḥusayn al-Ṣadūq, *A Shi'ite Creed: A Translation of Risālatu'l-I'tiqādāt*, trans. Asaf Ali Asghar Fyzee (London: Oxford University Press, 1942), 44. Al-Mufīd rejects this explanation, saying this was based on a rare tradition.

21 Takim, *Shi'ism Revisited*, 13.

22 See his *Faṣl al-khiṭāb fī taḥrīf kitāb Rabb al-arbāb* (Beirut: Markaz Dirāsat al-Fikriyya, 2020). See also Ja'far Subḥānī, *Maṣādir al-fiqh al-Islāmī wa-manābi'uhu* (Qom: Mu'assasat al-Imām al-Ṣādiq, 2007), 40–81.

23 Meir M. Bar-Asher, *Scripture and Exegesis in Early Imami Shiism* (Leiden: Brill, 1999), 16–17, 82–83, 90–91.

[in it].'[24] Another tradition cited by al-'Ayyāshī from al-Bāqir states: 'If God's book had not been subjected to additions and omissions, our rights would not have been hidden from any intelligent person. When our Qā'im rises and speaks, the Qur'an will verify what he says.'[25] Most Shī'ī scholars have refuted al-Nūrī's thesis and strenuously denied that there has been any interpolation or alteration in the contents of the Qur'an. They have also questioned the reliability of such traditions, claiming that the Imāms themselves have rejected the view that they were mentioned in the Qur'an.[26]

At times, the boundaries constructed by scholars are contested by their peers. This is because the borders are erected based on subjective interpretation of the sacred texts. In recent times, charges of extremism or deviation/misguidance have also been levelled by the *'ulamā'* against each other. Nematollah Salehi Najafabadi (d. 2006) in his *Shahīd-e jāwīd* tried to present al-Ḥusayn (d. 680), the grandson of the Prophet, as a human, pragmatic and political leader who was let down by his supporters when he tried to launch a bid for the caliphate. There were calls to ban the book and exile the writer. Najafabadi was forced into hiding in fear of his life[27] Another Shī'ī scholar, Musa al-Musawi (d. 1997) in his *al-Shī'a wa-l-taṣḥīḥ*, challenges not only Shī'ī practices but also core beliefs. He criticises the Shī'a, for example, for cursing the caliphs and is highly critical of other doctrines like those of *'iṣma* (infallibility), *raj'a* (the return of some Imāms before the end of time) and *taqiyya* (dissimulation).[28]

Ayatollah Mohammad Hussein Fadlallah (d. 2010) has also been subjected to a lot of criticism. He presents a more human presentation of the Imāms and Fāṭima, the Prophet's daughter. He casts doubts on some stories regarding Fāṭima, in particular on metaphysical aspects surrounding her creation and

24 Muḥammad ibn Muḥammad al-Mufīd, *al-Masā'il al-sarawiyya* (Qom: al-Mu'tamar al-'Ālamī li-Alfiyyat al-Shaykh al-Mufīd, 1993), 78–79. On other *ḥadīth* claiming distortion of Qur'anic verses, see Muḥammad ibn Mas'ūd al-'Ayyāshī, *Kitāb al-Tafsīr*, 2 vols. (Tehran: al-Maktaba al-'Ilmiyya al-Islāmiyya, 1961), 1:147–48, 180, 245, 285. See also 'Alī ibn Ibrāhīm al-Qummī, *Tafsīr al-Qummī* (Beirut: Maṭba'at al-Najaf, 1968), 1:129, 142, 159, 2:383.

25 *Encyclopedia of the Qur'ān*, s.v. 'Shī'ism and the Qur'ān' (Meir M. Bar-Asher), https://bit.ly/3GmANKo.

26 Hossein Modarressi, 'Early Debates on the Integrity of the Qur'an: A Brief Survey', *Studia Islamica*, no. 77 (1993): 29–30.

27 Evan Siegel, 'The Politics of *Shahīd-e Jāwīd*', in *The Twelver Shia in Modern Times: Religious Culture & Political History*, ed. Rainer Brunner and Werner Ende (Leiden: Brill, 2001), 151.

28 Rainer Brunner, 'A Shiite Cleric's Criticism of Shiism: Mūsa al-Mūsawī', in *The Twelver Shia in Modern Times*, 182–83.

marriage and the circumstances that led to her premature death.[29] Fadlallah was heavily criticised by Ja'far al-Murtaḍā al-'Āmilī especially on his recommendation that Shī'a should not recite 'Alī's name in the call to prayer and the excessive 'Āshūrā' rituals.[30] Subsequently, Fadlallah was labelled a deviant, a misguided person and one who will misguide others.[31]

Fatwas to kill or silence exhibit an inability to intellectually engage those who challenge the traditional narrative. Rather than responding to and rebutting their arguments, the *'ulamā'* choose to silence or marginalise those who challenge the dominant view. The different ways to silence interlocutors indicates that there are no clearly defined methods on how to restrict freedom of expression and to deal with those who purportedly held heretical views.

Labelling dissenting texts as books of misguidance would entail dismissing the works of many exegetes, jurists, philosophers, mystics and traditionists. Banning the works of others and silencing their voices assumes that one party knows and possesses the truth and has the divinely bestowed right to not only impose that truth but to also silence or obliterate those who differ.

Charges of heresy, apostasy and blasphemy are indicative of boundary violation. Boundaries of what constitute acceptable or unacceptable views are often fluid and subject to the proclivities of a scholar and the customs of the time. Muslim thinkers have often disagreed on the forms and demarcation of boundary lines. Since values change over time, boundaries reflect those changes. What is acceptable at one time or place is unacceptable at another. For example, in contemporary times, most people would ban and even prosecute those promoting slavery, child marriage, female genital mutilation (FGM) and polygamy. At one time these were all accepted practices. The question of constructing boundaries, their violation and implications on freedom of expression can be discerned from a discussion on the laws of blasphemy in Islam.

29 Stephan Rosiny, '"The Tragedy of Fāṭima al-Zahrā" in the Debate of Two Shiite Theologians in Lebanon', in *The Twelver Shia in Modern Times*, 210.

30 Ibid., 211, 241–45.

31 Ibid., 218–19.

4. Blasphemy

4.1 Definition

The right to free speech is not absolute. There are many restrictions on free speech especially on issues that could incite violence against a group. In the West, libel, defamation, obscenity and incitement to violence are excluded from the freedom of expression clause. So are racist and xenophobic and antisemitic remarks. Issues surrounding mapping boundaries and restrictions on freedom of expression can be better comprehended when considering the laws on blasphemy.

In the Islamic context, blasphemy can refer to acts such as using profane language, insulting or abusing what is considered sacred, a denial of the truth and the promulgation of falsehood. Blasphemy also includes deeds such as apostasy, attributing lies to, cursing or slandering God and the Prophet. It also covers the rejection of God, and His revelation.[32]

Qur'anic terms that denote blasphemy include *takdhīb* (imputing a lie) and *iftirā'* (proclamation of a false belief). The Qur'an also condemns polytheism and the worship of other gods besides God (Qur'an 6:24, 7:89, 10:18, 21:22, 28:75, 29:61–8). In Islamic juridical literature, *sabb* (insult) and *shatm* (abuse, vilification) are terms that are often used to describe the vilification of God and the Prophet.[33] To be sure, what is considered blasphemous is often malleable and varies depending on a scholar's proclivities. Significantly, although the Qur'an mentions and denounces the different genres of blasphemies, it does not prescribe any temporal punishment for any of them. Thus, there is no Qur'anic mandate for killing a blasphemer. According to Mohsen Kadivar, traditions that denounce a blasphemer as one whose blood may be lawfully shed (*mahdūr al-dam*) are invalid.[34]

4.2 Blasphemy against the Prophet Muḥammad

The Qur'an mentions many instances in which the Prophet's enemies insulted and reviled him especially when he was in Mecca (Qur'an 111:1, 69:44). They

32 *Encyclopedia of the Qur'ān*, s.v. 'Blasphemy' (Devin J. Stewart), https://bit.ly/3zovCh6.
33 Ibid.
34 Mohsen Kadivar, *Blasphemy and Apostasy in Islam: Debates in Shi'a Jurisprudence*, trans. Hamid Mavani (Edinburgh: Edinburgh University Press, 2021), 146–65.

claimed that the Prophet was a soothsayer, sorcerer and was possessed. The Jews reportedly said to the Prophet *al-sām ʿalaykum* (death to you).[35] Rather than pronouncing the death penalty on them, the Qur'an asks the Prophet to remain patient and steadfast.

Significantly, in the early literature, blasphemy against the Prophet and his Companions is not mentioned as a punishable crime. In their juridical texts, neither Mālik (d. 795) in his *al-Muwaṭṭa'*, or Saḥnūn ibn Saʿīd (d. 854) in his *al-Mudawwana al-kubrā*, or al-Shāfiʿī (d. 820) in *Kitāb al-Umm* or al-Shaybānī (d. 805) in *Kitāb al-Aṣl* state that insulting the Prophet or his Companions were offences that constitute the charge of apostasy and hence deserve the capital punishment.[36] Moreover, neither al-Shāfiʿī nor his student Ismāʿīl ibn Yaḥyā ibn Muslim al-Muzanī (d. 877) mention that a blasphemer should be considered an apostate and be killed.

In the legal texts, *sabb* as a punishable offense is mentioned around the end of the ninth/early tenth centuries. Muḥammad ibn Shanūn (d. 878), a Mālikī *faqīh*, was probably the first to write on the punishment for blasphemy.[37] Later on, the Shāfiʿī scholar Ibn al-Mundhir (d. 930) mentions the vilification of the Prophet in his book on *ijmāʿ*. Ibn al-Mundhir states that scholars agree that one who uses foul language to refer to God, the angels or prophets is a great sinner.[38] A study of the early legal texts indicates that the penalty for blasphemy was instituted only in the late ninth century.

If a Muslim abused the Prophet, most jurists consider him to be an apostate and hence to be condemned to death. Some jurists see insulting the Prophet as worse than reviling God. This is because the Prophet is not able to avenge his vilification whereas insulting God is violating rights for which only God can punish.[39]

35 Mohammad Hashim Kamali, *Freedom of Expression in Islam* (Kuala Lumpur: Berita Publishing, 1994), 225, 244.

36 Abdullah Saeed, 'Blasphemy Laws in Islam: Towards a Rethinking?', in *Freedom of Expression in Islam: Challenging Apostasy and Blasphemy Laws*, ed. Muhammad Khalid Masud, Kari Vogt, Lenal Larsen and Christian Moe (London: I.B. Tauris, 2021), 21.

37 Muhammad Khalid Masud, 'Reading Ibn Taymiyya's *al-Sarim*: Hermeneutic Shifts in the Definition of Blasphemy', in *Freedom of Expression in Islam*, ed. Masud et al., 79.

38 Lutz Wiederhold, 'Blasphemy against the Prophet Muhammad and His Companions (*Sabb al-Rasūl, Sabb al-Sahābah*): The Introduction of the Topic into Shāfiʿī Legal Literature and Its Relevance for Legal Practice under Mamluk Rule', *Journal of Semitic Studies* 42, no. 1. (1997): 41.

39 Abdullah Saeed and Hassan Saeed, *Freedom of Religion, Apostasy and Islam* (Burlington:

With the emergence of various sectarian groups and polemics the boundaries of blasphemy were expanded to protect the Prophet's Companions (*ṣaḥāba*) from vilification. This view probably arose in the late ninth century when some Shīʿī groups disparaged the *ṣaḥāba*. Extending the laws of blasphemy to cover the *ṣaḥāba* was part of the Sunnī response to Shīʿī polemics. This was also after an agreement regarding the collective righteousness and impeccability of the *ṣaḥāba* had been reached. This view can be further corroborated from the fact that some jurists considered insulting ʿĀʾisha, the wife of the Prophet, to be blasphemous but not the other wives.[40] The construction and subsequent extension of the boundaries of blasphemy can be gauged by the fact that many scholars did not agree that abusing the Companions was blasphemous. ʿAbd Allāh ibn Wahb (d. 812) states that the caliph ʿUmar ibn ʿAbd al-ʿAzīz (r. 717–20) stated that only the vilification of the Prophet is to be punished.[41]

4.3 Extension of the Laws of Blasphemy

Since blasphemy is not clearly defined in the sacred sources, sectarian and doctrinal disputes within the Muslim community afforded scholars the opportunity to further add to the list of blasphemous views and practices. Those who claimed their own position to be 'normative' characterised recalcitrant Muslims as apostates, blasphemers or even unbelievers. Accusations of blasphemy and apostasy were used to assert or refute certain doctrines or theological positions.

For example, between the ninth and eleventh centuries the Muslim community was polarised regarding the createdness of the Qur'an. Ashʿarīs asserted that the Qur'an was not created, whereas the Muʿtazilīs held the opposite view. Both sides charged the other with blasphemy. During the inquisition (*miḥna*, 833–48) instituted by the caliph al-Ma'mūn, many were imprisoned and even flogged if they denied that the Qur'an was created. The inquisition was finally abandoned in 848, fifteen years after it began. Under the caliph al-Qādir (r. 991–1031) his creed, which espoused the opposite view to that of al-Ma'mūn, dictated that anyone who believed that the Qur'an was created

Ashgate, 2005), 39.

40 Taqī al-Dīn Ibn Taymiyya, *al-Ṣārim al-maslūl ʿalā shātim al-rasūl*, ed. Muḥammad Muḥyī al-Dīn ʿAbd al-Ḥamīd (Beirut: Dār al-Kitāb, 1978), 566–67.

41 Saeed, 'Blasphemy Laws in Islam', 21.

was now considered a non-believer. Such formulations further indicate how boundaries shifted and were often tied to the political entity.

Along the same lines, Muʿtazilī beliefs regarding the attributes of God, the early Shīʿī claims regarding interpolation in the Qur'an and the Sufi belief in oneness with God (*waḥdat al-wujūd*) elicited charges of blasphemy or heresy. Clearly, terms connected to blasphemy developed over time and were subjected to various polemical and political forces. The fluidity of the boundaries of surrounding blasphemy is seen by the fact that gradually, a plethora of 'blasphemous list' was formulated. The list was malleable and often ambiguous. It was also contingent on where one was located and the school of law one followed. The preceding discussion demonstrates that terms associated with blasphemy were often vague and that scholars were not in agreement as to what constituted blasphemy.

4.4 Blasphemy and Apostasy

In legal discourse, blasphemy is also equated with apostasy (*ridda*) and unbelief (*kufr*). Although the Qur'an mentions and condemns apostasy it does not prescribe any temporal punishment for it. The Prophet is reported to have forgiven a number of apostates like ʿAbd Allāh ibn Sarḥ and Ḥārith ibn Suwayd. Early scholars debated and disagreed among themselves whether apostasy is a criminal offence. Seventh-century scholars like Sufyān al-Thawrī (d. 772) and Ibrāhīm al-Nakhaʿī (d. 713) stated that apostates must be invited to accept Islam but should not to be killed.[42] It has to be remembered that in the early period of Islam, apostasy had political ramifications since it threatened and challenged the Islamic polity. Stated differently, apostasy was a political rather than a purely religious offense as it was deemed to be subverting and confronting the state. Hence, there is a need to differentiate between the political and religious dimensions of blasphemy and apostasy.[43]

Later on, most schools of law (*madhāhib*, sing. *madhhab*) ruled that an apostate is to be killed. Jurists also maintained that Muslims who insult the Prophet must be treated as apostates and must therefore receive the same punishment, namely, capital punishment. It is assumed that one who blasphemes against

42 Kamali, *Freedom of Expression in Islam*, 93–94.

43 *Mawsūʿat al-fiqh al-Islāmī: ṭibqan li-madhhab Ahl al-Bayt*, ed. Muḥammad Hāshim al-Shāhrūdī (Qom: Mu'assasat Dā'irat Maʿārif al-Fiqh al-Islāmī, 2007), 8:364–67.

the Prophet or major Islamic beliefs is renouncing them and can therefore be treated as an apostate.[44] Since apostasy and heresy challenge and subvert authoritarian structures and can lead to social chaos they are deemed to have violated religious and political boundaries and are liable to punishment.[45]

The punishment for blasphemy was predicated on some incidents during the Prophet's lifetime when some Muslims are reported to have killed those who vilified the Prophet or God. For example, the poet Ka'b ibn al-Ashraf had composed pejorative poems against the Prophet. By abusing the Prophet, it was argued that the transgressors had waged war on Islam and could therefore be legitimately killed.[46]

4.5 The Punishment for Blasphemy

The preceding discussion indicates that the association of blasphemy with apostasy and the punishment associated with them was a later juridical construction and that the parameters of what constituted blasphemy were flexible and predicated on the penchant of scholars. These included topics like the createdness of the Qur'an, interpolation in the Qur'an,[47] God's attributes or the doctrine of the oneness of existence. Later jurists decreed that a blasphemer should be liable to criminal punishment to be decided by the head of state or a judicial authority.[48] By constructing such superficial parameters, jurists were able to curb freedom of expression and silence dissenting voices.

The changes and evolution in the laws on blasphemy are seen also in the punishment for a blasphemer. Not only was blasphemy considered a criminal act, the forms of punishment for the crime varied depending on one's *madhhab*. This is further proof that the boundaries surrounding the laws of blasphemy were humanly constructed and malleable.

44 Kamali, *Freedom of Expression in Islam*, 213.

45 See the discourse on apostasy in the legal work of Muḥammad al-Ḥasan al-Najafī, *Jawāhir al-kalām fī sharā'i' al-Islām* (Qom: Mu'assasat al-Nashr al-Islāmī, 2012), 42:946–95.

46 Kamali, *Freedom of Expression in Islam*, 213.

47 Early scholars had differed on whether parts of the Qur'an had been omitted or interpolated. See the discussion on this in al-Sayyid Abū al-Qāsim al-Mūsawī al-Khū'ī, *The Prolegomena to the Qur'an*, trans. Abdulaziz A. Sachedina (New York: Oxford University Press, 1998).

48 Kamali, *Freedom of Expression in Islam*, 244.

Importantly, just like the question of what constituted blasphemy, the early jurists did not agree on the death penalty for it. Most jurists opined that if a Muslim blasphemes, s/he is to be treated like an apostate and must be killed. Others argued that a Muslim who blasphemes may be executed even though s/he still remains a Muslim. If a non-Muslim blasphemes, s/he will incur the death penalty even though s/he cannot be considered an apostate.

The punishment for blasphemy is also dependent upon the *madhhab* one follows. Differences arise not only between the schools of law but also within a school. The Ḥanafī stance, for example, is nuanced and comprises different positions. Generally speaking, Ḥanafīs define blasphemous statements as acts of infidelity (*kufr*). A blasphemer's marriage is declared invalid and all claims to property or inheritance are nullified. Ḥanafīs also offer the offender a chance to repent and if s/he chooses to do so all her/his rights will be reinstated.[49]

The Mālikīs, on the other hand, treat blasphemy as a form of apostasy. The offender must be killed without being given a chance to repent. Female blasphemers, on the other hand, are to be punished but not executed.[50] Interestingly, in his *al-Muwaṭṭa'*, Mālik does not discuss the question of insulting the Prophet. The Shāfi'īs and Ḥanbalīs maintained differing views: some agreed with the Ḥanafīs whereas others accepted the Mālikī stance.[51] It is the later jurists who decreed that a blasphemer should be treated like an apostate and is liable to criminal punishment.[52]

Ibn Taymiyya's (d. 1328) interpretation was quite different. He equated Qur'anic verses regarding annoyance or insulting with hostility, acrimony and disobedience. Citing verses out of context, he concludes that the capital punishment is applicable to anyone who annoys God or the Prophet.[53] Although the Qur'an does not stipulate any earthly punishment for blasphemy, Ibn Taymiyya decreed that the blasphemer should be killed. His claim for a consensus of the community on the issue is incorrect.[54] Once again, the doctrine of *ijmā'* was used to impose a penalty for blasphemy even though there was no juristic consensus, neither was it a punishable offense in the scripture.

49 Encyclopedia.com, s.v. 'Blasphemy: Islamic Concept', www.encyclopedia.com/environment/encyclopedias-almanacs-transcripts-and-maps/blasphemy-islamic-concept.

50 Ibid.

51 Kamali, *Freedom of Expression in Islam*, 233.

52 Ibid., 244.

53 See his arguments in Ibn Taymiyya, *al-Ṣārim al-maslūl*, 515–27.

54 Ibid.

In the Shīʿī case, rulings on apostasy entered it through Sunnī sources.[55] Like the Sunnī jurists, most Shīʿī scholars agree that anyone who insults the Prophet must be killed. Some Shīʿī scholars further maintain that it is not essential to seek a jurist's permission to carry out the punishment. Shīʿī jurists extend this ruling to vilifying the Imāms and Fāṭima.[56]

The Shīʿī view for the punishment of apostasy is more nuanced. An apostate who is born of Muslim parent(s) (called *fiṭrī*) must be killed even if he repents. A convert who apostatises (called *millī*) is given three days to repent. If he does not do so, he should be killed on the fourth. A female apostate is not to be killed; rather, she is to be given a chance to repent. If she does not do so, then she should be imprisoned and punished at the time of prayer.[57]

Not all Shīʿī scholars agree on this point. Some maintain that the *ḥudūd* (punishment) is to be implemented by an infallible Imām only, whereas others claim that it is not possible to rely on singular traditions (*khabar al-wāḥid*) in matters relating to the capital punishment.[58] Jurists also point to cases where ʿAlī ibn Abī Ṭālib (d. 661) forgave a blasphemer.[59] The contemporary jurist Abdul-Karim Mousavi Ardebili (d. 2016) categorically states that apostasy was a punishable offence in the past as it could destabilise and threaten the Muslim political order. Since that is no longer the case, there is no justification for applying it now.[60] Hence, for him, neither the blasphemer nor an apostate can be killed.

Differences in juristic opinions on the issues discussed highlight the fact that far from being monolithic Islamic law and theology are quite flexible and open to diverse interpretations. There is much freedom to dissent and to disagree with 'normative positions' which were, after all, predicated on scholarly interpretive exercises and juristic consensus. These were humanly constructed rather than divinely bestowed.

55 Two such traditions are quoted by Ṭūsī. See Muḥammad ibn al-Ḥasan Ṭūsī, *al-Khilāf* (Qom: Mu'assasat al-Nashr al-Islāmī, 1987), 5:354. See also the examples cited in Kadivar, *Blasphemy and Apostasy in Islam*, 232.

56 Abū al-Qāsim al-Khū'ī, *Minhāj al-ṣāliḥīn*, 9th ed. (n.p., n.d.), 2:55 ('Kitāb al-Ḥudūd').

57 Ibid., 2:55–56.

58 Kadivar, *Blasphemy and Apostasy*, 110–11.

59 Sharīf al-Rāḍī, *Nahj al-balāgha* (Mashhad: al-ʿAtaba al-ʿAlawiyya al-Muqaddassa, n.d.), sermon 206.

60 'Abd al-Karīm Mūsawī Ardabīlī, *Fiqh al-ḥudūd wa-l-taʿzīrāt* (Qom: Mu'assasat al-Nashr li-Jāmiʿat al-Mufīd, 2006), 4:143–46. See also Nasir Makarim Shirazi, 'Latest Lecture about the Punishment for *Fiṭrī* Apostates' [in Persian], *Maktab-e Islām* (1984): 17.

Boundaries were constructed, contested and then rigidly applied even though initially there were none. These boundaries often fluctuate between countries and *madhāhib*, sometimes even within a *madhhab*. Punishments were imposed even though none were prescribed in the scripture. In doing so, jurists invoked various exegetical techniques like *ijmāʿ* or by citing historical anecdotes. In many instances accusations of blasphemy were meant to curtail people's freedom to differ or dissent. Offenders were accused of blasphemy even though they did not deny the basic propositions of Islam. Rather, they challenged rulings of *ʿulamāʾ* or the political authorities. In the process, freedom to express was replaced by freedom to ban and silence.

5. Books of Misguidance

Freedom of expression goes beyond matters relating to apostasy and blasphemy. The term *ḍalla* is used to refer to deviant views and appears 191 times in the Qur'an. It has assumed a wide range of moral and spiritual meanings related to the straight way.[61] One way of restricting freedom is by compiling a list of 'misguiding books'.[62] As has been shown by Hobballah in the present volume, the idea of banning misguiding books is a later scholarly invention. After examining the Qur'anic stance on misguiding works, he concludes that the Qur'an does not address the topic. He also notes that traditions do not support the notion of compiling or banning books of misguidance.

Despite this, under the principle of *ḍalāl* (misguidance) scholars contrived ways to censor what people read and viewed. For example, Ibn Qudāma al-Maqdisī (d. 1223), a Ḥanbalī scholar, wrote *Taḥrīm al-naẓar fī ʿilm al-kalām*, a work that criticised what Ibn Qudāma deemed to be the excessive rationalism of Ibn ʿAqīl (d. 1119). This led to the burning of books on philosophy.[63]

An important way to silence a dissenter or opponent is to accuse him of being misguided or of misguiding others. In compiling a list of books of misguidance it is assumed that the laity can be easily misled and have little capability in deciding what is proper and correct. Therefore, they have to be protected from

61 *Encyclopedia of the Qur'ān*, s.v. 'Astray' (James A. Toronto), https://bit.ly/3aqNPu5.

62 For more on the historical development of the question of the books of misguidance, see Muḥammad 'Alī Sulṭānī, 'Kutub Ḍalla', in *Kitāb-e Naqd wa-naqd-e kitāb* (Iran: Mu'assasa-ye Khāne-ye Kitāb, 2007).

63 See Haidar Hobballah's paper in the present volume.

such literature. Among the advocates of banning books is the contemporary jurist Ayatollah Makarim Shirazi (d. 1927). According to him, a jurist or the ruling authority can ban any publication or site that is likely to weaken or challenge people's beliefs or threaten the essentials of Islam. Under the principle of *ikhlāl* any act that weakens or creates doubts must be banned. This broad definition of misguidance is quite ambiguous and open to misuse by judicial authorities. At one point, Shirazi's website even prohibited using Facebook or installing satellite dishes because they could be used to spread corruption or engage in different types of sins.[64] Shirazi also allows the circulation of fake news if it favours an Islamic government.[65]

However, such views are not shared by all scholars. The eighteenth-century Akhbārī scholar Yūsuf al-Baḥrānī argues that, 'In my opinion, the ruling [of banning books of misguidance] is baseless due to a lack of textual proof [on it]. Prohibition and obligatoriness are rulings that can be contested based on proofs. The justifications deployed by them [jurists] are not enough to establish [such] a legal judgment.'[66]

Religious edicts that restrict freedom to act or speak also have major socio-political ramifications. In Indonesia fatwas have been used by lawmakers to formulate state policies. These can have adverse effects especially on minorities or secularists in Indonesia. When the police deal with the Aḥmadīs or Shī'īs they often refer to fatwas of the MUI (Majelis Ulama Indonesia, or Council of Indonesian Scholars), which characterise such groups as deviant sects in Islam. In many instances state laws policies and social norms are influenced by the fatwas of the MUI.[67]

In closing, it is appropriate to quote Morteza Motahhari (d. 1979). He states: 'I advise the youths and proponents of Islam: do not imagine that the way of protection of Islam is negation of freedom of expression. Islamic beliefs and philosophy are not preserved by prohibiting others to express their ideas. No! let them talk, do not let them betray. Keep in your mind that Islam cannot be guarded by preventing others to express their thoughts and beliefs. The only

64 Kadivar, *Blasphemy and Apostasy*, 354–56.

65 Ibid., 356–57.

66 Yūsuf al-Baḥrānī, *al-Ḥadā'iq al-nāḍira* (Najaf, 1960), 18:141.

67 Syafiq Hasyim, 'Politics of Fatwa, "Deviant Groups" and *Takfir* in the Context of Indonesian Pluralism: A Study of the Council of Indonesian Ulama', in *Freedom of Expression in Islam*, ed. Masud et al., 158–59.

way that we can guard Islam is [by] *logic*, regarding freedom [of expression], and encountering opposite thoughts explicitly, frankly, and clearly.'[68]

Conclusion

Even though Islam did not posit an ecumenical council or the papacy, Muslim jurists have constructed and expressed a normative evaluation of 'orthodoxy' that is employed by the juristic communities. Initially there are a wide range of views on a given topic but gradually a consensus is formed as to what the canonical or orthodox position is. This becomes entrenched in the juristic community and is posited as authoritative. Anyone who expresses a different stance is seen as a deviant and even a blasphemer. In this way, in the name of Islam, freedom to think or express an opinion is replaced by freedom to silence.

The present paper has argued that the laws of blasphemy are often misused to censor, protect the status quo and the dominant religious groups, symbols and powers. Accusations of heresy and blasphemy stifle religious discourse and enhance religious despotism since any challenge to the religious authority is equated with challenging God. In the process, freedom of expression is replaced by freedom to ban. A text is denied an independent voice and is manipulated according to the dictates of the dominant interpretive communities. Gradually the difference between the voice of God and that of human beings disappears in the minds of the laity.

68 See Mohsen Kadivar's paper in the present volume.

Lightning Source UK Ltd.
Milton Keynes UK
UKHW020629101022
410232UK00007B/500

9 781915 550019